THE BIGGEST BOOK OF BRAINTEASERS Ever!

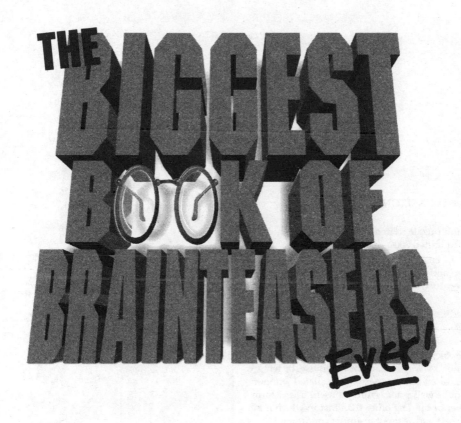

THIS IS A CARLTON BOOK

Text and puzzle content copyright © British
Mensa Limited 2000

Design and artwork copyright © Carlton Books
Limited 2000

This edition published by Carlton Books Limited
in 2000

A CIP catalogue record for this book is available
from the British Library

ISBN 1 84222 047 0

Project Editor: Lara Maiklem
Art Director: Paul Oakley
Puzzle Checking: John Paines
Original Puzzles Created by: John Bremner, Phil
Carter, Dave Chatton, Harold Gale, Peter Jackson,
Ken Russell, Carolyn Skitt
Production: Sarah Corteel

Printed in Great Britain

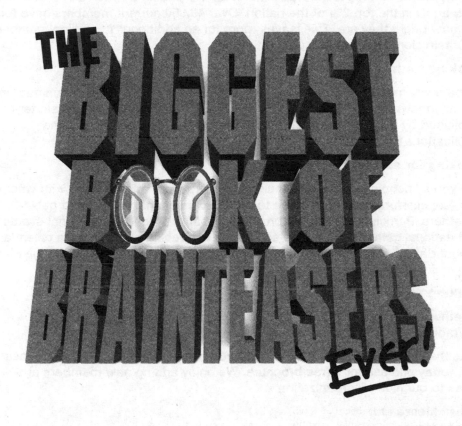

THE BIGGEST BOOK OF BRAINTEASERS Ever!

Compiled by Robert Allen

CARLTON
BOOKS

British Mensa Limited

British Mensa Limited is an organization for individuals who have one common trait: an IQ in the top 2% of the nation. Over 40,000 current members have found out how bright they are. This leaves room for an additional 1.5 million members in Britain alone. You may be one of them.

Looking for mental stimulation?

If you enjoy mental exercise, you'll find lots of good "workout programmes" in our national monthly magazine. Voice your opinion in one of the newsletters published by our many local chapters. Learn from the many books and publications that are available to you as a member.

Looking for social interaction?

Are you a "people person", or would you like to meet other people with whom you feel comfortable? Then come to our local meetings, parties and get-togethers. Participate in our lectures and debates. Attend our regional events and national gatherings. There's something happening on the Mensa calendar almost daily. So, you have lots of opportunities to meet people, exchange ideas and make interesting new friends.

Looking for others who share your special interest?

Whether yours is as common as crossword puzzles or as esoteric as Egyptology, there's a Mensa Special Interest Group (SIG) for it.

Take the challenge. Find out how smart you really are. Contact British Mensa Ltd. today and ask for a free brochure. We enjoy adding new members and ideas to our high-IQ organization.

British Mensa Ltd.
Mensa House
St John's Square
Wolverhampton WV2 4AH

Or, if you don't live in Great Britain and you'd like more details, you can contact:

Mensa International
15 The Ivories
628 Northampton Street
London N1 2NY
England

who will be happy to put you in touch with your own national Mensa organization.

Mental Meltdown

• •

It is customary to start books like this with some easy little puzzles to get you in the mood and break you in gently. Not this time. This section contains over 400 puzzles similar to the type used in IQ tests. Fun? Of *course* it's going to be fun.

1. Find the starting point and move from square to adjoining square, horizontally or vertically, but not diagonally, to spell a 12-letter word, using each letter once only. What are the missing letters?

See answer page 222

2. Find two words with different spellings, but sound alike, that can mean:

FROLIC / CHANCE

See answer page 222

3. What number should replace the question mark?

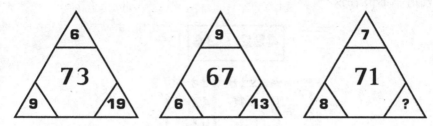

See answer page 222

4.

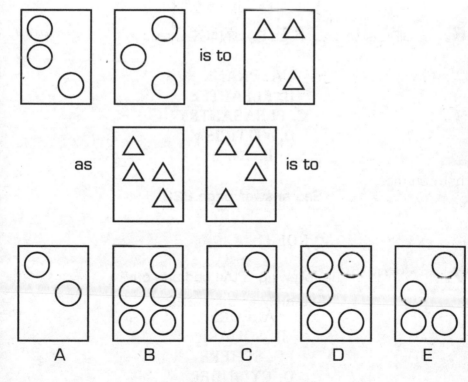

is to

as

is to

A   B   C   D   E

See answer page 222

5.   Which two numbers below have the same relationship as the two in the box?

482 : 34

A. 218 : 24
B. 946 : 42
C. 687 : 62
D. 299 : 26
E. 749 : 67

See answer page 222

6.   GIBE is to TAUNT as BADINAGE is to:

A. PRANK
B. REPARTEE
C. PLEASANTRY
D. WITTICISM
E. JOKE

See answer page 222

7.   Which of the following is the odd one out?

A. CUBE
B. SQUARE
C. SPHERE
D. CYLINDER
E. OCTAHEDRON

See answer page 222

8. If you divide 552 by 1/4, and then divide the result by half the original figure, what is the answer?

See answer page 222

9. What figure below will continue the sequence on the right?

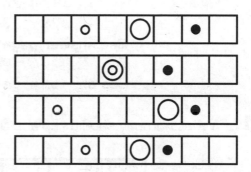

A

B

C

D

E

See answer page 222

10. What word is opposite in meaning to EVASIVE?

A. ZEALOUS
B. EXACT
C. OPEN
D. CAUSTIC
E. BRAVE

See answer page 222

11. What number should replace the question mark below?

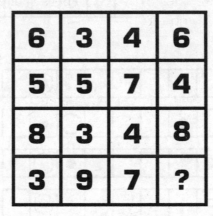

See answer page 222

PLEAD   LABEL   ALBUM   LUSTY?

12.   What word continues the above sequence?

A. FROWN
B. UTTER
C. LUNCH
D. DREAM
E. CHARM

See answer page 222

13.   What is the answer if, from the numbers below, you multiply by five the number of even numbers that are immediately followed by an odd number?

4 7 8 5 3 1 9 7 8 4 4 7 8 9 2 3

See answer page 222

14.   Which of the five boxes below is most like the box on the right?

A   B   C   D   E

See answer page 222

15. SEA PIGEON is an anagram of what nine-letter word?

See answer page 222

16. Which of the following is the odd one out?

A. SKIT
B. EMERITUS
C. LAMPOON
D. CLERIHEW
E. PARODY

See answer page 222

17. Find a six-letter word made up of only the following four letters.

G M

N O

See answer page 223

18. What number should replace the question mark?

34 7 29 11 23 16 16 22 ?

A. 3
B. 5
C. 8
D. 11
E. 13

See answer page 223

19. What word can be placed in front of the other five to form five new words? Each dot represents a letter.

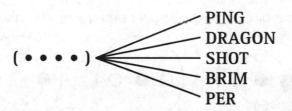

(• • • •)

PING
DRAGON
SHOT
BRIM
PER

See answer page 223

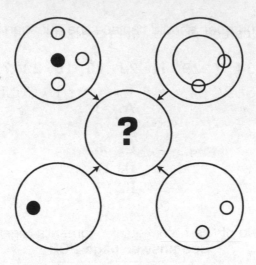

20. Each line and symbol that appears in the four outer circles, above, is transferred to the middle circle according to how many times it appears, as follows:

One time — it is transferred
Two times — it is possibly transferred
Three times — it is transferred
Four times — it is not transferred

Which of the circles below should appear as the middle circle?

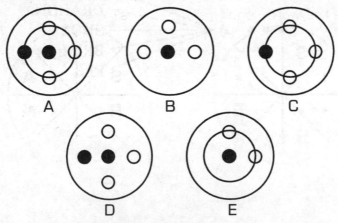

See answer page 223

21. A word can be placed in the brackets that has the same meaning as the words outside. What is it?

ENCLOSURE (• • • • • • • •) COMBINE

See answer page 223

22. Place two of the three-letter segments together to make a six-letter bug.

ANT   BEE   SCA   TLY   RAB   FLY

See answer page 223

23. If the missing letters in the two circles below are correctly inserted they will form synonymous words. The words do not have to be read in a clockwise direction, but the letters are consecutive. What are the words and missing letters?

See answer page 223

24. What number should replace the question mark?

A. 30
B. 32
C. 34
D. 36
E. 38

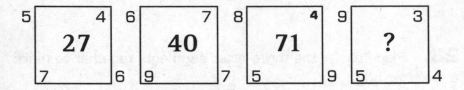

See answer page 223

25. If the missing letters in the circle below are correctly inserted they will form an eight-letter word. The word will not have to be read in a clockwise direction, but the letters are consecutive. What is the word and missing letters?

See answer page 223

26. What circle will continue the sequence and replace the question mark?

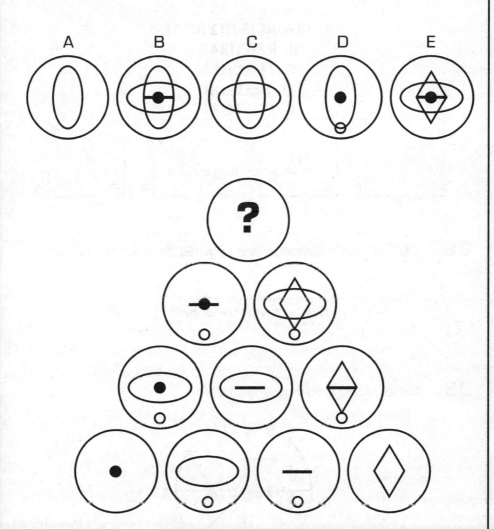

See answer page 223

27. Which of the following has the same meaning as MENDICANT?

A. CHURCH OFFICIAL
B. REPAIRER
C. TEACHER
D. BEGGAR
E. CHEMIST

See answer page 223

28. CUT PERM is an anagram of what seven-letter word?

See answer page 223

29. Simplify the following and find x.

$$\frac{8 \times 7}{2/7 - 2/14} = x$$

See answer page 223

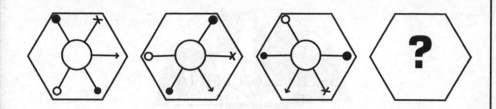

30. Which of A, B, C, D, or E, bottom should replace the question mark above?

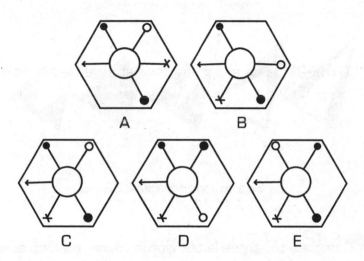

See answer page 223

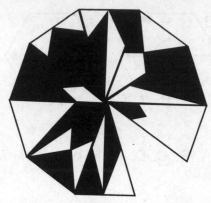

31.　Which of the segments below is missing from the diagram above?

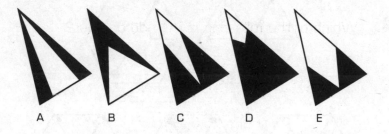

A　　B　　C　　D　　E

See answer page 223

32.　Complete the three-letter words which, reading down, will reveal a country.

T E (•)
N I (•)
F O (•)
T I (•)
B A (•)
O B (•)
E R (•)

See answer page 223

33. 2 1 7 3 8 9 5   is to   9 7 2 5 3 8 1   as
9 6 7 4 8 1 2 is to:

A. 7 1 9 2 4 8 6
B. 7 9 1 4 2 6 8
C. 2 1 4 7 9 6 8
D. 1 7 9 2 4 8 6
E. 7 1 9 4 2 6 8

See answer page 223

34. Which of the following is the odd one out?

A. MISSAL
B. LEXICON
C. LECTERN
D. PSALTER
E. THESAURUS

See answer page 223

35. What number will replace the question mark?

	72			19			73	
83	7	55	25	3	13	39	?	3
	37			4			28	

See answer page 223

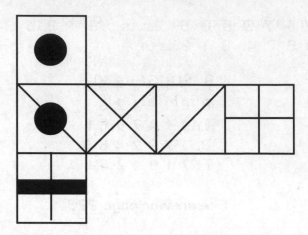

36. When the above is folded to form a cube, just one of the following can be produced. Which one is it?

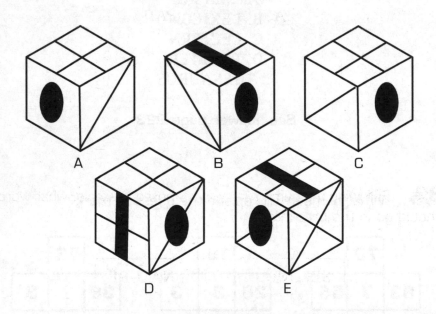

See answer page 224

37. Which word is a synonym of EXPRESSIVE?

A. PARTICULAR
B. SUGGESTIVE
C. POSITIVE
D. INSCRUTABLE
E. ELEGANT

See answer page 224

38. Complete the two words using the letters of the following once only.

CASE A DOOR PAD

• E • • R • T • •   • E • • R • T • •

See answer page 224

39. Following the same rules as the boxed example, what word should go in the brackets?

SECOND (ARDENT) NATURE

VALISE (• • • • • •) OPENLY

See answer page 224

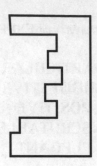

40. Which piece, below, can be put with the one above to form a perfect square?

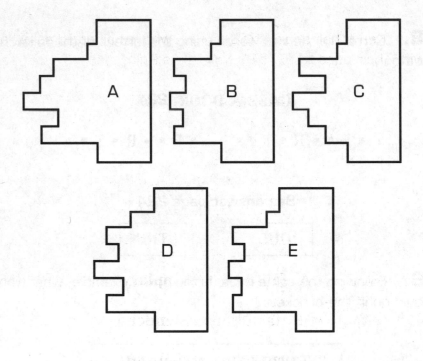

See answer page 224

41. What two words are opposite in meaning?

A. EXPAND
B. DELIGHT
C. UPSURGE
D. OFFEND
E. UPEND
F. EQUATE

See answer page 224

42. Ken is half again as old as Phil, who is half again as old as David. Their ages total 152? How old is Phil?

See answer page 224

43. Which two words below have the same relationship as the two words in the box?

DOUBT : CONVICTION

A. faultless : exemplary

B. fastidious : slender

C. courage : resolution

D. instinct : constancy

E. routine : abnormal

See answer page 224

44. Which of the following is the odd one out?

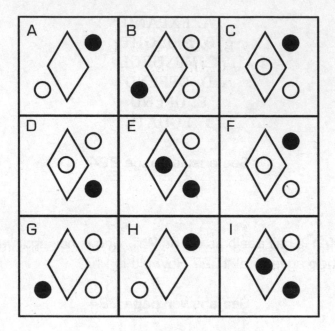

See answer page 224

45. What number should replace the question mark?

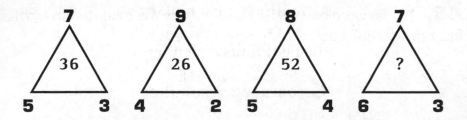

See answer page 224

46. Which of the following is not an anagram of a fruit?

A. MINK PUP
B. BURY REBEL
C. USA MAST
D. MANS GUT
E. DAMN RAIN

See answer page 224

47. Find a six-letter word made up of only the following four letters?

L O

G I

See answer page 224

48. What word can be placed in front of the other five to form five new words? Each dot represents a letter.

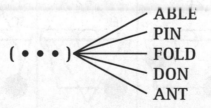

(● ● ●) — ABLE
PIN
FOLD
DON
ANT

See answer page 224

49. DEAD LIVER is an anagram of what nine-letter word?

See answer page 224

50. Each of the nine squares in the grid marked 1A to 3C should incorporate all of the items which are shown in the squares of the same letter and number, at the left and top, respectively. For example, 2B should incorporate all of the symbols that are in squares 2 and B. One square, however, is incorrect. Which one is it?

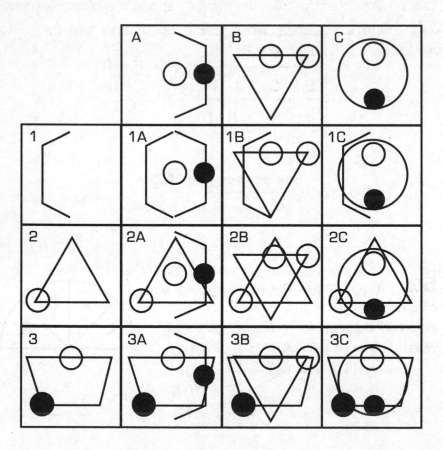

See answer page 224

51. What word is a synonym of PAROXYSM?

A. SEIZURE
B. SUPERABUNDANCE
C. SPASMODIC
D. SPACE
E. PARODY

See answer page 224

52. Which of the following should replace the question mark?

6	2	5	7
8	3	17	7
9	2	9	9
7	4	10	?

A. 24
B. 30
C. 18
D. 12
E. 26

See answer page 224

53. If the missing letters in the circle on the right are correctly inserted they will form an eight-letter word. The word will not have to be read in a clockwise direction, but the letters are consecutive. What is the word and missing letters?

See answer page 225

54. A word can be placed in the brackets that has the same meaning as the words outside. What is it?

SEARCH (• • • • • •) POLECAT

See answer page 225

55. Place two three-letter segments together to form a shade

ISE   SCA   YEL   LEW   CER   LET

See answer page 225

56. What word is an antonym of LAMBENT?

A. FLICKERING
B. TWINKLING
C. STEADY
D. SLUGGISH
E. HEAVINESS

See answer page 225

57. Which of the following is the odd one out?

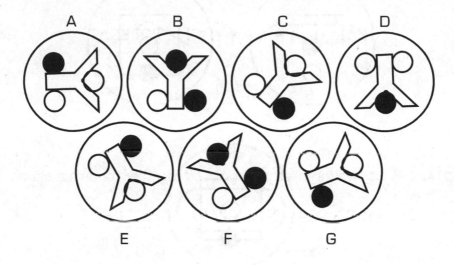

A   B   C   D

E   F   G

See answer page 225

58. If the missing letters in the two circles below are correctly inserted they will form synonymous words. The words do not have to be read in a clockwise direction, but the letters are consecutive. What are the words and missing letters?

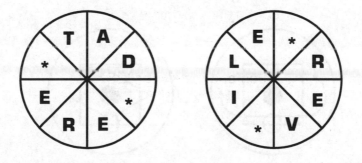

See answer page 225

59.

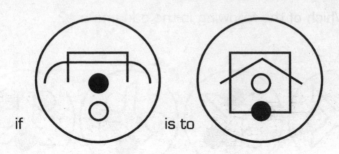

if ... is to

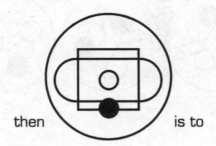

then ... is to

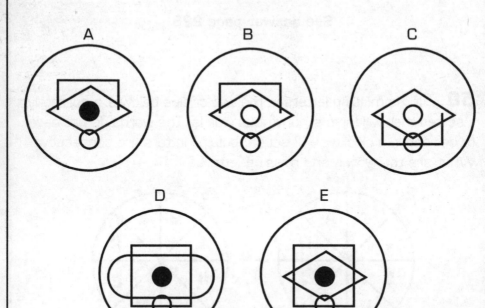

A B C

D E

See answer page 225

60. Which of the following is the odd one out?

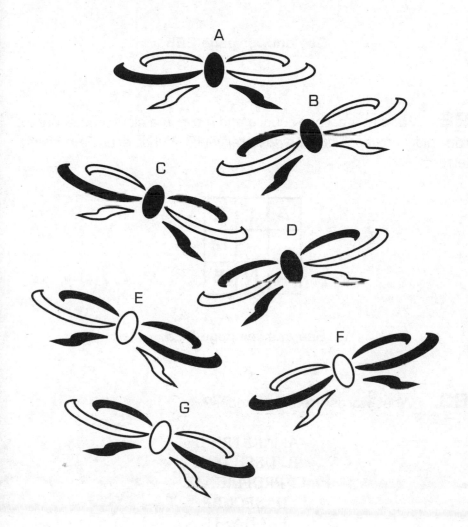

See answer page 225

61. GLOSSY METALS is an anagram of which well-known three-word phrase (3, 7, 2) which could also be "ready for the off?"

See answer page 225

62. Start at a corner square and move in a clockwise spiral to the middle to spell out a nine-letter word. What are the missing letters?

See answer page 225

63. What words are antonymous?

A. ABSTRUSE
B. DEFICIENT
C. PROFLIGATE
D. SECURE
E. CHASTE
F. EXOTIC

See answer page 225

64. What number should replace the question mark?

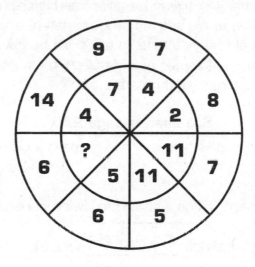

See answer page 225

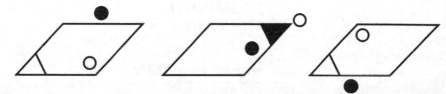

65. Which of the following, below, will continue the series above?

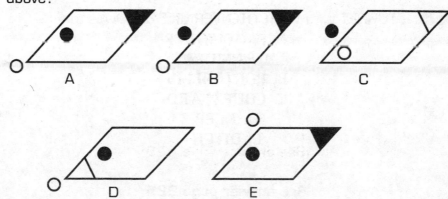

See answer page 225

66. A man returned from his greenhouse with a small basket of cherries. To his first friend he gave half his cherries, plus half a pair of cherries, to his second he gave half of what he had left, plus half a pair of cherries, and to the third he gave half of what he had left, plus half a pair of cherries. This meant he had no cherries left. How many did he start with?

See answer page 225

67. What word will go with the following series?

GAMMON   ACHE   TRACK   ?

A. MEAT
B. WARD
C. FIND
D. SMOOTH
E. KIND

See answer page 225

68. TURRET is to WATCHTOWER as DONJON is to:

A. RAMPART
B. PORTCULLIS
C. COURTYARD
D. KEEP
E. DITCH

See answer page 225

69. What number will replace the question mark?

1   2   3   7   22   ?

A. 52
B. 68
C. 126
D. 154
E. 155

See answer page 225

70. Which of the following is the odd one out?

A. CASKET
B. CARBOY
C. DECANTER
D. DEMIJOHN
E. AMPULLA

See answer page 225

71. What word is a synonym of LOGISTICS?

A. VALIDITY
B. MANAGEMENT
C. STRENGTH
D. RESOURCES
E. RECORD

See answer page 225

72.

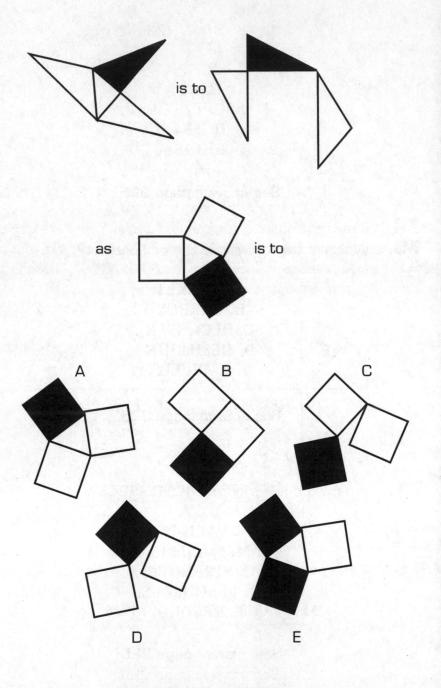

See answer page 226

73. What number should replace the question mark?

```
1  7  5  9  5  7
6  4  8  1  4  4
2  3  2  ?  9  2
9  1  2  3  3  5
2  6  5  4  3  7
```

See answer page 226

74. If the missing letters in the two circles below are correctly inserted they will form antonymous words. The words do not have to be read in a clockwise direction, but the letters are consecutive. What are the words and missing letters?

See answer page 226

75. What number should replace the question mark?

91   735/8   561/4   387/8   ?

See answer page 226

76. A word can be placed in the brackets that has the same meaning as the words outside. What is it?

VIOLIN (• • • • • •) SWINDLE

See answer page 226

77. Which of the following is always an ingredient of CURACAO?

A. PLUMS
B. LEMON PEEL
C. ORANGE PEEL
D. CHERRIES
E. LIME

See answer page 226

78. Find a six-letter word made up of only the following four letters?

P O
E H

See answer page 226

79. Which of the following will replace the question mark and complete the series?

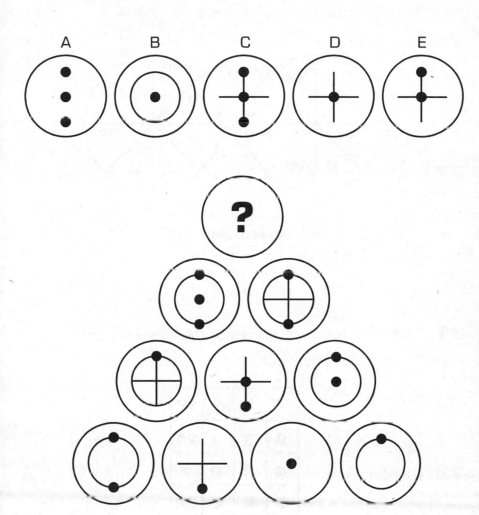

See answer page 226

80. If the missing letters in the two circles below are correctly inserted they will form synonymous words. The words do not have to be read in a clockwise direction, but the letters are consecutive. What are the words and missing letters?

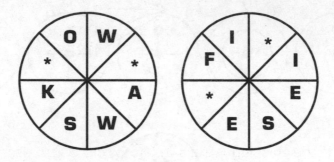

See answer page 226

81. What number should replace the question mark?

7	5	9	18
6	3	7	21
4	3	9	?
7	4	8	24

See answer page 226

82. What word can be placed in front of the other five to form five new words? Each dot represents a letter.

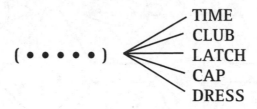

(• • • • •)
TIME
CLUB
LATCH
CAP
DRESS

See answer page 226

83. If the missing letters in the circle below are correctly inserted they will form an eight-letter word. The word will not have to be read in a clockwise direction, but the letters are consecutive. What is the word and missing letters?

See answer page 226

84. What number should replace the question mark?

2   −5 7/8   −13 3/4   ?   −29 1/2   −37 3/8

See answer page 226

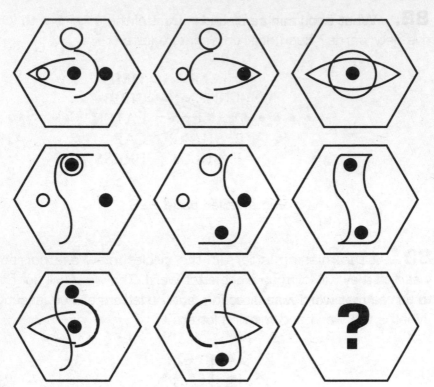

85. Which of the hexagons below should replace the question mark above?

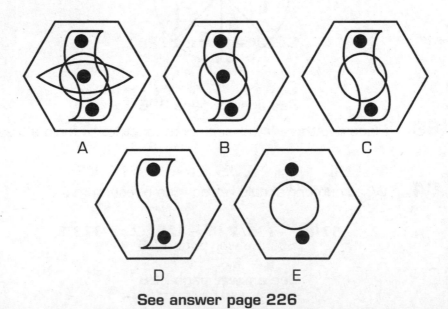

A

B

C

D

E

See answer page 226

86. What two words are antonymous?

A. GRAND
B. BALEFUL
C. ECONOMICAL
D. CLEAN
E. SHARP
F. SULLY

See answer page 226

87. What word is closest in meaning to feisty?

A. HOLY
B. MALEVOLENT
C. MEAN
D. GENEROUS
E. EXCITABLE

See answer page 226

88. Place two three-letter segments together to form a tree.

CHE   DEN   OAK   LOW   LIN   POP

See answer page 226

89.

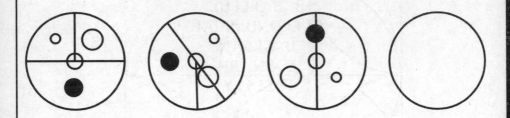

Which of the circles below will continue the sequence above?

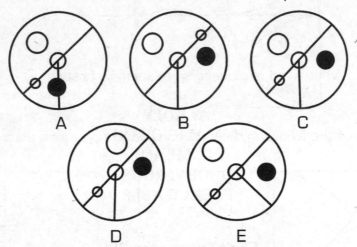

A   B   C

D   E

See answer page 226

90.

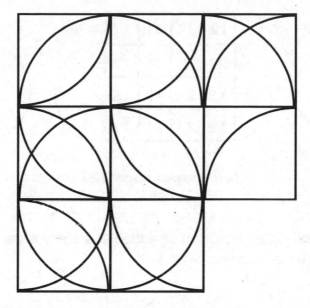

Which of the following tiles will complete the square above?

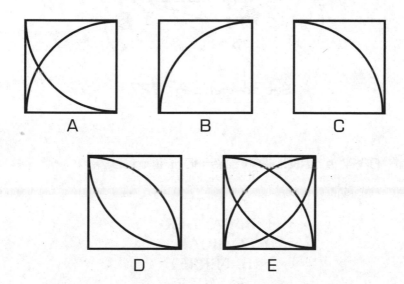

See answer page 226

91. What number should replace the question mark?

12	33	21	12
27	?	31	27
15	25	10	15
12	33	21	12

See answer page 227

92. A four-letter word can be added at the end of the following to make five new words. What is it?

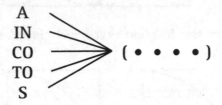

See answer page 227

93. DREY is to SQUIRREL as HOLT is to:

A. OTTER
B. BADGER
C. BOAR
D. FERRET
E. MOLE

See answer page 227

94.   What is the value of $^7/_9 \div {}^1/_3$?

See answer page 227

95.   Start at a corner square and move in a clockwise spiral to the middle to spell out a nine-letter word. What are the missing letters?

O		E
E	C	T
	I	R

See answer page 227

96.   What number should replace the question mark?

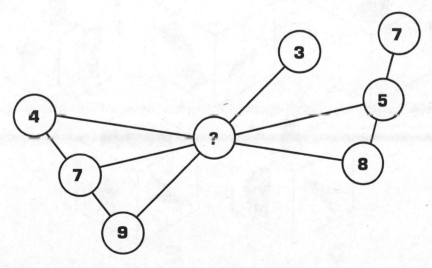

See answer page 227

97.

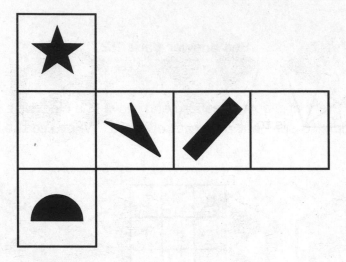

When the above is folded into a cube, only one of the following can be produced. Which one is it?

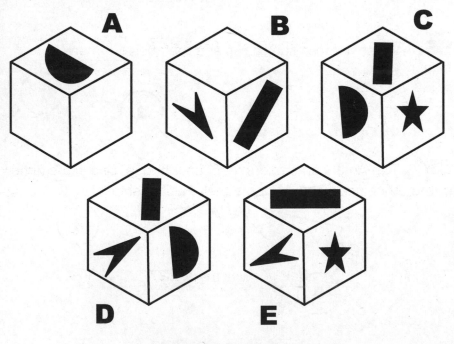

See answer page 227

98.

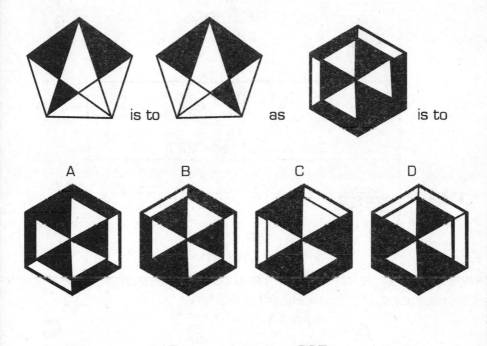

is to   as   is to

A   B   C   D

See answer page 227

99. Two American soldiers meet on a bridge. One is the father of the other one's son. What is their relationship?

See answer page 227

100. What two words are antonymous?

A. ONEROUS
B. EFFICACIOUS
C. FIRM
D. SAD
E. UNAVAILING
F. CORRUPT

See answer page 227

101. What word is the odd one out?

A. MILKSOP
B. COWARD
C. TRAITOR
D. WEAKLING
E. NAMBY-PAMBY

See answer page 227

102. What number will replace the question mark?

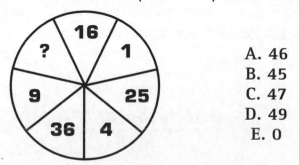

A. 46
B. 45
C. 47
D. 49
E. 0

See answer page 227

103. What two words are closest in meaning?

> A. HASTY
> B. INDIRECTLY
> C. CARELESSLY
> D. OBLIQUELY
> E. CAREFULLY
> F. SLICK

See answer page 227

104. What word is the odd one out?

> A. REGENERATE
> B. REGURGITATE
> C. REVITALIZE
> D. RESUSCITATE
> E. REANIMATE

See answer page 227

105. What number should replace the question mark?

5   1   21/2   21/2   0   4   −21/2   ?

See answer page 227

106. A word can be placed in the brackets that has the same meaning as the words outside. Each dot represents a letter. What is it?

MANAGER (• • • •) STUD

See answer page 227

107. What number should replace the question mark?

See answer page 227

108. Which of the following is not a type of wind?

A. MISTRAL
B. PAVANE
C. ZEPHYR
D. SIROCCO
E. MONSOON

See answer page 227

109.

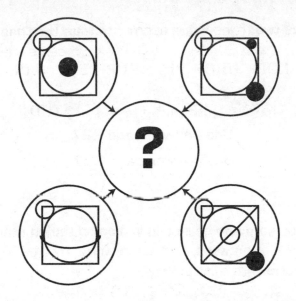

Each line and symbol that appears in the four outer circles, above, is transferred to the middle circle according how many times it appears, as follows:

One time – it is transferred
Two times – it is possibly transferred
Three times – it is transferred
Four times – it is not transferred

Which of the circles below should appear in the middle circle?

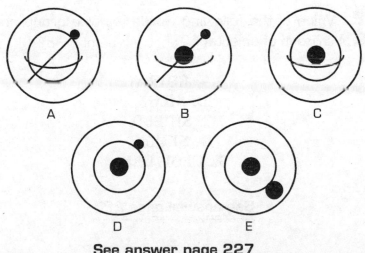

A   B   C

D   E

See answer page 227

110. Place two three-letter segments together to form a coin.

KOP   UDO   PIA   RUP   ESC   LIR

See answer page 227

111. What word can be placed in front of the other five to form five new words or phrases, and some words may be hyphenated? Each dot represents a letter.

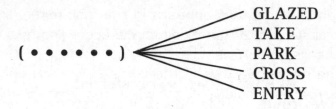

(• • • • • •)
GLAZED
TAKE
PARK
CROSS
ENTRY

See answer page 227

112. Which of the following words is not a group noun (the name of a group of objects)?

A. COVEY
B. SIEGE
C. SHIELD
D. SKULK
E. CLOWDER

See answer page 227

113. What number should replace the question mark?

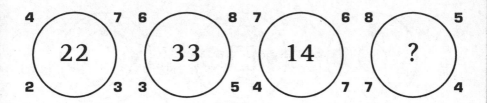

See answer page 227

114. If the missing letters in the circle below are correctly inserted they will form an eight-letter word. The word will not have to be read in a clockwise direction, but the letters are consecutive. What is the word and missing letters?

See answer page 228

115.

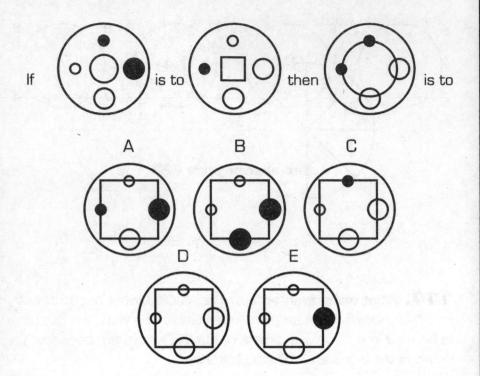

If ... is to ... then ... is to

A   B   C

D   E

See answer page 228

116. If the missing letters in the two circles below are correctly inserted they will form synonymous words. The words do not have to be read in a clockwise direction, but the letters are consecutive. What are the words and missing letters?

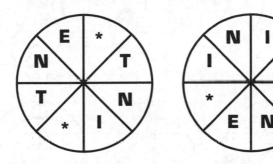

See answer page 228

117. What word is an antonym of NOCUOUS?

A. SYSTEMATIC
B. PAROCHIAL
C. HARMLESS
D. MERCURIAL
E. TRAUMATIC

See answer page 228

118. Simplify the following and find x?

$$\frac{64 - 32}{1/8 - 1/16} = x$$

See answer page 228

119.

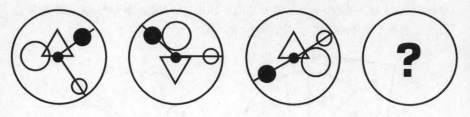

Which of the circles below will continue the sequence above?

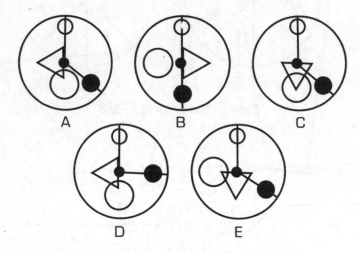

A   B   C

D   E

See answer page 228

120. Four of the five pieces below can be fitted together to form a perfect square. What piece is the odd one out?

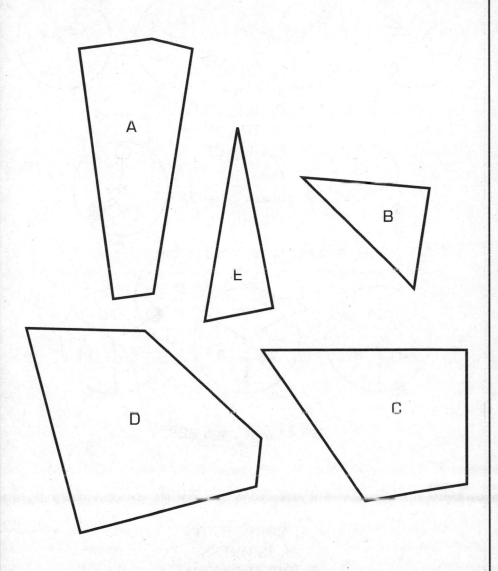

See answer page 228

121.

ANGER   TENDER   DIRECT   RENTED   RANGE

What word is missing from above?

A. GREEN
B. FINAL
C. CREDIT
D. TRAIN
E. DETECT

See answer page 228

122. What number should replace the question mark?

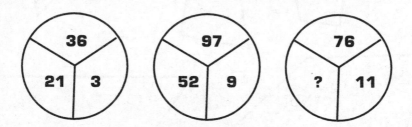

See answer page 228

123. What word is a synonym of rectitude?

A. CORRUPTION
B. REDRESS
C. RESTORATION
D. HONESTY
E. REINSTATEMENT

See answer page 228

124. Bill's house is 10th from one end of the block and sixth from the other end. How many houses are there in the block?

See answer page 228

125. A three-word phrase, below, has had each word's initial letter removed. What is the phrase?

OATCHN

See answer page 228

126.

NUMBER (RETURN) LETTER

Following the same rules as above, what word should go in the brackets?

TENDON (• • • • • •) LILIES

See answer page 228

127.

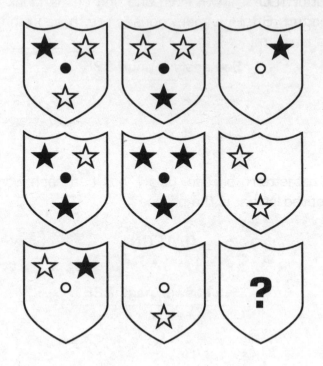

Which shield, below, will replace the question mark above?

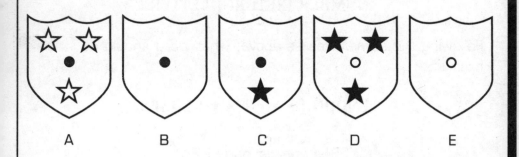

A   B   C   D   E

See answer page 228

128. Out of 100 people surveyed, 86 had an egg for breakfast, 75 had bacon, 62 had toast, and 82 had coffee. How many people, as least, must have had all four items?

See answer page 228

129. What letter is immediately to the left of the letter three to the right of the letter immediately to the left of the letter three to the right of the letter B?

A   B   C   D   E   F   G   H

See answer page 229

130. What two words are antonymous?

A. CLUMSY
B. SLOW
C. CLOSE
D. EXOTIC
E. EXPERT
F. APPREHENSIVE

See answer page 229

131. Which of the following is the odd one out?

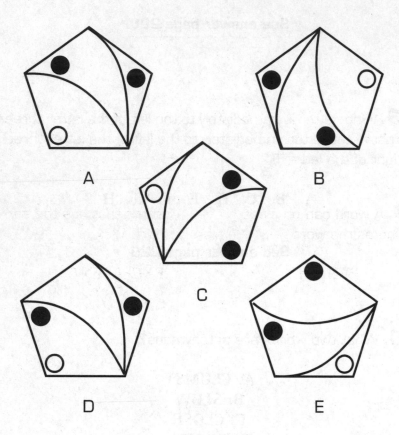

A

B

C

D

E

See answer page 229

132. What is the odd one out?

A. MAJOR
B. ADMIRAL
C. COLONEL
D. BRIGADIER
E. GENERAL

See answer page 229

133. A word can be placed in the brackets that has the same meaning as the words outside. What is it?

PENALTY (• • • •) EXCELLENT

See answer page 229

134. What number should replace the question mark?

7 –5 2 1 –3 7 –8 13 ? 19

See answer page 229

135.

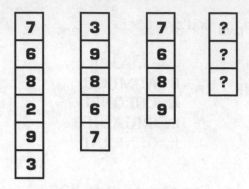

Which of the boxes below will follow the sequence above?

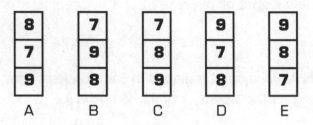

A   B   C   D   E

See answer page 229

136.

A   B   C   D   E

Into which of the boxes A, B, C, D, or E, can a dot be placed so that both dots will meet the same conditions as in the top box?

See answer page 229

137. Place two three-letter segments together to form a profession.

BUR   SOL   GAR   DEN   SAR   VAN

See answer page 229

138. What word can be placed in front of the other five to form five new words or phrases? Each dot represents a letter.

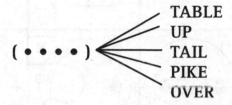

(• • • •)

TABLE
UP
TAIL
PIKE
OVER

See answer page 229

139. Find a six-letter word made up of only the following four letters?

T E

P O

See answer page 229

140. Each of the nine squares in the grid marked 1A to 3C should incorporate all of the items which are shown in the squares of the same letter and number, at the left and top, respectively. For example, 2B should incorporate all of the symbols that are in squares 2 and B. One square, however, is incorrect. Which one is it?

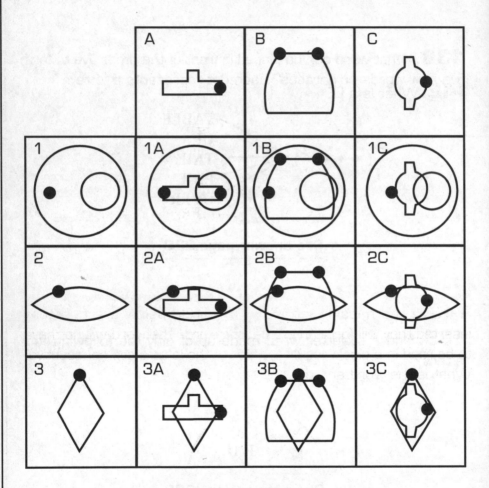

See answer page 229

141. What number should replace the question mark?

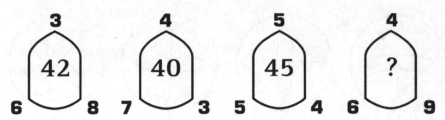

See answer page 229

142. What is a LEMAN?

A. A PARAMOUR
B. AN ANIMAL
C. A NOOSE
D. A BODICE
E. A SPINNAKER

See answer page 229

143. If the missing letters in the circle below are correctly inserted they will form an eight-letter word. The word will not have to be read in a clockwise direction, but the letters are consecutive. What is the word and missing letters?

See answer page 229

144. Which of the following is the odd one out?

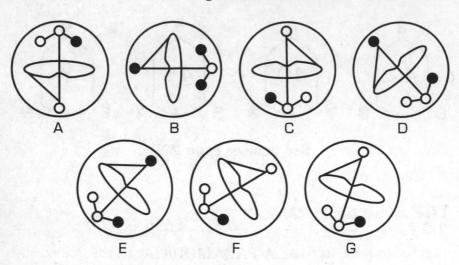

See answer page 229

145. What number should replace the question mark?

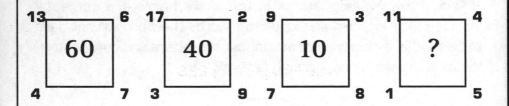

See answer page 229

146. What word is a synonym of bathos?

A. DIFFIDENT
B. DEPTH
C. NADIR
D. DEFLATE
E. DEFECTION

See answer page 229

147. If the missing letters in the two circles below are correctly inserted they will form synonymous words. The words do not have to be read in a clockwise direction, but the letters are consecutive. What are the words and missing letters?

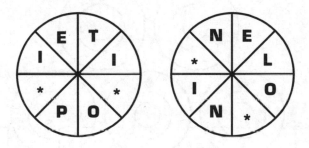

See answer page 229

148. MOOD TANS is an anagram of what eight-letter word?

See answer page 229

149. Which of the circles A, B, C, D, or E, should replace the question mark below?

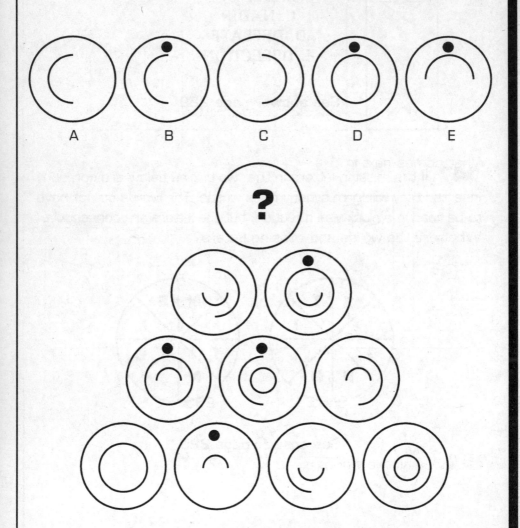

A B C D E

See answer page 229

150.

What comes next in this sequence?

A   B   C   D   E

See answer page 230

151. What two words are antonyms?

A. BARE
B. TINY
C. SAFE
D. PRODIGIOUS
E. ABUSIVE
F. FRUGAL

See answer page 230

152. What number is the odd one out?

A. 382618
B. 589411
C. 213787
D. 528572
E. 654346

See answer page 230

153. Find the starting point and move from square to adjoining square, horizontally or vertically, but not diagonally, to spell a 12-letter word, using each letter once only. What are the missing letters?

A		P
R	T	O
N	I	L
I	S	

See answer page 230

154. Simile is to comparison as onomatopoeia is to:

A. REPETITION
B. SOUND
C. VERSION
D. UNDERSTATEMENT
E. EXAGGERATION

See answer page 230

155. Which of the following is the odd one out?

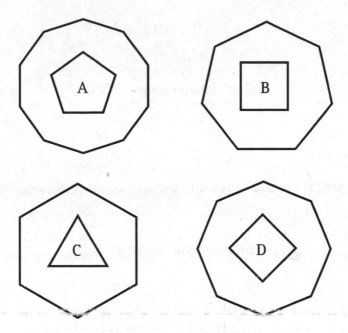

See answer page 230

156. What letter should replace the question mark?

A		E		J
D		?		M
H		L		Q

See answer page 230

157. What number comes next in this sequence?

1   3   8   19   42   ?

See answer page 230

158. HALTED CAR is an anagram of what nine-letter word?

See answer page 230

159. What number should replace the question mark?

	72	
46	16	51
	34	

	96	
38	18	43
	12	

	28	
14	?	16
	11	

See answer page 230

160.

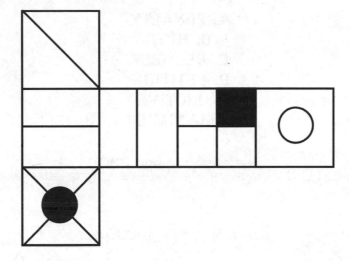

When the above is folded to form a cube, just one of the following below can be produced. What one is it?

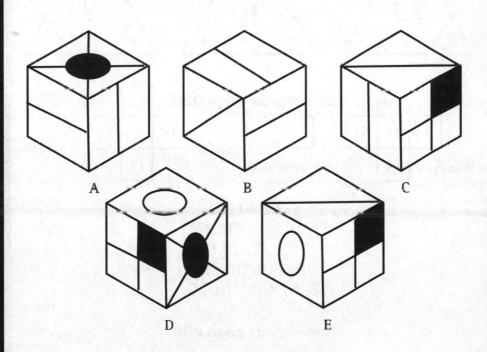

A   B   C

D   E

See answer page 230

161. What two words are synonymous?

A. PENALTY
B. HINT
C. REQUEST
D. PETITION
E. MOTIVE
F. MAXIMUM

See answer page 230

162.

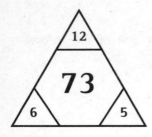 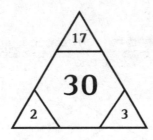 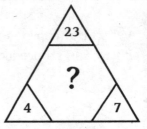

See answer page 230

163. What is the odd one out?

A. CHATEAU
B. MINSTER
C. CITADEL
D. FORTRESS
E. STRONGHOLD

See answer page 230

164. Find two words with different spellings, but sound alike, that can mean:

PORTICO / WALK

See answer page 230

165. What number should replace the question mark?

$$22 \quad 14\tfrac{1}{4} \quad 6\tfrac{1}{2} \quad ? \quad -9$$

6cc oncwor page 230

166. Insert a word in the brackets that completes the first word and starts the second one. Each dot represents a letter.

TRAM (• • • •) AGE

See answer page 230

167. Place two three-letter segments together to form a vehicle.

TER   WAY   SKY   DRO   VER   CAR

See answer page 230

168. A word can be placed in the brackets that has the same meaning as the words outside. What is it?

AVERAGE   (• • • •)   STINGY

See answer page 231

169. Find a six-letter word made up of only the following four letters.

L   E
O   G

See answer page 231

170. Which of the hexagons at the bottom, A, B, C, D, or E, should replace the question mark below?

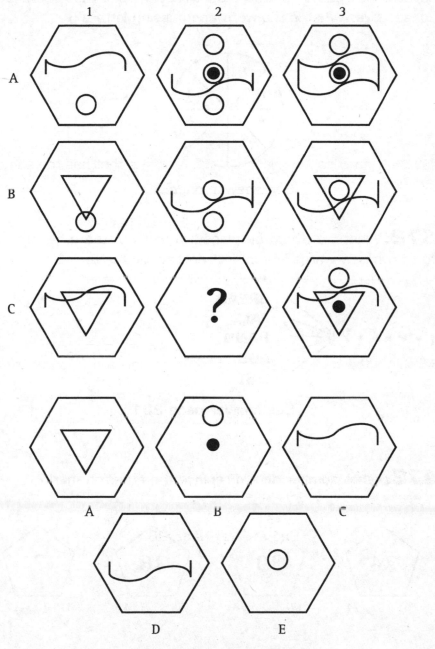

See answer page 231

171. If the missing letters in the circle below are correctly inserted they will form an eight-letter word. The word will not have to be read in a clockwise direction, but the letters are consecutive. What is the word and missing letters?

See answer page 231

172. What word can be placed in front of the other five to form five new words? Each dot represents a letter.

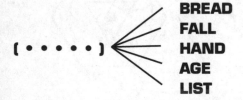

BREAD
FALL
HAND
AGE
LIST

See answer page 231

173. What number should replace the question mark?

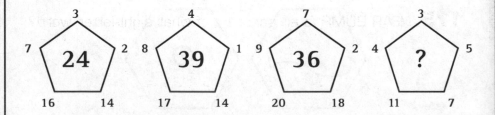

See answer page 231

174. Which of the following is the odd one out?

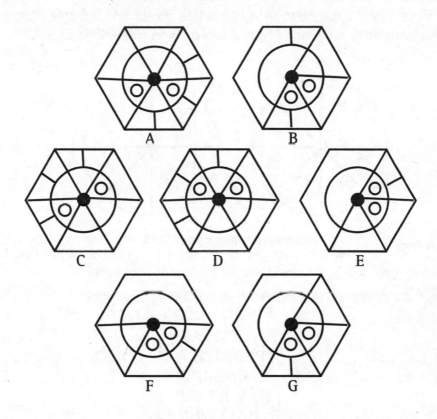

A

B

C

D

E

F

G

See answer page 231

175. NEAR BUMP is an anagram of what eight-letter word?

See answer page 231

176. If the missing letters in the two circles below are correctly inserted they will form synonymous words. The words do not have to be read in a clockwise direction, but the letters are consecutive. What are the words and missing letters?

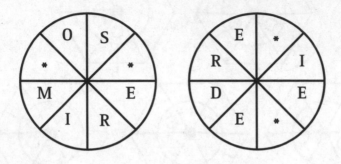

See answer page 231

177. Which of the following is not an occupation?

A. VESPIARY
B. BAILIFF
C. COURIER
D. VINTNER
E. BALLERINA

See answer page 231

178. What is a GIMCRACK?

A. BLOW
B. BAUBLE
C. JAUNTY
D. CRACKER
E. PRESS

See answer page 231

179. Which of the circles below should replace the question mark below?

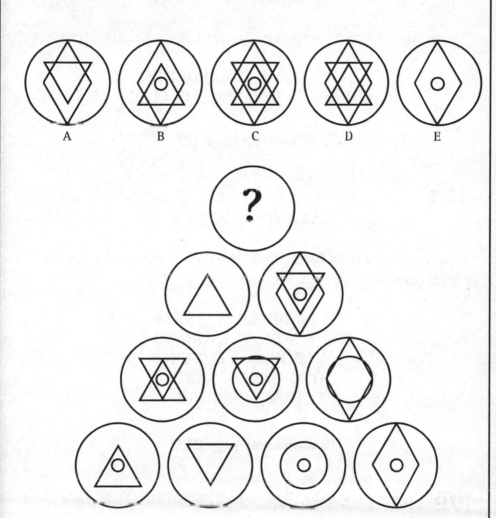

See answer page 231

180.

ROWS	(SOFTWARE)	FATE
?	(COMPLETE)	MELT

Which word below should replace the question mark above?

A. COME   B. POET
C. COPE   D. LOPE   E. CODE

See answer page 231

181.

ISLAND : WATER

Which pair of words below have the same relationship as the words above?

A. ORCHARD : TREES
B. MEADOW : GRASS
C. BOOK : COVER
D. OASIS : SAND
E. HEM : FRINGE

See answer page 231

182. What word is an antonym of ARISTOCRATIC?

A. UNKIND
B. PATRICIAN
C. LIBERAL
D. POOR
E. PLEBIAN

See answer page 231

183. How many minutes is it before 10.00 pm if, 50 minutes ago, it was four times as many minutes past 7.00 pm?

See answer page 231

184.

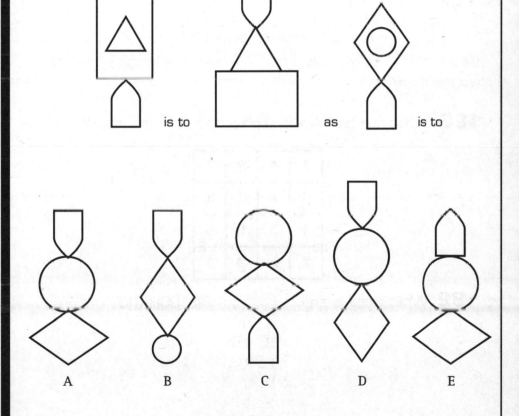

is to ... as ... is to

A   B   C   D   E

See answer page 231

185.

Which of the five boxes below is most like the box above?

A   B   C   D   E

See answer page 231

186. What number should replace the question mark?

7	4	9	2
3	1	1	3
4	7	6	5
2	2	?	4

A. 0
B. 1
C. 2
D. 3
E. 4

See answer page 231

187.

Which of the pentagons below will replace the question mark above?

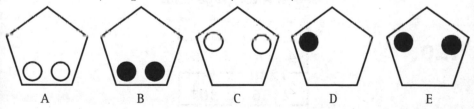

A   B   C   D   E

See answer page 232

188. What would describe STERNUTATION?

A. Heavy breathing
B. The act of sneezing
C. Shouting loudly
D. A strict upbringing
E. Bringing up the rear

See answer page 232

189. In how many ways can the word MENSA be read? Start at the central letter M and move to an adjoining letter vertically or horizontally, but not diagonally.

```
                          A
              A     A     S     A
        A     S     S     N     S     A
   A    S     S     N     E     N     S     A
A  S A  N S   E N   M E   E N   N S   A S A  A
   A    S     N     E     N     S     A
        A     S     N     E     N     S     A
              A     S     N     S     A
                    A     N     A
                          S
                          A
```

See answer page 232

190.

7240 : 905
2456 : 307

Which pair of numbers below have the same relationship as the numbers above?

A. 8056 : 98
B. 3216 : 402
C. 4824 : 36
D. 9872 : 108

See answer page 232

191.

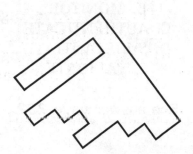

Which of the shapes below, when fitted to the piece above, will form a perfect square?

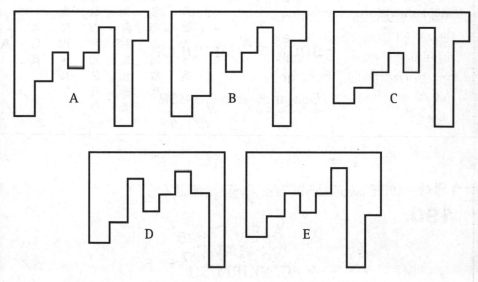

A

B

C

D

E

See answer page 232

192. What word is the odd one out?

A. VERIFY
B. MONITOR
C. AUTHENTICATE
D. SUBSTANTIATE
E. VALIDATE

See answer page 232

193. Find two words with different spellings, but sound alike, that can mean:

BOUNTY / MEDDLES

See answer page 232

194. What two words are synonymous?

A. FRACAS
B. PALAVER
C. SKIRMISH
D. PAROXYSM
E. COERCION
F. FRACTURE

See answer page 232

195. What number should replace the question mark?

$$2 \quad -\tfrac{1}{3} \quad \tfrac{1}{18} \quad ? \quad \tfrac{1}{648}$$

A. $\tfrac{1}{108}$

B. $\tfrac{1}{324}$

C. $-\tfrac{1}{324}$

D. $-\tfrac{1}{108}$

E. $\tfrac{1}{36}$

See answer page 232

196. Place two three-letter segments together to form an item of clothing.

ORA   TER   GOT   ROS   FED   RUF

See answer page 232

197. If the missing letters in the circle below are correctly inserted they will form an eight-letter word. The word will not have to be read in a clockwise direction, but the letters are consecutive. What is the word and missing letters?

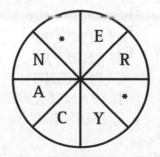

See answer page 232

198. What word can be placed in front of the other five to form five new words? Each dot represents a letter.

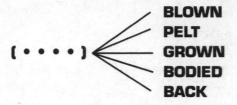

(• • • •)

BLOWN
PELT
GROWN
BODIED
BACK

See answer page 232

199. If the missing letters in the two circles below are correctly inserted they will form synonymous words. The words do not have to be read in a clockwise direction, but the letters are consecutive. What are the words and missing letters?

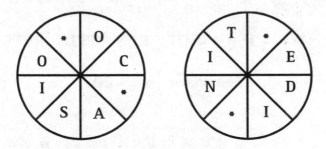

See answer page 232

200. What word is a synonym of RAILLERY?

A. CENSURE
B. SHELVES
C. FENCING
D. BANTER
E. VEHEMENCE

See answer page 232

201.

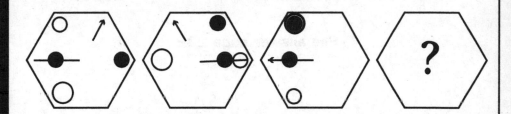

Which of the hexagons below should replace the question mark above?

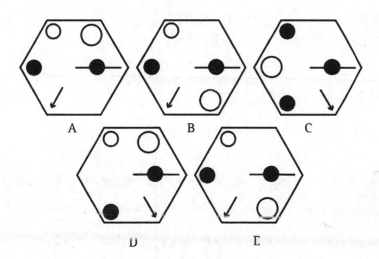

See answer page 232

202. A word can be placed in the brackets that has the same meaning as the words outside. What is it?

COMPUTER INSTRUMENT (• • • • •) RODENT

See answer page 232

203. What is the odd one out?

A. BEETLE
B. BEE
C. WASP
D. SPIDER
E. ANT

See answer page 232

204. Find a six-letter word made up of only the following four letters?

O W
L I

See answer page 232

205. Which of the circles, A, B, C, D, or E, should replace the question mark below?

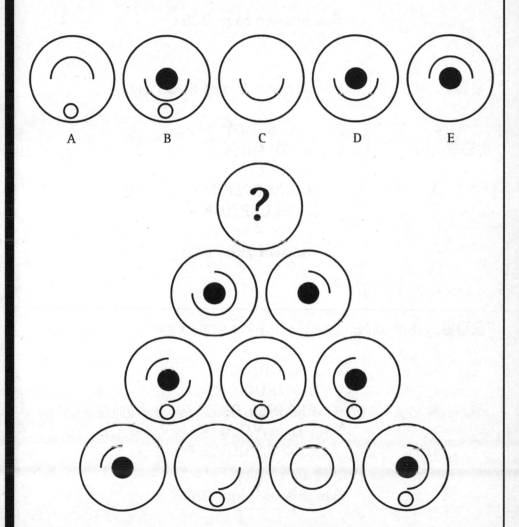

See answer page 232

206. What is the value of x?

$$(3 \times 14 \div 2) + 6 + 56 = x$$

See answer page 232

207. What word is a synonym of LUCUBRATION?

A. STUDY
B. OIL
C. DELIGHT
D. DECEPTION
E. PERCEPTION

See answer page 232

208. What word is an antonym of HEINOUS?

A. ODIOUS
B. ATROCIOUS
C. PRAISEWORTHY
D. AWFUL
E. NEFARIOUS

See answer page 232

209.

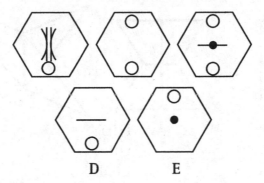

D   E

Which of the hexagons above should replace the question mark below?

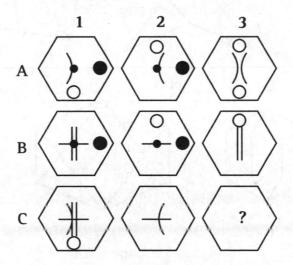

See answer page 233

210.

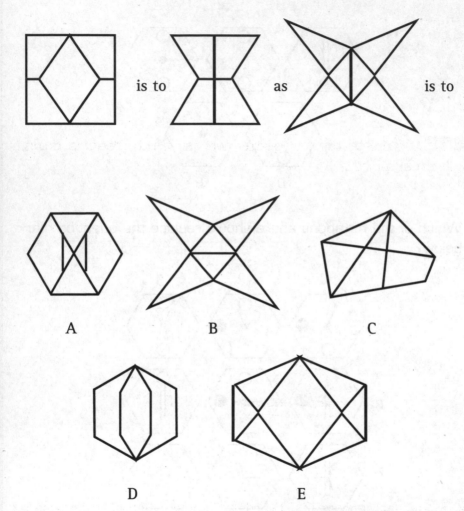

is to ... as ... is to

A B C

D E

See answer page 233

211. If one letter in each of the four words below is changed, a phrase can be found. What is it?

AN   SHE   ODE   LAND

See answer page 233

212. Complete the three-letter words, which, reading down, will reveal a bird.

E L (•)
A I (•)
S E (•)
G E (•)
S K (•)
D I (•)
P E (•)
D U (•)

See answer page 233

213. A farmer with 240 yards of fencing wishes to enclose a rectangular area of the greatest possible size. What will be the greatest area surrounded?

See answer page 233

214. Four of the pieces below can be fitted together to form a square. What is the odd one out?

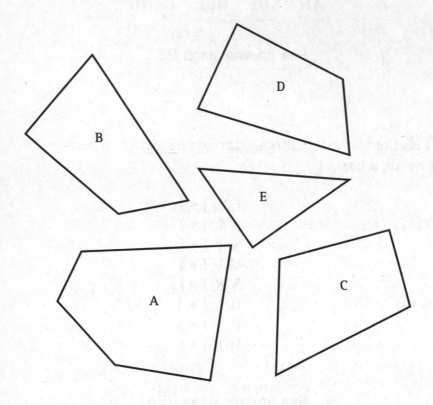

See answer page 233

215. Start at a corner square and move in a clockwise spiral to the middle to spell out a nine-letter word.
What are the missing letters?

F		S
	E	C
A	N	I

See answer page 233

216. What word is a synonym of PRINCIPLE?

A. MAJESTY
B. AXIOM
C. COST
D. CAPITAL
E. LEADER

See answer page 233

217. Find two words with different spellings, but sound alike, that can mean:

RESIDUE / FORCE AWAY

See answer page 233

218. What number should replace the question mark?

5	6	1
?	4	8
7	2	3

A. 0
B. 1
C. 2
D. 3
E. 4

See answer page 233

219. A three-word phrase, below, has had each word's initial letter removed. What is the phrase?

ETTASE

See answer page 233

220. What is the odd one out?

A. PEW
B. PULPIT
C. FONT
D. BELFRY
E. AISLE

See answer page 233

221. Which of the above hexagons is the odd one out?

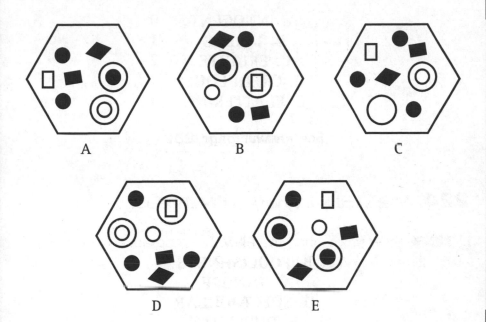

A   B   C

D   E

See answer page 233

222. What number should replace the question mark?

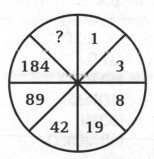

See answer page 233

223. What word is an antonym of CULPABLE?

A. INNOCENT
B. LIABLE
C. ERUDITE
D. CREDULOUS
E. FLATTERING

See answer page 233

224. What word is a synonym of IMBROGLIO?

A. ENVY
B. FOOLISHNESS
C. TANGLE
D. SPECTACULAR
E. DUPLICITY

See answer page 233

225. What word can be placed in front of the other five to form five new words or phrases? Each dot represents a letter.

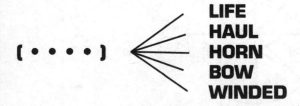

(• • • •)
LIFE
HAUL
HORN
BOW
WINDED

See answer page 233

226.

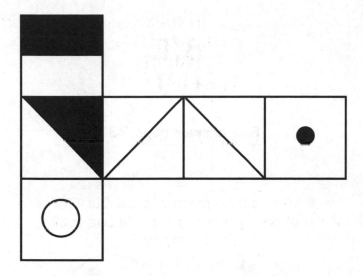

When the above is folded to form a cube, one of the figures below can be produced. What is it?

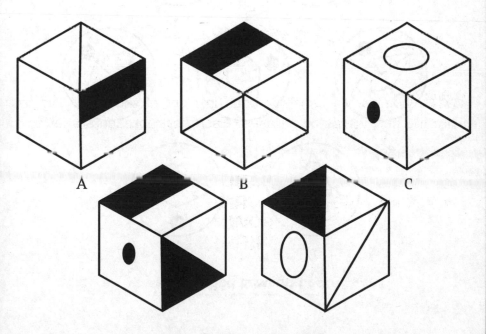

A   B   C

See answer page 233

227. Find a six-letter word made up of only the following four letters?

B E

U J

See answer page 233

228. Which of the following is the odd one out?

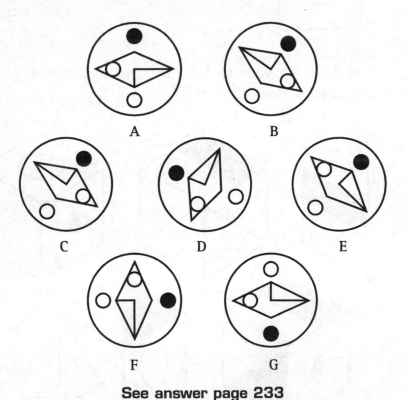

A   B

C   D   E

F   G

See answer page 233

229. Place two three-letter segments together to form a weather term.

HYR   MET   COM   ISO   ZEP   THE

See answer page 234

230. Which of the following is the opposite of TORPID?

A. SHALLOW
B. DROWSY
C. SLUGGISH
D. LETHARGIC
E. ENERGETIC

See answer page 234

231. Which of the following words is the odd one out?

A. CAPRICIOUS
B. FICKLE
C. UNSTABLE
D. SPURIOUS
E. INCONSTANT

See answer page 234

232. Which of the circles below should replace the question mark below?

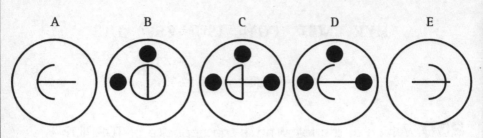

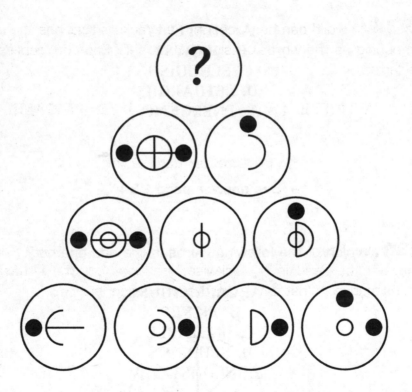

See answer page 234

233. What number should complete the series and replace the question mark?

73614   4637   764   ?

See answer page 234

234. A word can be placed in the brackets that has the same meaning as the words outside. What is it? Each dot represents a letter.

A TRIFLE (• • • • • • • • •) BALL GAME

See answer page 234

235. If the missing letters in the circle below are correctly inserted they will form an eight-letter word. The word will not have to be read in a clockwise direction, but the letters are consecutive. What is the word and missing letters?

See answer page 234

236.

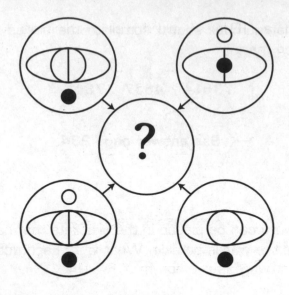

Each line and symbol that appears in the four outer circles, above, is transferred to the middle circle according to how many times it appears, as follows

One time – it is transferred
Two times – it is possibly transferred
Three times – it is transferred
Four times – it is not transferred

Which of the circles below should appear in the middle circle?

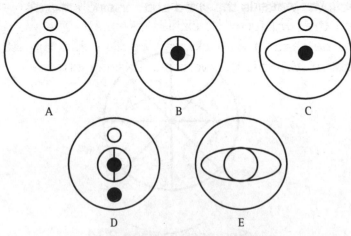

See answer page 234

237. Find a 10-letter word using adjoining letters once

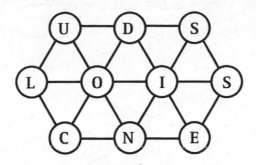

See answer page 234

238. What word is a synonym of FARRAGO?

A. A MIXTURE
B. A DANCE
C. A PLAIN
D. A TYPE OF WHEAT
E. A DINGO

See answer page 234

239. If the missing letters in the circle below are correctly inserted they will form an eight-letter word. The word will not have to be read in a clockwise direction, but the letters are consecutive. What is the word and missing letters?

See answer page 234

240. Four of the five pieces below can be fitted together to form a decagon. Which is the odd one out?

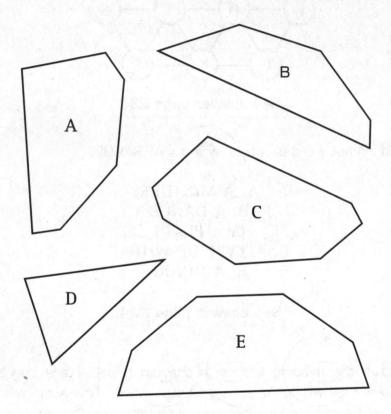

See answer page 234

241. Which of the circles, A, B, C, D, or E, should replace the question mark below?

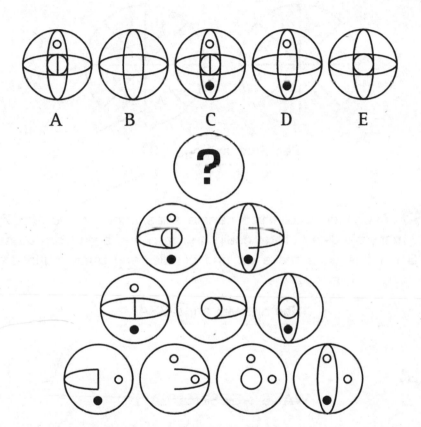

A   B   C   D   E

See answer page 234

242. If the missing letters in the two circles below are correctly inserted they will form synonymous words. The words are read in a clockwise direction, and the letters are consecutive. What are the words and missing letters?

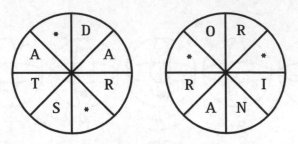

See answer page 234

243. A chandler collected candle ends until he had 2197. How many candles in total could he make and burn from these if 13 candles ends make up one candle, and these ends are collected and reused?

See answer page 234

244.

WAVE : GESTICULATE

Which pair of words below have the same relationship as the words above?

A. RUN : SAUNTER
B. KICK : GENUFLECT
C. SNORE : ANNOY
D. LAUGH : CHANT
E. WINK : NICTITATE

See answer page 234

245.

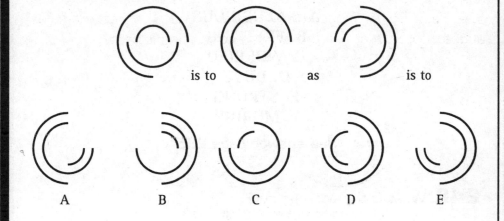

is to   as   is to

A   B   C   D   E

See answer page 234

246. What number is missing from the third column?

18   24   54

15   40   15

6   3   ?

See answer page 234

247. What two words are antonymous?

A. SALUBRIOUS
B. FRETTING
C. WORRIED
D. BUSY
E. STRONG
F. MORBID

See answer page 235

248. What is the odd one out?

A. HOLE
B. ICE
C. ELEPHANT
D. LEG
E. SEA

See answer page 235

249.

4986 : 1314 : 45

What series has the same relationship as the one above?

A. 2386 : 1314 : 45
B. 7842 : 1513 : 64
C. 7217 : 1862 : 34
D. 9875 : 1217 : 83
E. 8795 : 1514 : 65

See answer page 235

250.

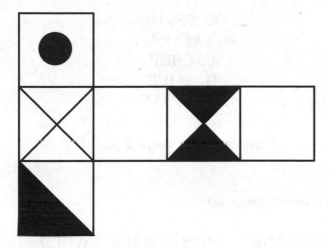

When the above is folded to form a cube, one of the figures below can be produced. What is it?

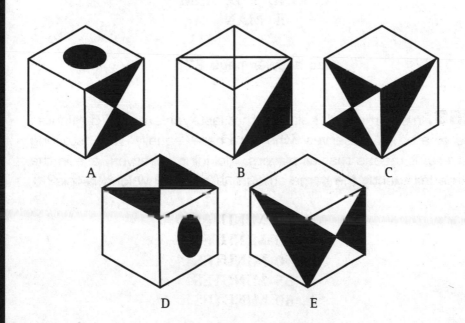

A   B   C

D   E

See answer page 235

251. KNIFE is to CUT as CLEAVER is to?

A. SEVER
B. LACERATE
C. CHOP
D. SLICE
E. IMPALE

See answer page 235

252. What word goes with:

AGE   PORT   ABLE   WORD

A. LIKE   B. OVER
C. KIND   D. ARM
E. MAN

See answer page 235

253. In a game of 12 players that lasts for exactly 75 minutes there are six reserves who alternate equally with starting players. It means that all players, including reserves, are in the game for exactly the same amount of time. How long is this?

A. 30 MINUTES
B. 40 MINUTES
C. 50 MINUTES
D. 55 MINUTES
E. 60 MINUTES

See answer page 235

254. What two words are synonymous?

A. NOISY
B. WORTHY
C. LOWLY
D. LAUDABLE
E. COMPLIMENTARY
F. FROTHY

See answer page 235

255.

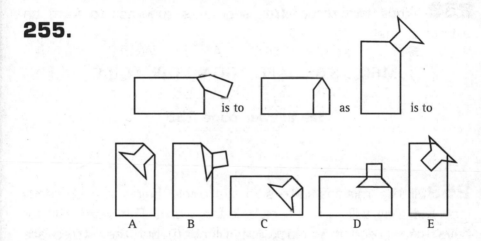

See answer page 235

256. What is the group noun for a number of LEOPARDS?

A. CHIP
B. HUNT
C. STRIDE
D. PACK
E. LEAP

See answer page 235

257. What two words are synonymous?

A. JAUNT
B. JUMP
C. INSULT
D. OUTING
E. PROMISE
F. IMAGINE

See answer page 235

258. Place two three-letter segments together to form an extinct animal.

MBO   STU   AFE   GGA   GIR   QUA

See answer page 235

259. If the missing letters in the circle below are correctly inserted they will form an eight-letter word. The word will not have to be read in a clockwise direction, but the letters are consecutive. What is the word and missing letters?

See answer page 235

260.

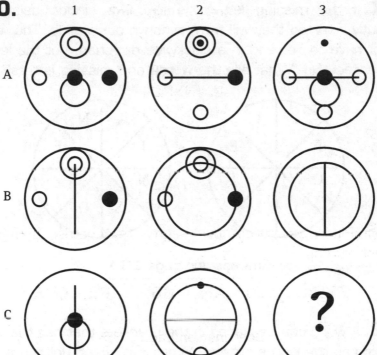

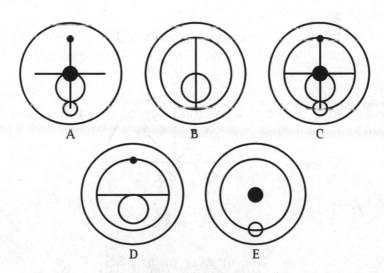

Which of the circles below should replace the question mark above?

See answer page 235

261. If the missing letters in the two circles below are correctly inserted they will form synonymous words. The words do not have to be read in a clockwise direction, but the letters are consecutive. What are the words and missing letters?

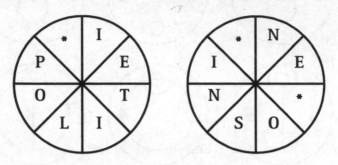

See answer page 235

262. A word can be placed in the brackets that has the same meaning as the words outside. What is it? Each dot represents a letter.

TREE (• • • •) YEARN

See answer page 235

263. Find a six-letter word made up of only the following four letters?

S H
A R

See answer page 235

264. What word is an antonym of LIEGE?

A. LORD
B. VASSAL
C. SOVEREIGN
D. FORTRESS
E. NUNCIO

See answer page 235

265. What word is a synonym of NUBILE?

A. LITHE
B. MARRIAGEABLE
C. INEBRIATED
D. LISSOM
E. SUPPLE

See answer page 235

266. What word can be placed in front of the other five to form five new words or phrases? Each dot represents a letter.

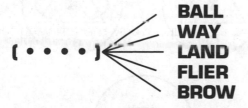

BALL
WAY
LAND
FLIER
BROW

See answer page 235

267.

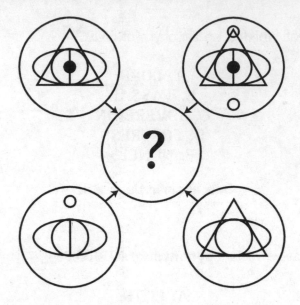

Each line and symbol that appears in the four outer circles, above, is transferred to the middle circle according to how many times it appears, as follows:

One time — it is transferred
Two times — it is possibly transferred
Three times — it is transferred
Four times — it is not transferred

Which of the options below should appear as the middle circle?

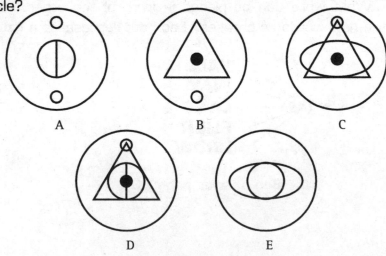

See answer page 235

268. If the missing letter in the circle below is correctly inserted it will form an eight-letter word. The word will not have to be read in a clockwise direction, but the letters are consecutive. What is the word and missing letter?

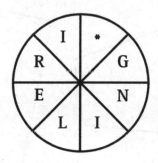

See answer page 235

269. What is a SHADOOF?

A. A SHADOWY FIGURE
B. A RESERVOIR
C. A DAM
D. A WATER-RAISING CONTRAPTION
E. A RUNNING STREAM

See answer page 235

270.

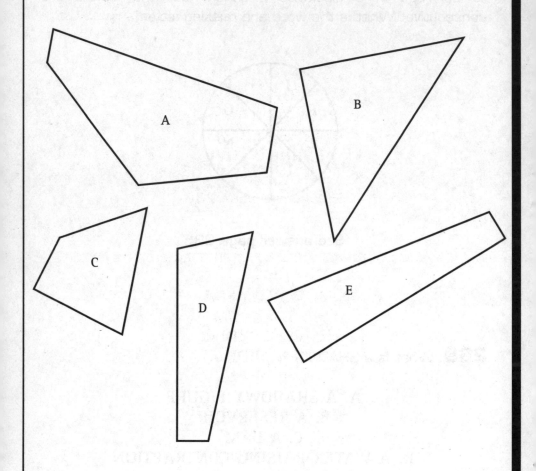

See answer page 236

271.

PHILANDER : FLIRT

Which pair of words below have the same relationship as the words above?

A. OBTAIN : FIND
B. MISTRUST : MISTREAT
C. PROSAIC : UNUSUAL
D. GREET : SALUTE
E. HUG : LOVE

See answer page 236

272. Which of the following is not an anagram of a reptile?

A. ON CANADA
B. TIN ROOM
C. COOL CIDER
D. CAROB
E. BIT HAUL

See answer page 236

273. What number is the odd one out?

A. 36119
B. 22515
C. 57624
D. 28918
E. 90030

See answer page 236

274.

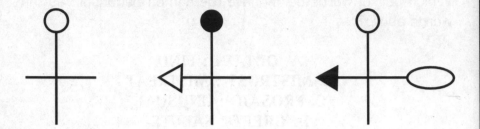

Which of the figures below will continue the sequence above?

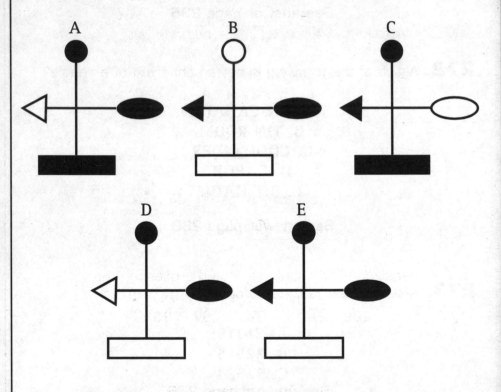

See answer page 236

275. What words are antonymous?

A. CHANGE
B. ADMIRE
C. SOOTHE
D. STIR
E. VEX
F. EXPAND

See answer page 236

276. Which of the following is the odd one out?

A. FEMUR
B. PATELLA
C. FIBULA
D. ULNA
E. TIBIA

See answer page 236

277. What number should replace the question mark?

100   99.5   90.5   97   95   ?

See answer page 236

278. Complete the two words using the letters of the following once only.

IDLING TURN

• A • • T • E •   • A • • T • E •

See answer page 236

279. CRISIS (PRAISE) SPREAD

Following the same rules as above, what word should go in the brackets?

REPOSE (• • • • • •) ARENAS

See answer page 236

280. What number replaces the question mark?

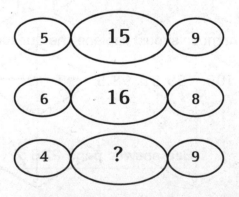

See answer page 236

281.

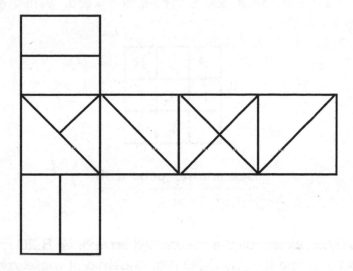

When the above is folded to form a cube, one of the figures below can be produced. What is it?

A   B   C

D   E

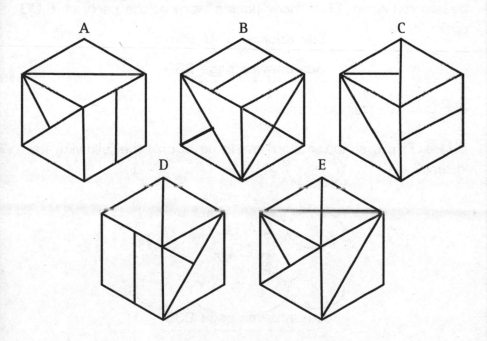

See answer page 236

282. Start at a corner square and move in a clockwise spiral to the middle to spell out a nine-letter word. What are the missing letters?

E		H
F	T	E
	R	A

See answer page 236

283. By 8.00 pm, all the guests had arrived. By 8.30 pm, one-third of them had left. By 9.30 pm, one-third of those remaining had also departed. By 11.00 pm, the same had happened again, and one-third of those remaining had gone. After this, only 16 guests remained. How many guests were at the party at 8.00 pm?

See answer page 236

284. Find a six-letter word made up of only the following four letters?

E L
T Y

See answer page 236

285.

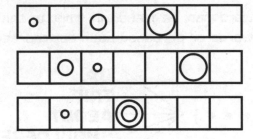

What should continue the sequence above?

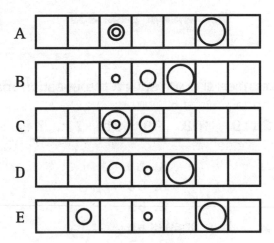

A

B

C

D

E

See answer page 236

286. If the missing letters in the circle below are correctly inserted they will form an eight letter word. The word will not have to be read in a clockwise direction, but the letters are consecutive. What is the word and missing letters?

See answer page 237

287. What word can be placed in front of the other five to form five new words or phrases? Each dot represents a letter.

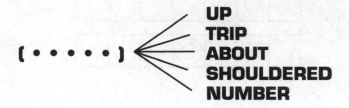

(• • • • •)

UP
TRIP
ABOUT
SHOULDERED
NUMBER

See answer page 237

288. What number should replace the question mark?

119   108   99   81   72   ?

A. 63
B. 64
C. 65
D. 66
E. 67

See answer page 237

289. A word can be placed in the brackets that has the same meaning as the words outside. What is it? Each dot represents a letter.

HORSE STRAP (• • • • • • • • • •) GAMBLING
TERM

See answer page 237

290.

If 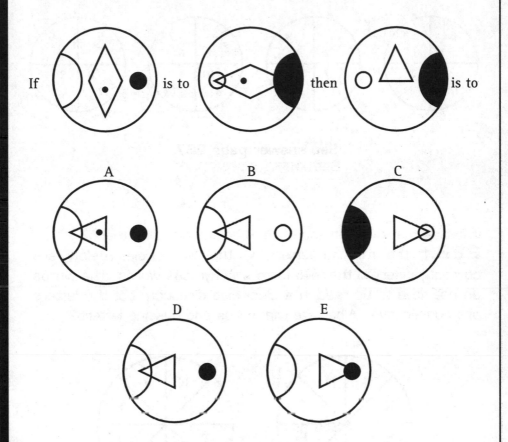 is to ... then ... is to

See answer page 237

291. What number should replace the question mark?

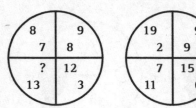 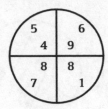

See answer page 237

292. If the missing letters in the two circles below are correctly inserted they will form synonymous words. The words do not have to be read in a clockwise direction, but the letters are consecutive. What are the words and missing letters?

 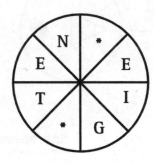

See answer page 237

293. Place two three-letter segments together to form a fish.

ENT   LET   PIK   MUL   GER   PAR

See answer page 237

294. Which of the following is the odd one out?

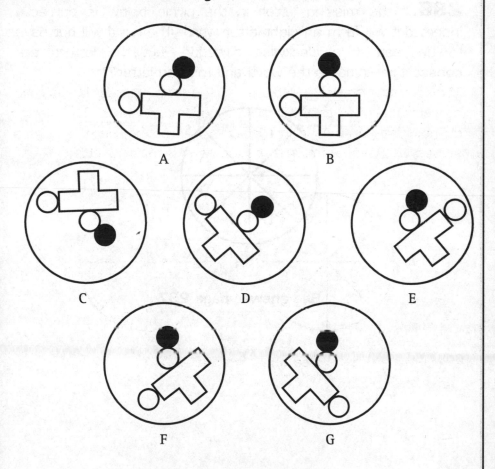

A

B

C   D   E

F   G

See answer page 237

295. If one letter in each of the four words below is changed, a phrase can be found. What is it?

SIN   OF   SHE   HENCE

See answer page 237

296. If the missing letter in the circle below is correctly inserted it will form an eight-letter word. The word will not have to be read in a clockwise direction, but the letters are consecutive. What is the word and missing letter?

See answer page 237

297. Which number continues this sequence?

1		3	6		10		12
	3	5		3		3	?

See answer page 237

298. What word is a synonym of JOCOSE?

A. MISERLY
B. MISERABLE
C. COMICAL
D. GENEROUS
E. IMPARTIAL

See answer page 237

299. Which of the hexagons at the bottom should replace the question mark below?

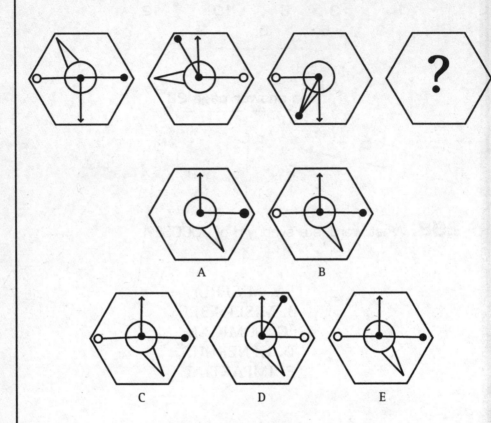

A   B

C   D   E

See answer page 237

300. Which three of the five pieces below can be fitted together to form a cuboid?

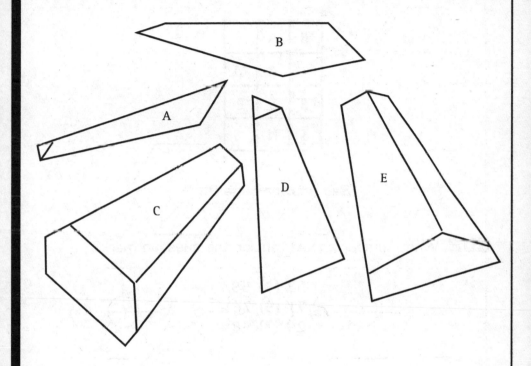

A. ACD
B. ABC
C. CDE
D. BCD
E. ADE

See answer page 237

301. Find the starting point and move from square to adjoining square, horizontally or vertically, but not diagonally, to spell a 12-letter word, using each letter once only. What are the missing letters?

R	A	
	A	M
S	S	E
I	N	

See answer page 237

302. What number should replace the question mark?

53 (3) 59
71 (9) 79
29 (?) 98

See answer page 237

303. THREE MEN EXIT is an anagram of a three-word phrase that could also be "the highest degree". What is the phrase?

See answer page 238

304. Find two words with different spellings, but sound alike, that can mean:

SCREEN / HURRIED

See answer page 238

305. What number should replace the question mark?

3   9   11   33   35   ?

See answer page 238

306. What two words are antonymous?

A. REFRESHING
B. INVITING
C. KIND
D. SENSIBLE
E. WISE
F. INVIDIOUS

See answer page 238

307.

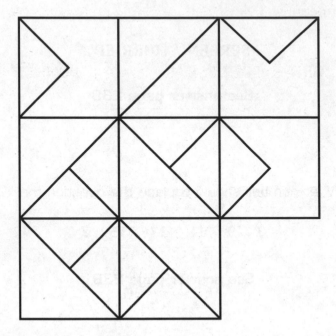

Which of the squares below will go in the blank space above?

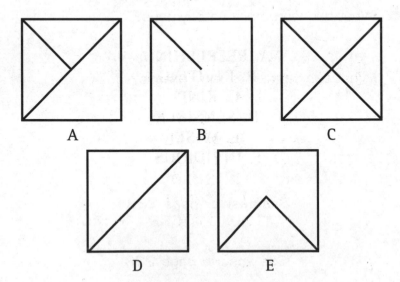

A   B   C

D   E

See answer page 238

308. A word can be placed in the brackets that has the same meaning as the words outside. What is it? Each dot represents a letter.

GREEK GODDESS (• • • •) PONDER

See answer page 238

309. CLIP is to BROOCH as TORQUE is to?

A. CROWN
B. NECKCHAIN
C. HEADBAND
D. EARRING
E. RING

See answer page 238

310. What two words are synonymous?

A. BAN
B. BANAL
C. FIT
D. HOLD
E. PERMIT
F. PROSCRIBE

See answer page 238

311. What positive number replaces the question mark?

2	4	2
16	12	48
8	12	?

See answer page 238

312. What word is the odd one out?

A. VARIETY
B. SPECIES
C. BREED
D. STOCK
E. STRAIN

See answer page 238

313. What is the essential ingredient of SAUERKRAUT?

A. PEPPERS
B. CHEESE
C. SQUID
D. SAUSAGE
E. CABBAGE

See answer page 238

314.

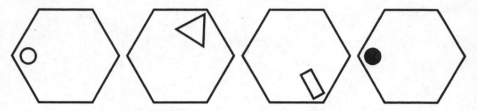

Which of the hexagons below will continue the above sequence?

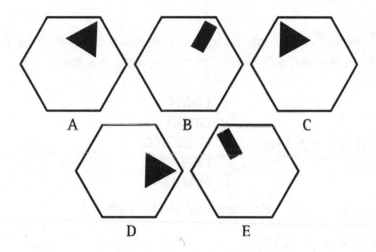

315. What number replaces the question mark?

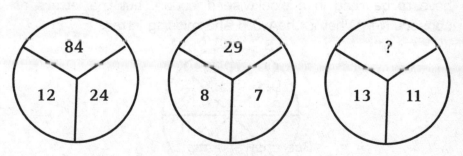

See answer page 238

316. Find a six-letter word made up of only the following four letters?

L B
P E

See answer page 238

317. What word can be placed in front of the other five to form five new words? Each dot represents a letter.

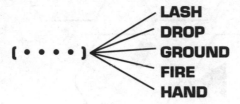

(• • • •)

LASH
DROP
GROUND
FIRE
HAND

See answer page 238

318. If the missing letters in the circle below are correctly inserted they will form an eight-letter word. The word will not have to be read in a clockwise direction, but the letters are consecutive. What is the word and missing letters?

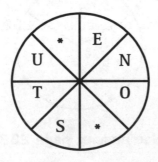

See answer page 238

319. Which of the following is the odd one out?

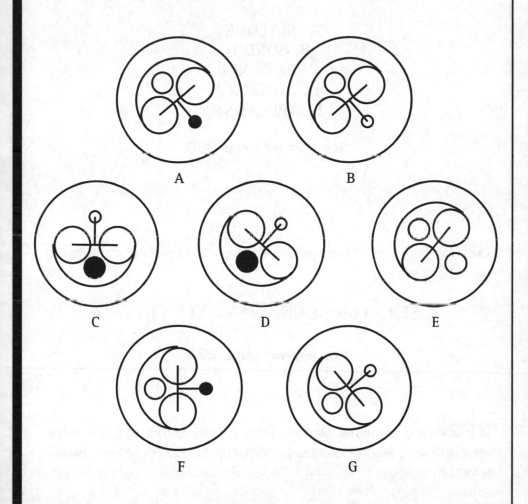

See answer page 238

320. What word has the same meaning as ECLAT?

A. JEALOUSY
B. SORDID
C. PATIENCE
D. MYSTERY
E. APPLAUSE

See answer page 238

321. Place two three-letter segments together to form a nautical item.

SER   FUN   GUN   VAN   ELS   HAW

See answer page 238

322. A word can be placed in the brackets that has the same meaning as the words outside. What is it? Each dot represents a letter.

MOVE ON ITS AXIS (• • •) COOKING UTENSIL

See answer page 238

323. If the missing letters in the two circles below are correctly inserted they will form synonymous words. The words do not have to be read in a clockwise direction, but the letters are consecutive. What are the words and missing letters?

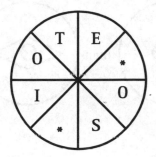 

See answer page 238

324. What is the difference between the lowest cube number and the highest square number?

10	17	80	41
36	4	10	26
25	14	7	8
19	11	190	23

See answer page 238

325.

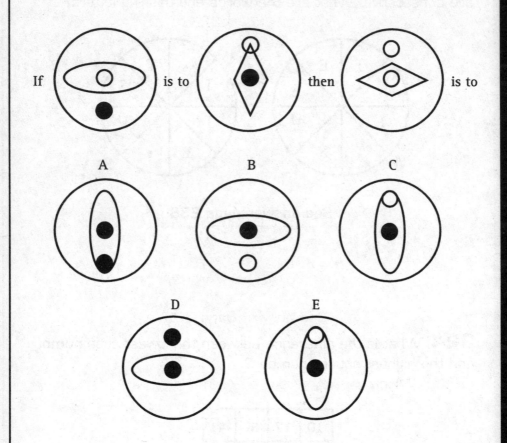

See answer page 238

326. What is the group noun for a number of OWLS?

A. GAGGLE
B. FLOCK
C. PARLIAMENT
D. MURMURATION
E. FLIGHT

See answer page 239

327. What is a synonym of GENUFLECT?

A. ACCENTUATE
B. BREATHE HEAVILY
C. GIVE WAY
D. CLEAR THE THROAT
E. BEND THE KNEE

See answer page 239

328. Which two words are antonymous?

A. ENTANGLE
B. COVERT
C. ASSUAGE
D. IRRITATE
E. BRANDISH

See answer page 239

329.

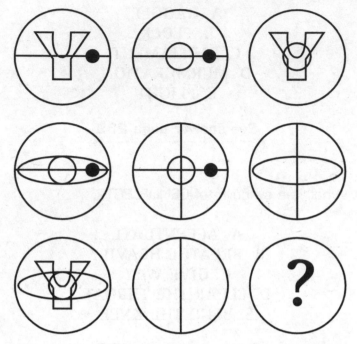

Which of the circles above should replace the question mark below?

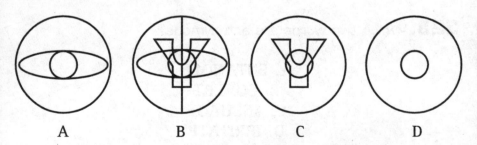

A   B   C   D

See answer page 239

330. Which three of the five pieces below can be fitted together to form a perfect square?

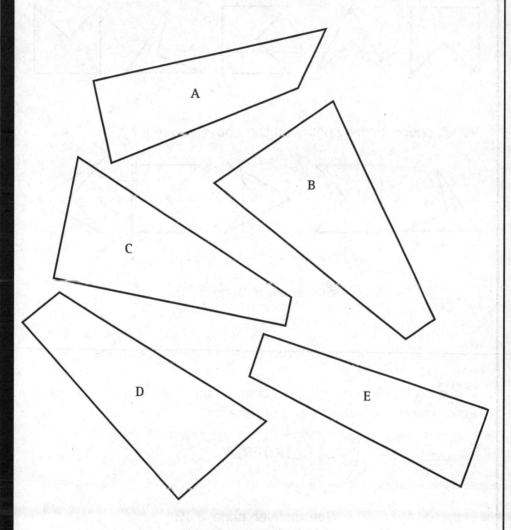

A. ABC
B. BDE
C. BCD
D. ADE
E. ACD

See answer page 239

331.

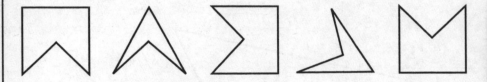

What option below continues the above sequence?

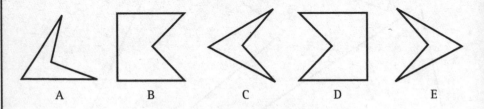

A   B   C   D   E

See answer page 239

332.

A three-word phrase, below, has had each word's initial letter removed. What is the phrase?

IRDFREY

See answer page 239

333. What number should replace the question mark?

$$0 \quad 1 \quad 5 \quad 14 \quad 30 \quad ?$$

See answer page 239

334. If one letter in each of the four words below is changed, a phrase can be found. What is it?

TALE FAR I RUDE

See answer page 239

335. A train, 0.25 miles long, going at a speed of 40mph enters a tunnel that is 2.25 miles long. How long does it take for all of the train to pass through the tunnel from the moment the front enters it, to the moment the rear emerges?

See answer page 239

336.

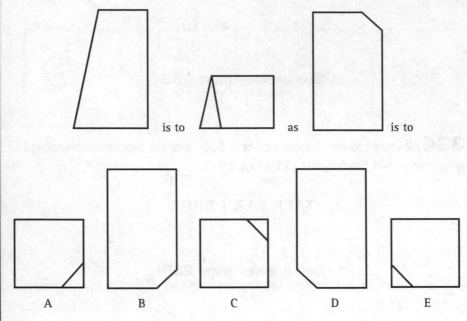

is to ... as ... is to

A   B   C   D   E

See answer page 239

337. To which square from the five at the bottom can a dot be added so that it meets the same conditions as the box below?

A   B   C   D   E

See answer page 239

338. Which of the following is the odd one out?

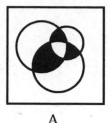 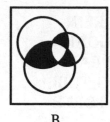  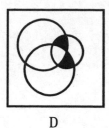

A   B   C   D

See answer page 239

339. Start at a corner square and move in a clockwise spiral to the middle to spell out a nine-letter word. What are the missing letters?

T	E	R
	D	E
E		F

See answer page 239

340. Which of the following is not an anagram of a form of transport?

A. RAIL REIN
B. NOD GOAL
C. OLD PEAR
D. AIM LOO TUBE
E. CARVE FORTH

See answer page 239

341. WIMBLE is to DRILL as ROUTER is to?

A. SAW
B. SHAPE
C. WRENCH
D. HIT
E. CUT

See answer page 240

342. What word is a synonym of SALUTARY?

A. WELCOMING
B. SINGULAR
C. GLOWING
D. CRINGING
E. BENEFICIAL

See answer page 240

343.

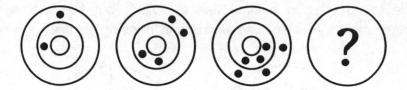

What figure below continues the sequence above?

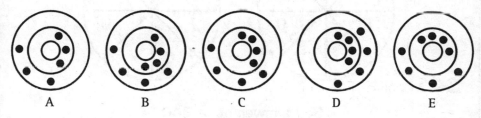

A   B   C   D   E

See answer page 240

344. What number replaces the question mark

7	3	4	8
9	11	?	5
6	9	4	1
4	1	1	4

See answer page 240

345. If the missing letters in the two circles below are correctly inserted they will form related words. The words do not have to be read in a clockwise direction, but the letters are consecutive. What are the words and missing letters?

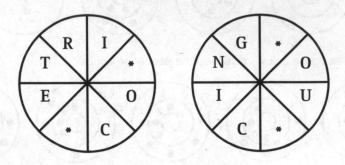

See answer page 240

346. Find a six-letter word made up of only the following four letters?

L B
F E

See answer page 240

347. Place two three-letter segments to form a bird?

RAN   LEW   ROW   TIT   CUR   SPA

See answer page 240

348. What word can be placed in front of the other five to form five new words? Each dot represents a letter.

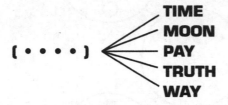

(• • • •)

TIME
MOON
PAY
TRUTH
WAY

See answer page 240

349. Which word is a synonym of SPINDRIFT?

A. FLOTSAM
B. SEA-SPRAY
C. SPINNAKER
D. TOPSAIL
E. RUDDER-BEARING

See answer page 240

350. A word can be placed in the brackets that has the same meaning as the words outside. What is it? Each dot represents a letter.

BASKET (• • • • • •) IMPEDE

See answer page 240

351.

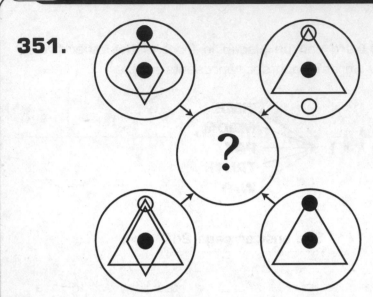

Each line and symbol that appears in the four outer circles, above, is transferred to the middle circle according to how many times it appears, as follows:

One time — it is transferred
Two times — it is possibly transferred
Three times — it is transferred
Four times — it is not transferred

Which of the circles below should appear in the middle circle?

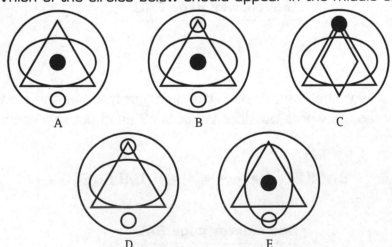

See answer page 240

352. What number should replace the question mark?

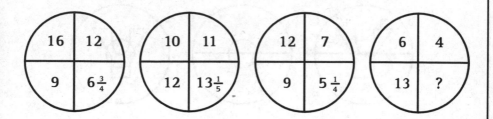

See answer page 240

353. If the missing letters are inserted they will form a word describing location. What is it?

See answer page 240

354.

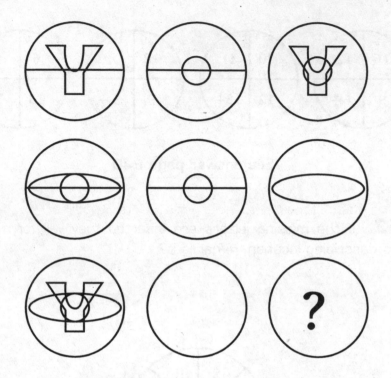

What circle should replace the question mark?

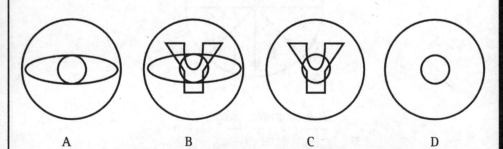

| A | B | C | D |

See answer page 240

355. What is a CARBONADE?

A. NECKWEAR
B. POACHER'S GUN
C. BEEF STEW
D. SOFT DRINK
E. BELT FOR BULLETS

See answer page 240

356. Place three two-letter segments together to form another word for falseness.

DE   MB   SW   UG   IN   HU   DL

See answer page 240

357. What is the group noun for a number of PARTRIDGES?

A. COVEY
B. SEDGE
C. WEDGE
D. FLOCK
E. DRIFT

See answer page 240

358. What word is a synonym of EXIGENCY?

A. INNUENDO
B. CIRCUITOUSLY
C. NECESSITY
D. DELUSION
E. DEVOUTNESS

See answer page 240

359.

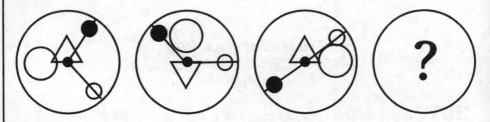

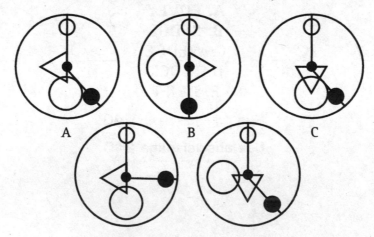

What circle will continue the sequence?

A   B   C

See answer page 240

360.

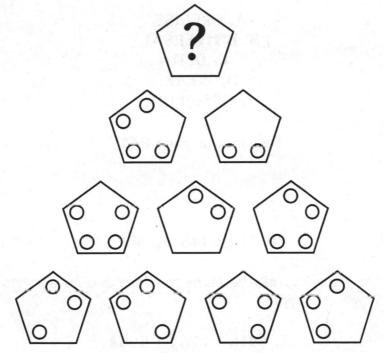

Which of the pentagons below should replace the question mark?

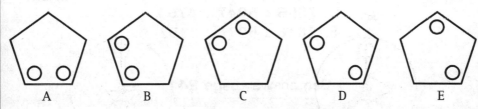

A   B   C   D   E

See answer page 240

361. What word is a synonym of GENERIC?

A. PRECISE
B. UNIVERSAL
C. OLD
D. WEAK
E. COMPLETE

See answer page 241

362.

4627 : 6445 : 8263

Which series below has the same relationship as the series above?

A. 5916 : 7734 : 9552
B. 4763 : 3854 : 2945
C. 1234 : 3214 : 4123
D. 7856 : 6947 : 4769
E. 2846 : 5971 : 8352

See answer page 241

363. EPIC PROSE is an anagram of what nine-letter word?

See answer page 241

364. Start at a corner square and move in a clockwise spiral to the middle to spell out a nine-letter word. What are the missing letters?

	O	
A	L	A
C	I	N

See answer page 241

365. Which of the following pentagons in the odd one out?

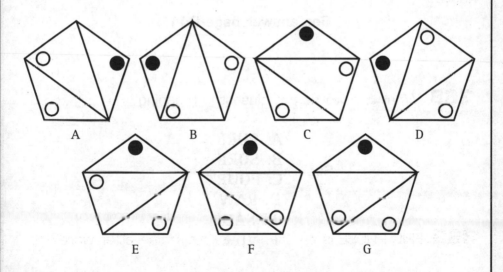

A   B   C   D

E   F   G

See answer page 241

366. If one letter in each of the three words below is changed, a phrase can be found. What is it?

ALL AS BASE

See answer page 241

367. Which of the following is the odd one out?

A. MOCHA
B. TAWNY
C. TEAL
D. UMBER
E. BEIGE

See answer page 241

368. What two words are closest in meaning?

A. PURE
B. SORE
C. POUR
D. RAW
E. SAD
F. VILE

See answer page 241

369. What word is an antonym of WOOLLY?

A. FLEXIBLE
B. REGULAR
C. PRECISE
D. RARE
E. NEBULOUS

See answer page 241

370. EGGPLANT is to AUBERGINE as ZUCCHINI is to?

A. BREADFRUIT
B. SORREL
C. CAPSICUM
D. COURGETTE
E. ARTICHOKE

See answer page 241

371. Find two words with different spellings, but sound alike, that can mean:

WAN / BUCKET

See answer page 241

372. Which three of the five pieces below can be fitted together to form a perfect square?

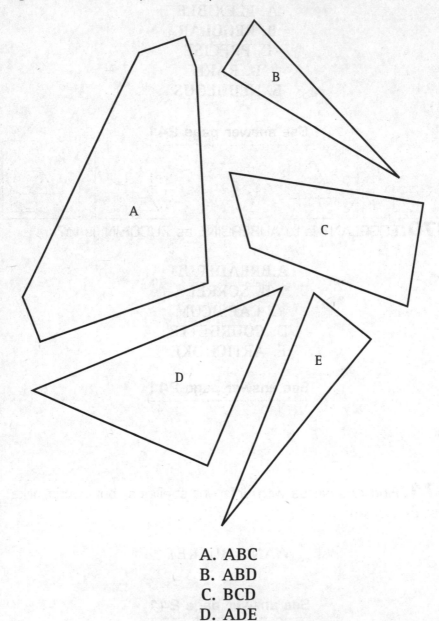

A. ABC
B. ABD
C. BCD
D. ADE
E. CDE

See answer page 241

373. To which square at the bottom, A, B, C, D, or E, can a dot be added so that it meets the conditions in the box above them?

A　　　　B　　　　C　　　　D　　　　E

See answer page 241

374. What word goes with the following?

RED　KING　TAN

A. LET
B. ROW
C. CAT
D. MAT
E. PAT

See answer page 241

375. Place three two-letter segments together to form a word for a system of magic.

RO OD AS VO ST OO LO

See answer page 241

376. What number should replace the question mark?

6 7 2 9 −2 11 ?

See answer page 241

377. A word can be placed in the brackets that has the same meaning as the words outside. What is it? Each dot represents a letter.

POST (• • • • •) ANTE

See answer page 241

378. If the missing letters in the circle below are correctly inserted they will form an eight-letter word. The word will not have to be read in a clockwise direction, but the letters are consecutive. What is the word and missing letters?

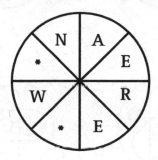

See answer page 241

379. If the missing letters in the two circles below are correctly inserted they will form synonymous words. The words do not have to be read in a clockwise direction, but the letters are consecutive. What are the words and missing letters?

See answer page 241

380.

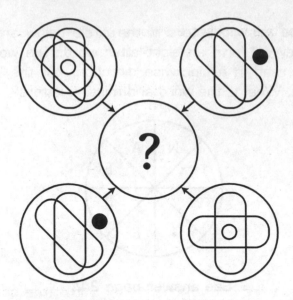

Each line and symbol that appears in the four outer circles, above, is transferred to the middle circle according to how many times it appears, as follows:

One time — it is transferred
Two times — it is possibly transferred
Three times — it is transferred
Four times — it is not transferred

Which of the circles below should appear as the middle circle?

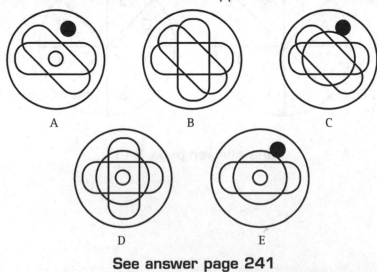

See answer page 241

381. What two words are antonymous?

A. ANXIETY
B. ARISTOCRACY
C. PRELUDE
D. CELEBRATED
E. PROLETARIAT

See answer page 241

382. What word can be placed in front of the other five to form five new words? Each dot represents a letter.

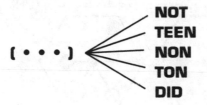

(• • •)
NOT
TEEN
NON
TON
DID

See answer page 241

383. Find a six-letter word made up of only the following four letters?

H E
C R

See answer page 241

384.

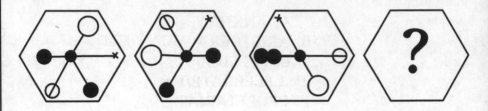

Which of the hexagons below should replace the question mark above?

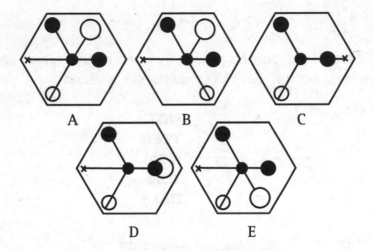

A
B
C

D
E

See answer page 241

385. What word is a synonym of FLACCID?

A. TENUOUS
B. SPASMODIC
C. FLABBY
D. ROBUST
E. FASTIDIOUS

See answer page 242

386. Place two three-letter segments together to form a weapon.

GEL   PIS   DAG   CUD   GON   GIT

See answer page 242

387. What is the group noun given to a number of HERMITS?

A. COLLECTION
B. CLAN
C. DWELLING
D. GATHERING
E. OBSERVANCE

See answer page 242

388. What word is the antonym of LACONIC?

A. SENTENTIOUS
B. SUCCINCT
C. LOQUACIOUS
D. SCANTINESS
E. APPREHENSIVE

See answer page 242

389. Each of the nine squares in the grid marked 1A to 3C should incorporate all of the items which are shown in the squares of the same letter and number, at the left and top, respectively. For example, 2B should incorporate all of the symbols that are in squares 2 and B. One square, however, is incorrect. Which one is it?

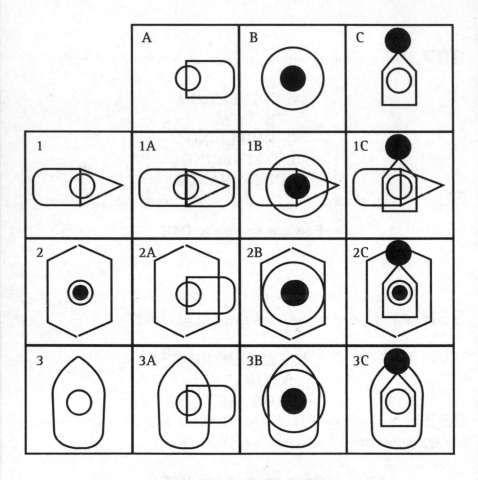

See answer page 242

390. Find two synonymous words in the inner and outer spirals of the circle below, one reading clockwise, the other anti-(counter) clockwise. What are the words and missing letters ?

See answer page 242

391. Complete the two words using the letters of the following once only.

FIND MRS BILGE

• • S • E • • E •   • • S • E • • E •

See answer page 242

392. What number should continue the sequence and replace the question mark?

1 2 5 14 41 122 ?

See answer page 242

393. What word is an antonym of PSEUDO?

A. NORMAL
B. ARTIFICIAL
C. PRUDENT
D. AUTHENTIC
E. PROVISION

See answer page 242

394. Which of the following in the odd one out?

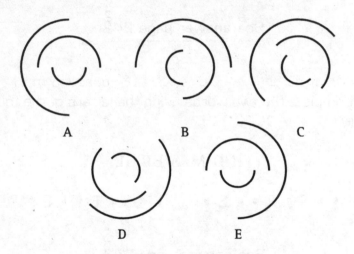

See answer page 242

395. Which of the following is the odd one out?

A. GOAT
B. BULL
C. CHICKEN
D. LION
E. RAM

See answer page 242

396. Complete the three-letter words which, reading down, will reveal an animal.

H E (•)
F O (•)
L E (•)
S I (•)
H A (•)
A R (•)
W O (•)
B A (•)

See answer page 242

397. What number should replace the question mark?

9768   7488   3744 ?

A. 2516
B. 2732
C. 2814
D. 2816
E. 2852

See answer page 242

398. What word is a synonym of DISINTERESTED?

A. IMPARTIAL
B. STRONG
C. STAUNCH
D. IMPETURBABLE
E. ODD

See answer page 242

399. Start at a corner square and move in a clockwise spiral to the middle to spell out a nine-letter word. What are the missing letters?

U		S
T	E	I
A	N	

See answer page 242

400.

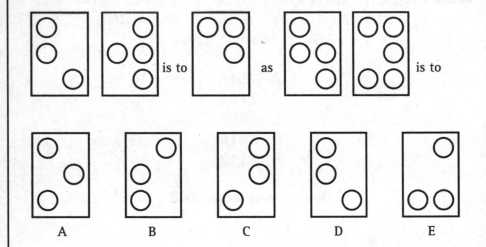

A	B	C	D	E

See answer page 242

401.

EPISTLE : LETTER

Which pair of words below has the same relationship as the pair above?

A. HOMILY : FAREWELL
B. ACRONYM : OPPOSITE
C. LEXICON : ORIGIN
D. EPITHET : NAME
E. SYNTAX : REVENUE

See answer page 242

402.

SUDDEN MOMENT TUMULT WEANING

What comes next?

A. CHARMING
B. PRECIPITATION
C. THEME
D. HARMONY
E. CONGRATULATE

See answer page 242

403. If one letter in each of the three words below is changed, a phrase can be found. What is it?

FIND ANY CANDY

See answer page 242

404.

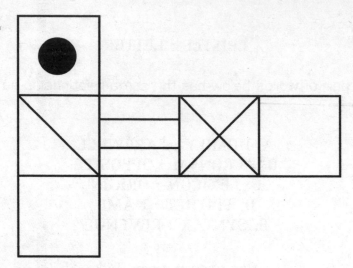

When the above is folded to form a cube, just one of the following can be produced. Which one is it?

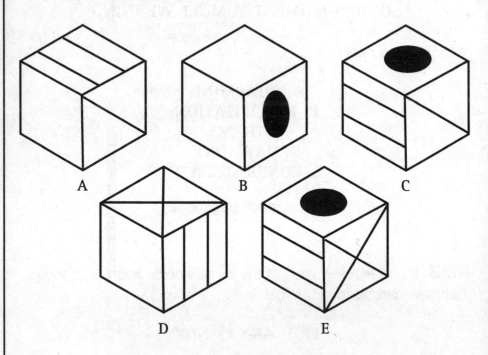

A   B   C

D   E

See answer page 242

405. Find a six-letter word made up of only the following four letters?

V O
L E

See answer page 242

406. What word can be placed in front of the other five to form five new words? Each dot represents a letter.

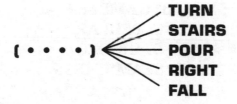

(• • • •) TURN
STAIRS
POUR
RIGHT
FALL

See answer page 242

407. If the missing letters in the two circles below are correctly inserted they will form synonymous words. The words do not have to be read in a clockwise direction, but the letters are consecutive. What are the words and missing letters?

See answer page 243

408. What two words are antonymous?

A. SPIRITUAL
B. POLLUTED
C. DEPRAVITY
D. CORPOREAL
E. HARMONY

See answer page 243

409. What word is a synonym of HUCKSTER?

A. MECHANIC
B. GAMBLER
C. PEDLAR
D. GIGOLO
E. SEAMSTRESS

See answer page 243

410. What number should replace the question mark?

See answer page 243

411. Each of the nine squares in the grid marked 1A to 3C should incorporate all of the items which are shown in the squares of the same letter and number, at the left and top, respectively. For example, 2B should incorporate all of the symbols that are in squares 2 and B. One square, however, is incorrect. Which one is it?

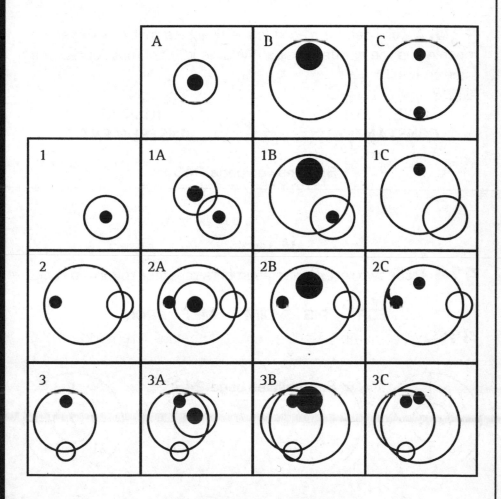

See answer page 243

412. Place two three-letter segments together to form a boat.

TER   MAS   GAL   IRE   CUT   EON

See answer page 243

413. A word can be placed in the brackets that has the same meaning as the words outside. What is it? Each dot represents a letter.

DWELL ON CONSTANTLY   (• • • •)   MUSICAL INSTRUMENT

See answer page 243

414. Place two three-letter segments together to form a rock.

EOR   PIG   DIM   MET   PON

See answer page 243

415.

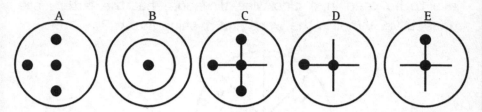

Which of the circles above should replace the question mark below?

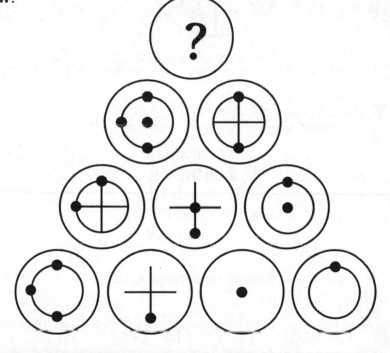

See answer page 243

416. If the missing letters in the circle below are correctly inserted they will form an eight-letter word. The word will not have to be read in a clockwise direction, but the letters are consecutive. What is the word and missing letters?

See answer page 243

417. What word is the odd one out?

A. GINKGO
B. JUNIPER
C. DEODAR
D. SISKIN
E. PAWPAW

See answer page 243

418. What word is synonym of DIFFIDENT?

A. BASHFUL
B. DEMENTED
C. CELEBRATED
D. UNCOUTH
E. ILLICIT

See answer page 243

419.

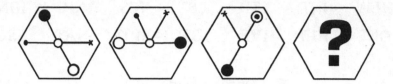

Which of the hexagons below should replace the question mark above?

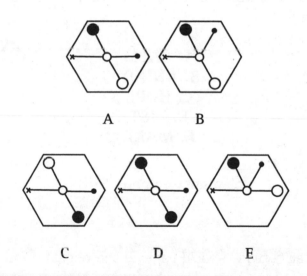

A   B

C   D   E

See answer page 243

420. Place four of the three-letter segments together to form two synonymous words?

HEW	INT	ETH	EST	ICS	NIC	ION
ONE	HID	IVE	STR	MOT	NAT	ESC

See answer page 243

421.

AGLOW   ENVY   GHOST   HINT   ?

Which one of the words below should replace the question mark above?

A. CALM
B. ANNOY
C. HOPE
D. FIST
E. MAKE

See answer page 243

422. What number should replace the question mark?

13   44   88   176   847   ?

See answer page 243

423. Which of the following words in the odd one out?

A. DULCET
B. SOFT
C. MELODIC
D. EUPHONIOUS
E. HARMONIOUS

See answer page 243

424. Find the starting point and move from square to adjoining square, horizontally or vertically, but not diagonally, to spell a 12-letter word, using each letter once only. What are the missing letters?

I		U
N	A	L
A		I
M	E	

See answer page 243

425. DEMONIC VIPER is an anagram of what 12-letter word?

See answer page 243

426.

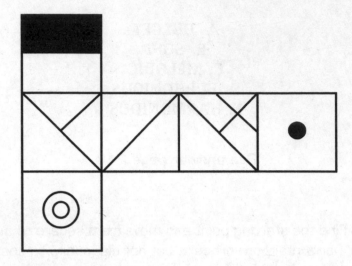

When the above is folded to form a cube, only one of the following can be produced. What one is it?

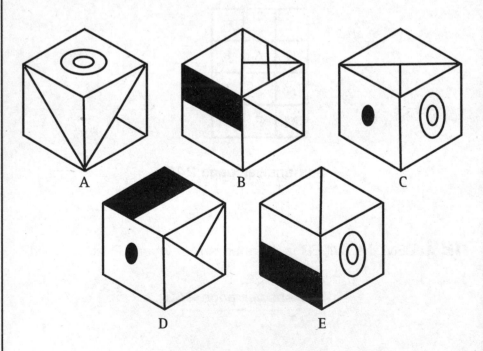

A   B   C

D   E

See answer page 243

427. Which of the following is the odd one out?

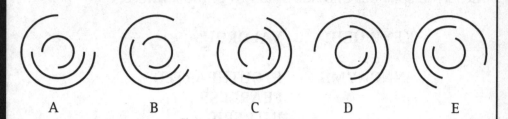

A   B   C   D   E

See answer page 243

428. What number should replace the question mark?

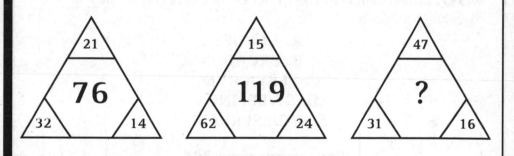

See answer page 244

429. Take one letter from each of the synonyms below, in order, to spell out another synonym of the keyword.

KEYWORD: VALOROUS

SYNONYMS: STOUTHEARTED
              FEARLESS
              INTREPID
              DOUGHTY
              VALIANT
              COURAGEOUS

See answer page 244

430. Which of the following words is the odd one out?

A. LARGE
B. BROAD
C. PERVASIVE
D. SWEEPING
E. WIDESPREAD

See answer page 244

431. CLAVIER is to PIANO as TAMBOUR is to:

A. PERCUSSION
B. DRUM
C. XYLOPHONE
D. ACCORDION
E. WOODWIND

See answer page 244

432. What number should replace the question mark?

1.5 0.5 3.5 10.5 7.5 2.5 ?

See answer page 244

433. A word can be placed in the brackets to go at the end of the left word and the start of the right one, creating two new words. Each dot represents a letter. What are the three words?

OFF (• • •) ANGER

See answer page 244

434. If a car had increased its average speed for a 180-mile journey by 5 mph, the journey would have been completed in 30 minutes less. What was the car's original average speed?

See answer page 244

435.

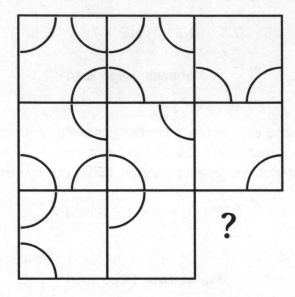

Which is of the squares below will replace the question mark above?

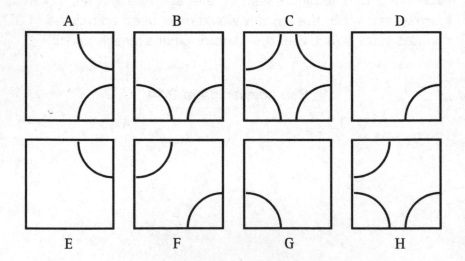

See answer page 244

436. What two words are opposite in meaning?

A. WORRIED
B. PIOUS
C. ANGRY
D. IRREVERENT
E. COVETOUS
F. DISTINGUISHED

See answer page 244

437. FOND MATES SALT JAM is an anagram of what three-word phrase that means wreckage?

See answer page 244

438. A word can be placed in the brackets that has the same meaning as the words outside. What is it? Each dot represents a letter.

OFTEN (• • • • • • •) HAUNT

See answer page 244

439. What number in the grid below is two places away from itself multiplied by five, two places away from itself minus two, four places away from itself doubled, three places away from itself plus five, and two places away from itself divided by two.

13	46	12	16	20	38
23	16	6	24	22	8
3	7	4	1	30	9
4	2	50	40	8	76
15	90	6	18	2	11
10	14	5	8	20	28

See answer page 244

440. Which is the odd one out?

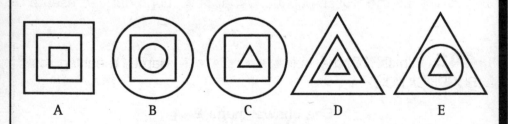

A   B   C   D   E

See answer page 244

441. Which of the following words is opposite to REFINED?

A. UNCOMFORTABLE
B. GAUCHE
C. BRITTLE
D. LOUD
E. ANNOYING

See answer page 244

442. Complete the six-letter words so that the last two letters of one word are the first two of the next and the last two of the fifth word are the first two of the first.

(• •) M O (• •)
(• •) R I (• •)
(• •) S I (• •)
(• •) V I (• •)
(• •) T H (• •)

See answer page 244

443. Which of the following has the same meaning as SUPPLICATION?

A. OVERNIGHT
B. REQUEST
C. ADDITION
D. MOVEMENT
E. CONFIRMATION

See answer page 244

444. Find two synonymous words in the inner and outer spirals of the circle below, one reading clockwise, the other anti-(counter) clockwise. What are the words and missing letters ?

See answer page 244

445. What is the meaning of an OREAD?

A. A MOUNTAIN NYMPH
B. A PRECIPICE
C. A PLAIN
D. A CLOCK
E. AN OBSERVATORY

See answer page 244

446. What is the decimal value of x in the following sum:

$$^7/_8 + {}^7/_{12} - {}^5/_6 = X$$

See answer page 245

447. Which of the following anagrams is not a BIRD?

A. LIGWATA
B. KYSRLAK
C. RAWSOPR
D. KITRALT
E. GONEDUD

See answer page 245

448. MENU MASCOT is an anagram of what 10-letter word?

See answer page 245

449. Which two words are the closest in meaning?

A. MASQUERADE
B. MAUNDER
C. MAUDLIN
D. MEANDER
E. MEDIATE
F. MOODY

See answer page 245

450.

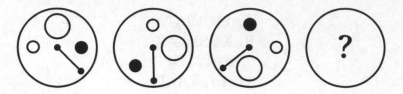

Which of the circles below should replace the question mark above?

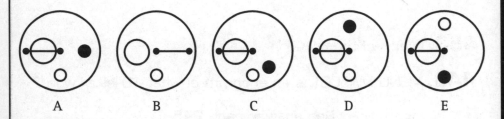

A   B   C   D   E

See answer page 245

451. What number should replace the question mark?

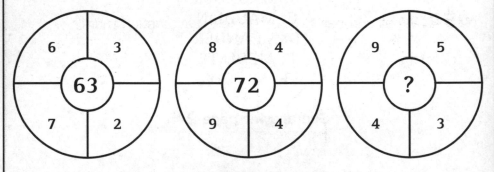

6	3
63	
7	2

8	4
72	
9	4

9	5
?	
4	3

See answer page 245

452. What is the name given to a group of KNAVES?

A. BAND
B. DECEIT
C. RAYFUL
D. SESSION
E. THRONG

See answer page 245

453. Which of the following is not a drink?

A. ANISETTE
B. FLUMMERY
C. MUSCATEL
D. EGG NOG
E. GRENADINE

See answer page 245

454. What number should replace the question mark?

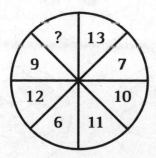

See answer page 245

455.

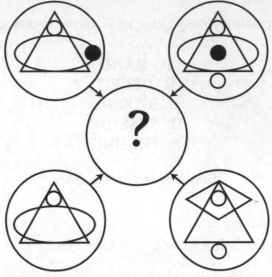

Each line and symbol that appears in the four outer circles, above, is transferred to the middle circle according to how many times it appears, as follows:

One time – it is transferred
Two times – it is possibly transferred
Three times – it is transferred
Four times – it is not transferred

Which of the circles below should appear as the middle circle?

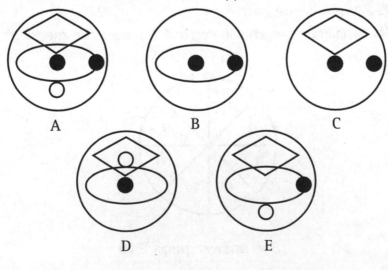

A   B   C

D   E

See answer page 245

456. A word can be placed in the brackets that has the same meaning as the words outside. What is it? Each dot represents a letter.

TREE (• • • • • •) COUNTRY

See answer page 245

457. What is a PILAFF?

A. A TURKISH DISH
B. A WEAPON
C. A DANCE
D. A SKATING MOVEMENT
E. A MUSICAL INSTRUMENT

See answer page 245

458. Which of the following is not a dance?

A. BEGUINE
B. PERCALINE
C. TARANTELLA
D. FARRANDOLE
E. POLONAISE

See answer page 245

459. Each of the nine squares in the grid marked 1A to 3C should incorporate all of the items which are shown in the squares of the same letter and number, at the left and top, respectively. For example, 2B should incorporate all of the symbols that are in squares 2 and B. One square, however, is incorrect. Which one is it?

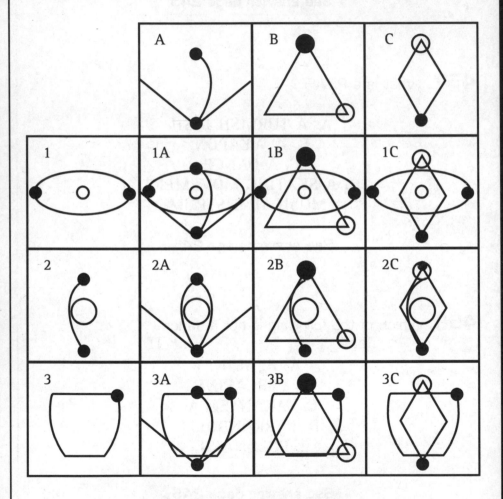

See answer page 245

460. Which two words are the closest in meaning?

A. MAGNIFICENT
B. VITUPERATIVE
C. SOLEMN
D. DEFAMATORY
E. BRISK
F. MALIGNANT

See answer page 245

461. TOURED FIT is an anagram of what nine-letter word?

See answer page 245

462. What is a PUNKAH?

A. A FISH
B. A SMOKING IMPLEMENT
C. A FAN
D. A FERN
E. A SERVANT

See answer page 245

463. What number should replace the question mark?

7	14	3	7
8	23	5	17
9	21	3	6
6	20	5	?

See answer page 245

464. What number should replace the question mark?

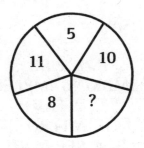

See answer page 245

465. Each of the nine squares in the grid marked 1A to 3C should incorporate all of the items which are shown in the squares of the same letter and number, at the left and top, respectively. For example, 1B should incorporate all of the symbols that are in squares 1 and B. One square, however, is incorrect. Which one is it?

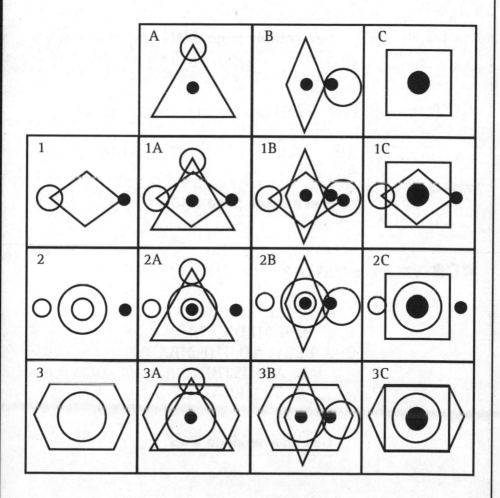

See answer page 245

466. Which of the following is not a weapon?

A. OERLIKON
B. DRUGGET
C. SJAMBOK
D. HARQUEBUS
E. CLAYMORE

See answer page 246

467. What number should replace the question mark?

1   10   26   ?   87   136

See answer page 246

468. What is a COLLOP?

A. A SLICE OF MEAT
B. A MEDICINE
C. A BLOW TO THE HEAD
D. A DUSTBIN
E. A MEDAL

See answer page 246

469.

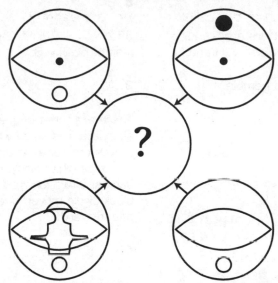

Each line and symbol that appears in the four outer circles, above, is transferred to the middle circle according to how many times it appears, as follows:

One time – it is transferred
Two times – it is possibly transferred
Three times – it is transferred
Four times – it is not transferred

Which of the circles below should appear as the middle circle?

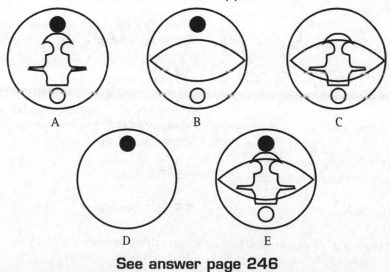

A   B   C

D   E

See answer page 246

1. Abbreviation.

The missing letters are, reading from top to bottom, V, B and N.

2. Gambol and gamble.

3. 15.

(Top × left) + right = middle.

(7 × 8) [56] + 15 = 71.

The others are (6 × 9) [54] + 19 = 73 and (9 × 6) [54] + 13 = 67.

4. E.

No figure in the same position in both rectangles is carried forward and figures change from triangle to circle and vice versa.

5. B (946 : 42).

Break down left number:

(First digit × second digit) + third digit = right number.

(9 × 4) [36] + 6 = 42.

The example was (4 × 8) [32] + 2 = 34.

6. B (Repartee).

Repartee is a synonym for badinage, as taunt is for gibe.

7. B (Square).

The others are three-dimensional; a square is two-dimensional.

8. 8.

552 ÷ $\frac{1}{4}$ = 2208; 2208 ÷ 276 (half of 552) = 8.

9. A.

There are three sequences, all alternate: the small white circle moves one forward and two back; the large white circle moves one back and two forward; the small black circle moves one back and one forward.

10. C (Open).

11. 6.

Reading down, the sum of numbers on each row increases by two.

12. Utter.

Each word starts with the second letter of the previous one.

13. 25.

There are five odd numbers which follow an even one, so 5 × 5 = 25.

14. E.

There are four circles, two black (medium-sized) and two white (one large, one small).

15. Espionage.

16. B. Emeritus.

The others are terms of lightly poking fun.

17. Gnomon (a pointer on a sundial).

18. C (8).

Alternate numbers go in different sequence:

– 5, – 6, – 7, and – 8; + 4, + 5, + 6.

19. Snap.

20. A.

21. Compound.

22. Scarab.

23. Misspend, squander. The missing letters are M and P (misspend), Q and D (squander).

24. C (34).

The sums are (top left × bottom right) – (bottom left – top right) = middle.

(9 × 4) [36] – (5 – 3) [2] = 34.

The others are

(5 × 6) [30] – (7 – 4) [3] = 27;

(6 × 7) [42] – (9 – 7) [2] = 40;

(8 × 9) [72] – (5 – 4) [1] = 71.

25. Henchman.

The missing letters are both H.

26. E.

Different symbols in adjoining

circles on the same row are carried into the circle between them in the row above. Similar symbols in the same place are dropped.

27. D (beggar).

28. Crumpet.

29. 392. 2/14 = 1/7, so 2/7 – 1/7 = 1/7. 8 × 7 = 56. 56 ÷ 1/7 = 56 × 7/1. 56 × 7 = 392.

30. C.

Every item rotates 60° clockwise each time.

31. E.

Opposite segments are mirror images except that black and white shading is reversed.

32. Algeria. The words are: teA, niL, foG, tiE, baR, obl, and erA.

33. D (179486).

The numbers were reordered as follows: sixth, third, first, seventh, fourth, fifth, second. Therefore the new order is:

A	B	C	D	E	F	G
9	6	7	4	8	1	2
F	C	A	G	D	E	B
1	7	9	2	4	8	6

34. C (lectern, a stand).

The others are all types of book.

35. 9.

(Top+Right) - (Bottom+Left) = Middle.

(73+3) - (39+28) = 76 - 67 = 9

Others are:
(72+55) - (83+37) = 127 - 120 = 7

and

(19+13) - (25+4) = 32 - 29 = 3

36. D.

37. Suggestive.

38. Separated and decorator.

39. Please. Three letters of the left and right words transfer to the middle as follows:

A	A	L	I	S	E
4				5	3
(P	L	E	A	S	E)
1	2	3	4	5	6
0	P	E	N	L	Y
1	6			2	

40. B.

41. Delight, offend.

42. Phil is 48 years old. Ken is 72 and David is 32.

43. E (routine : abnormal).

They are antonyms as are "doubt" and "conviction".

44. D.

The others all have identical pairs: A and H, B and G, C and F, and E and I.

45. 39.

The sums are (top + left) x right = middle. [7 + 6] [13] × 3 = 39.

Others are:
[7 + 5] [12] × 3 = 36;
[9 + 4] [13] × 2 = 26;
[8 + 5] [13] × 4 = 52.

46. MANS GUT (mustang).

The others are pumpkin (milk pup), blueberry (bury rebel), satsuma (USA mast) and mandarin (damn rain).

47. Gigolo.

48. Ten.

49. Daredevil.

50. 3A.

51. A (seizure).

52. C (18).

Reading from the left along each row, (first column × second column) – third column = fourth column.

[7 × 4] [28] – 10 = 18.

Others are:
[6 × 2] [12] – 5 = 7;
[8 × 3] [24] – 17 = 7;
[9 × 2] [18] – 9 = 9.

53. Sluggard. The missing letters are S and G.

54. Ferret.

55. Cerise.

56. C (steady).

57. D.

The others all have identical pairs: A and E, B and F, and C and G.

58. Adherent, believer. The missing letters are H and N (adherent) and B and E (believer).

59. A. The black and white dots change position; the full square becomes a half-square and vice versa; and the oval becomes a diamond and vice versa .

60. D.

The others all have identical pairs:

A and E, B and F, and C and G, except that black and white shading is reversed.

61. All systems go.

62. Abatement. The missing letters are B and T.

63. Profligate, chaste.

64. 4. The sum of diagonally opposite segments are the same. 6 + 4 = 8 + 2.

65. A.

At each stage, the black circle rotates 90° clockwise and goes in and out of the parallelogram; the white circle rotates 90°anti-(counter) clockwise and also goes in and out of the parallelogram; the triangle rotates 180° and changes from black to white and vice versa.

66. 7 pairs of cherries. He gave the 14 cherries to his friends as follows: To the first friend (half of 7) $3\frac{1}{2}$ pairs + $\frac{1}{2}$ a pair = 4 pairs (leaving 3 pairs).

To the second friend (half of 3) $1\frac{1}{2}$ pairs + $\frac{1}{2}$ a pair = 2 pairs (leaving 1 pair).

To the third friend (half of 1) $\frac{1}{2}$ a pair + $\frac{1}{2}$ a pair = 1 pair.

67. Ward.

Each word can be prefixed by BACK, making backgammon, backache, backtrack, and backward.

68. Keep.

69. 155.

Consecutive numbers are multiplied together and 1 is added to the answer.

1 x 1 [1] + 1 = 2; 1 x 2 [2] + 1 = 3; 2 x 3 [6] + 1 = 7; 3 x 7 [21] + 1 = 22; 7 x 22 [154] + 1 = 155.

70. Casket. It is a box, the others are jars, normally made of glass.

71. Management.

72. C.

The left part transfers across to lie touching the original, uppermost right side.

73. 6.

The sum of the columns are, reading left to right: 20, 21, 22, 23, 24, 25.

74. Intrepid, cautious.

The missing letters are: R and P (intrepid) and U twice (cautious).

75. $21\frac{1}{2}$.

The number decreases by $17\frac{3}{8}$ each time.

76. Fiddle.

77. C (orange peel).

78. Hoopoe (a bird).

79. D.

Different symbols in adjoining circles on the same row are carried into the circle between them in the row above. Similar symbols in the same place are dropped.

80. Waxworks, effigies.

The missing letters are X and R (waxworks) and F and G (effigies).

81. 9.

Reading from left to right (first column – second column) x third column = fourth column. [4 – 3] [1] x 9 = 9. The others are: (7 – 5) [2] x 9 = 18; (6 – 3) [3] x 7 = 21; (7 – 4) [3] x 8 = 24.

82. Night.

83. Hipflask.

The missing letters are F and K.

84. $-21\frac{5}{8}$.

The number decreases by $7\frac{7}{8}$ each time.

85. A.

Reading across rows and down columns, unique elements in the first two are transferred to the third (bottom or right). Common elements disappear.

86. F (sully) and D (clean).

87. E (Excitable).

88. Linden.

89. C. At each stage, the long line rotates 45° clockwise, the short line rotates 180° and all the circles rotate 90° clockwise.

90. C.

Reading across columns and down rows, unique elements in the first two are transferred to the third (bottom or right). Common elements disappear.

91. 58.

Looking across each row and down each column, the third and fourth numbers are the differences of the numbers in the two previous squares.

92. Ward. The words made are: award, inward, coward, toward, and sward.

93. Otter. A holt is an otter's home as a drey is a squirrel's home.

94. $2^1/_3$.

The sum can be rephrased as $^7/_9$ x $^3/_1$ (or 3); 3 x $^7/_9$ = $^{21}/_9$ (or $2^1/_3$).

95. Geometric.

The missing letters are G and M.

96. 8.

The sum of each row of three digits is 20.

97. A.

98. B. The two figures are mirror images of each other.

99. They are the son's mother and father.

100. B (efficacious) and E (unavailing).

101. C (traitor).

102. D (49).

Alternate sectors increase by 1, 3, 5, 7, 9, 11, and 13.

They are also squares of 1, 2, 3, 4, 5, 6, and 7.

103. B (indirectly) and D (obliquely).

104. B (regurgitate, to vomit).

The others are to restore or revive

105. $5^1/_2$.

There are two series that alternate:

one is – $2^1/_2$, the other is + $1^1/_2$.

Looking at the two series separately,
– $2^1/_2$ runs 5, $2^1/_2$, 0, –$2^1/_2$;
+ $1^1/_2$ goes 1, $2^1/_2$, 4, $5^1/_2$.

106. Boss.

107. 16.

The sum of inner and diagonally opposite outer segments totals 29.

108. Pavane (a dance).

109. B.

110. Escudo.

111. Double.

112. Shield.

113. 12.

In each case (top left x top right) – (bottom left x bottom right) =

middle. [8 x 5] [40] – [7 x 4] [28] = 12.

The others are:
[7 x 4] [28] – [2 x 3] [6] = 22;
[6 x 8] [48] – [3 x 5] [15] = 33;
[7 x 6] [42] – [4 x 7] [28] = 14.

114. Hijacker.

The missing letters are J and K.

115. E.

The circle becomes a square; a black circle on the top becomes white; and black and white swap left to right.

116. Ointment and liniment.

The missing letters are: O and M (ointment) and L and M (liniment).

117. C (harmless).

118. 512. 64 – 32 [32] ÷ $\frac{1}{8}$ ($\frac{2}{16}$) – $\frac{1}{16}$ [$\frac{1}{16}$] can be rephrased as 32 x $\frac{16}{1}$ (16) = 512.

119. C.

At each stage, the triangle rotates 180°, the large circle rotates 90° clockwise, the small white circle rotates 45° anti- (counter) clockwise, and the black circle rotates 90° anti- (counter) clockwise.

120. C.

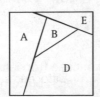

121. C (credit).

Credit is an anagram of direct as is anger of range, and tender is of rented.

122. 21. In each case (top – left) ÷ 5 = right.

(76 – 21) [55] ÷ 5 = 11.

The others are:
(36 – 21) [15] ÷ 5 = 3;
(97 – 52) [45] ÷ 5 = 9.

123. Honesty.

124. 15.

125. To catch on.

126. Silent. Three letters of the left and right words transfer to the middle as follows:

```
T E N D O N
6 4         5
(S I L E N T)
1 2 3 4 5 6
L I L I E S
  2 3     1
```

127. B.

Reading across columns and down rows of shields, common elements with the same shading in the first two are transferred to the third (bottom or right) and change shading. Unique elements disappear.

128. 5. Add the differences between 100 and 86, 75, 62 and 82, then subtract this total from the original 100.

(14 + 25 + 38 + 18) = 95; 100 – 95 = 5.

129. F.

130. A (clumsy) and E (expert).

131. D. The others all have identical pairs: A and B, and C and E.

132. B (admiral, a naval rank).

The others are all army ranks.

133. Fine.

134. –13. There are two alternate series, – 5 and + 6. The numbers are:

7, 2, –3, –8, –13; –5, 1, 7, 13, 19.

135. E. The order of the column is reversed and the lowest digit is removed each time.

136. D.

One dot will appear in a enclosed small circle and another in the link between two larger circles.

137. Bursar.

138. Turn.

139. Poppet.

140. 1C.

141. 60.

The sums are:

(top x left) + (top x right) = middle.

(4 x 6) [24] + (4 x 9) [36] = 60.

Others are:
(3 x 6) [18] + (3 x 8) [24] = 42;
(4 x 7) [28] + (4 x 3) [12] = 40;
(5 x 5) [25] + (5 x 4) [20] = 45.

142. A (a paramour).

143. Gangrene.

The missing letter is G twice.

144. B. The others all have identical pairs: A and C, D and E, and F and G.

145. 30.

The sums are: (top left – bottom right) x (bottom left + top right) = middle.

(11 – 5) [6] x (1 + 4) [5] = 30.

Others are:
(13 – 7) [6] x (4 + 6) [10] = 60;
(17 – 9) [8] x (3 + 2) [5] = 40;
(9 – 8) [1] x (7 + 3) [10] = 10.

146. C (nadir).

147. Impolite and insolent.

The missing letters are: M and L (impolite) and S and T (insolent).

148. Mastodon.

149. B. Different symbols/lines in

adjoining circles on the same row are carried into the circle between them in the row above. Similar symbols/lines in the same place are dropped.

150. D.

All three shapes move down one place at each stage and the star goes from black to white and vice versa.

151. B (tiny) and D (prodigious).

152. D (528572).

The others, if split in half and added as two three-digits numbers, would total 1000. 528 + 572 = 1100.

153. Trampolinist. The missing letters are, reading from top to bottom: M and T.

154. Sound.

155. B.

The number of sides of the inner figure should be half those of the outer ones. In the case of B, there is a square inside a seven-sided figure.

156. H.

Reading down each column, the letter advances three, then four places in the alphabet. Reading across, the difference is four, then five places.

157. 89.

Double the previous number, then add 1, 2, 3, 4, and 5, respectively.

158. Cathedral.

159. 12.

The sum of digits of the left and right numbers and also the top and bottom ones equals the middle number.

1 + 4 + 1 + 6 = 12; 2 + 8 + 1 + 1 = 12.

160. C.

161. C (request) and D (petition).

162. 88.

The sum is: $left^2 + right^2 + top = middle$.

4^2 [16] + 7^2 [49] + 23 = 88.

Others are:
6^2 [36] + 5^2 [25] + 12 = 73;
2^2 [4] + 3^2 [9] + 17 = 30.

163. B (minster). The rest are types of military buildings; a minster is a religious one.

164. Gate and gait.

165. $-1\frac{1}{4}$. Subtract $7\frac{3}{4}$ at each stage.

166. Line.

167. Drosky

(a Russian two- or four-wheeled cart).

168. Mean.

169. Goggle.

170. B.

Reading across columns and down rows, unique elements in the first two are transferred to the third (bottom or right). Common elements disappear.

171. Tribunal.

The missing letters are T and B.

172. Short.

173. 48.

The sums are (bottom left – bottom right) x (sum of top three numbers) = middle.

$(11 – 7) [4]$ x $(4 + 3 + 5) [12] = 48$.

Others are:
$(16 – 14) [2]$ x $(7 + 3 + 2) [12] = 24$;
$(17 – 14) [3]$ x $(8 + 4 + 1) [13] = 39$;
$(20 – 18) [2]$ x $(9 + 7 + 2) [18] = 36$.

174. C.

The others all have identical pairs: A and D, B and G, and E and F.

175. Penumbra.

176. Imposter and deceiver.

The missing letters are P and T (imposter) and C and V (deceiver).

177. A (vespiary, a wasp's nest).

178. B (bauble).

179. C.

Different symbols in adjoining circles on the same row are carried into the circle between them in the row above. Similar symbols in the same place are dropped.

180. C (cope).

The two words outside the brackets form an anagram so removing "melt" from "complete" will leave the letters to make "cope".

181. D (oasis : sand).

Sand entirely surrounds an oasis as water surrounds an island.

182. E (plebian).

183. 26 minutes.

184. A.

The top two items separate; the larger one rotates 90° clockwise and moves to the bottom, and the smaller one becomes large and goes in the middle. The bottom item rotates 180° and moves to the top.

185. C.

It is the only one with vertical, horizontal, and diagonal symmetry.

186. A (O).

The sum of the two left columns is

the same as the sum of the two right columns. Also, the 1st and 3rd columns have the same values as do the 2nd and 4th columns. The same applies to the rows.

187. C.

Identical symbols, including shading, in adjoining pentagons on the same row are carried into the pentagon between them in the row above. Different symbols in the same place are dropped.

188. B (the act of sneezing).

189. 60 ways.

190. B (3216 : 402).

The left pair of digits and the right pair of digits are both divided by eight.

191. B.

192. B (monitor). The others mean to prove; monitor is to check.

193. Prize and pries .

194. A (fracas) and C (skirmish).

195. D ($-{}^{1}/_{108}$) .

Multiply by $-{}^{1}/_{6}$ at each stage.

196. Fedora (a wide-brimmed hat).

197. Jerrycan.

The missing letters are J and R.

198. Full.

199. Occasion and incident. The missing letters are C and N in both cases.

200. D (banter).

201. A.

At each stage the large white circle rotates 60° clockwise, the small white circle rotates 120° clockwise, the black dot with a line rotates 180°, and the arrow and the small black circle both rotate 60° anti-(counter) clockwise.

202. Mouse.

203. D (spider, which has eight legs). The others are all bugs with six legs.

204. Willow.

205. C.

Different symbols in adjoining circles on the same row are carried into the circle between them in the row above. Similar symbols in the same place are dropped.

206. 83.

207. A (study).

208. C (praiseworthy).

209. A.

Reading across columns and down rows, unique elements in the first two are transferred to the third (bottom or right). Common elements disappear.

210. E. The right and left halves of the figure switch positions as illustrated below:

211. On the one hand.

212. Flamingo. The completed words are: elF, aiL, seA, geM, skI, diN, peG, duO.

213. 3600 yards². Divide the 240 yards by 4 to get 60 yards each side, so 60 x 60 = 3600.

214. D.

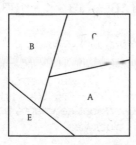

215. Fascinate. The missing letters are A and T.

216. B (axiom).

217. Rest and wrest.

218. A (O). The sum of each horizontal, vertical, and diagonal line equals 12.

219. Set at ease.

220. D (belfry).

The others are inside the main part of a church; the belfry is where the bells are.

221. D.

The others contain only one small white circle, while this one has two.

222. 375.

The previous number doubled, then at each stage 1, 2, 3, 4, 5, 6, and 7, respectively, is added.

1 + 1 + 1 = 3;
3 + 3 + 2 = 8;
8 + 8 + 3 = 19;
19 + 19 + 4 = 42;
42 + 42 + 5 = 89;
89 + 89 + 6 = 184;
184 + 184 + 7 = 375.

223. A (innocent).

224. C (tangle).

225. Long.

226. C.

227. Jujube.

228. G. The others form identical

pairs in different rotations: A&F, B&C, D&E.

229. Zephyr (a wind).

230. E (energetic).

231. D (spurious, which means false). The others mean irregular or unreliable.

232. C.

Different symbols in adjoining circles on the same row are carried into the circle between them in the row above. Similar symbols in the same place are dropped.

233. 67.

The order of numbers reverses and the lowest digit is dropped.

234. Bagatelle.

235. Maniacal.

The missing letters are M and I.

236. D.

237. Cloudiness.

238. A (a mixture).

239. Yashmaks.

The missing letters are Y and M.

240. B.

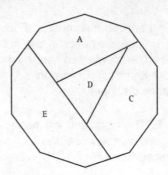

241. A.

Different symbols in adjoining circles on the same row are carried into the circle between them in the row above. Similar symbols in the same place are dropped.

242. Standard and ordinary. The missing letters are N and D (standard) and D and Y (ordinary).

243. 183. 2197 ÷ 13 = 169.

The 169 candle stubs can be reused, so 169 ÷ 13 = 13 and 13 ÷ 13 = 1.

Therefore 169 + 13 + 1 = 183.

244. E (wink : nictitate).

245. B.

The two innermost segments both rotate 90° clockwise.

246. 18.

In each column (top ÷ bottom) x 5 = middle. (54 ÷ 18) [3] x 5 = 15.

Others are:

[18 ÷ 6] [3] x 5 =15;
[24 ÷ 3] [8] x 5 = 40.

247. A (salubrious) and F (morbid).

248. Elephant. The others can all be prefixed by "black".

249. E (8795 : 1514 : 65).

The sum of the first two digits and the sum of the last two digits are put together and the process is repeated.

250. A.

251. C (chop).

A cleaver chops as a knife cuts.

252. B (over).

All the words can be prefixed by pass to make new words.

253. C (50 minutes).

The game lasts 75 minutes and 12 players can be in the game for its duration, so there are a total of 900 player minutes (75 minutes x 12 players) If 18 players are involved, the sum is [75 x 12] [900] ÷ 18 = 50.

254. B (worthy) and D (laudable).

255. A.

The top figure is folded along its adjoining line and moves into the lower one.

256. E (leap).

257. A (jaunt) and D (outing).

258. Quagga.

259. Outhouse.

The missing letters are O and H.

260. C.

Reading across columns and down rows, unique elements in the first two are transferred to the third (bottom or right). Common elements disappear.

261. Impolite and insolent.

The missing letters are M (impolite) and L and T (insolent).

262. Pine.

263. Harass.

264. B (vassal).

265. B (marriageable).

266. High.

267. B.

268. Hireling.

The missing letter is H.

269. D (a water-raising contraption).

270. D.

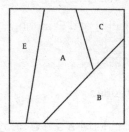

271. D (greet : salute).

272. E (bit haul) which makes halibut, a fish. The other anagrams are: ON CANADA (anaconda), TIN ROOM (monitor), COOL CIDER (crocodile), and CAROB (cobra).

273. D (28918).

The first three digits of the other numbers is the square of the last two digits: 361 is the square of 19, 225 is the square of 15, 576 is the square of 24, and 900 is the square of 30.

274. D.

A new and different white symbol is added to one of the arms at each stage. The symbol then alternates between black and white at each stage.

275. C (soothe) and E (vex).

276. D (ulna, a bone in a human's arm). The others are bones in a human's leg.

277. 92.5.

At each stage the numbers reduce

by 0.5, 1, 1.5, 2, and 2.5, respectively.

278. Gauntlet and daintier.

279. Reason.

Three letters of the left and right words transfer to the middle as follows:

```
R  E  P  O  S  E
   2     5  4
(R  E  A  S  O  N)
 1  2  3  4  5  6
A  R  E  N  A  S
 1        6  3
```

280. 12. In each case the sum is (left x right) ÷ 3 = middle. (4 x 9) [36] ÷ 3 = 12.

The others are:
(5 x 9) [45] ÷ 3 = 15;
(6 x 8) [48] ÷ 3 = 16.

281. D.

282. Heartfelt.

The missing letters are T and L.

283. 54 guests at 8.00 pm.

284. Eyelet.

285. D.

At each stage, the small circle moves two squares right and one left; the medium circle moves one left and two right; and the large circle moves one right and two left.

286. Objector.

The missing letters are J and T.

287. Round.

288. A (63). The sum of digits is removed from the first number to create the second and the sequence continues. 72 – 7 – 2 = 63.

The sequence starts:
119 – 1 – 1 – 9 = 108;
108 – 1 – 8 = 99;
99 – 9 – 9 = 81;
81 – 8 – 1 = 72.

289. Martingale.

290. E.

The middle figure rotates 90° clockwise and the outer figures rotate 180° and change from black to white and vice versa.

291. 4.

In each case the sums of numbers in diagonally opposite sectors are the same.

292. Increase and heighten. The missing letters are C and S (increase) and H twice (heighten).

293. Mullet.

294. E.

The others all have identical pairs in different rotations: A and F, B and D, and C and G.

295. Sit on the fence.

296. Guidance.

The missing letters are G and N.

297. 6. The lower numbers indicate the number of letters in each preceeding upper number.

298. C (comical).

299. A. In each case, the white circle and black arrow both rotate 180°, the white arrow rotates 60° anti- (counter) clockwise, and the black dot rotates 120° anti- (counter) clockwise.

300. A (ACD).

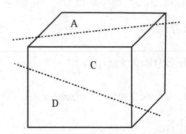

301. Embarrassing.

The missing letters are, reading from top to bottom, B, R and G.

302. 4.

The sums are: (right digits multiplied) ÷ (left digits multiplied) = middle. (9 x 8) [72] ÷ (2 x 9) [18] = 4.

The others are:
(5 x 9) [45] ÷ (5 x 3) [15] = 3;
(7 x 9) [63] ÷ (7 x 1) [7] = 9.

303. In the extreme.

304. Hide and hied.

305. 105.

The sequence alternates:

x3, +2. 3 x 3 = 9;
9 + 2 = 11; 11 x 3 = 33;
33 + 2 = 35; 35 x 3 = 105.

306. C (kind) and F (invidious).

307. D.

Reading across columns and down rows, unique elements in the first two squares are transferred to the third (bottom or right). Common elements disappear.

308. Muse.

309. B (neckchain).

310. A (ban) and F (proscribe).

311. 24.

In each row (left x middle) ÷ 4 = right. (8 x 12) [96] ÷ 4 = 24.

The others are: (2 x 4) [8] ÷ 4 = 2; (16 x 12) [192] ÷ 4 = 48.

312. B (species, a general word).

The others are types of species.

313. E (cabbage).

314. A.

The figures rotate 120° clockwise and the circle, triangle, and rectangle are white first time, black second time.

315. 46.

The sums are: (top – left) ÷ 3 = right.

(46 – 13) [33] ÷ 3 = 11.

The others are:
(84 – 12) [72] ÷ 3 = 24;
(29 – 8) [21] ÷ 3 = 7.

316. Pebble.

317. Back.

318. Outshone.

The missing letters are O and H.

319. E. The others are all pairs in different rotations, A and F, B and G, and C and D.

320. E (applause).

321. Hawser.

322. Pan.

323. Toilsome and tiresome.

The missing letters are L and M (toilsome) and R and M (tiresome).

324. 28.

The lowest cube number is 8, the highest square number is 36; 36-8 = 28.

325. A.

The oval becomes a diamond and vice versa, and rotates 90° clockwise. The circles change from black to white and vice versa, and rotate 180°.

326. C (parliament).

327. E (bend the knee).

328. C and D (assuage and irritate).

329. B.

Reading across columns and down rows, unique elements in the first two circles are transferred to the third (bottom or right). Common elements disappear.

330. B (BDE).

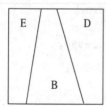

331. A.

There are alternate sequences, the right-angled figure rotates 90° clockwise, and the pointed figure rotates 120° clockwise.

332. Bird of prey.

333. 55.

At each stage progressive square numbers are added.

$0 + 1^2 (1) = 1$;
$1 + 2^2 (4) = 5$;
$5 + 3^2 (9)\ 14$;
$14 + 4^2 (16) = 30$;
$30 + 5^2 (25) = 55$.

334. Take for a ride.

335. 3 minutes, 45 seconds.

Add the train length (0.25 miles) to the tunnel length (2.25 miles) and multiply by the number of minutes per mile covered (60/40, or 1.5). 2.5 x 1.5 = 3.75.

336. A.

The top half is folded across the middle and placed over the bottom half.

337. C.

The dot appears in the large circle and the triangle.

338. D.

In the others all areas common to only two circles are shaded. In D, one such area is not covered.

339. Reflected.

The missing letters are L and C.

340. C (OLD PEAR or leopard).

The others are:
RAIL REIN (airliner),
NOD GOAL (gondola),
AIM LOO TUBE (automobile),
and CARVE FORTH (hovercraft).

341. E (cut).

342. E (beneficial).

343. C.

At each stage two dots are added; outer dots rotate 45° clockwise; inner dots rotate 45° anti- (counter) clockwise.

344. 7.

The sums are: (first column + third column) = (second column + fourth column). $(9 + 7) = (11 + 5)$.

The others are:
$(7 + 4) = (3 + 8)$;
$(6 + 4) = (9 + 1)$;
$(4 + 1) = (1 + 4)$.

345. Ricochet and bouncing.

The missing letters are C and H (ricochet) and B and N (bouncing).

346. Feeble.

347. Curlew.

348. Half.

349. B (sea-spray).

350. Hamper.

351. D.

352. $8^2/_3$.

The sums are:
(bottom left x top right) =(top left x bottom right).

(13×4) [52] $= (6 \times 8^2/_3)$ [52].

The others are:
(9×12) [108] x $(16 \times 6^3/_4)$ [108];
(12×11) [132] $= (10 \times 13^1/_5)$ [132];
(9×7) [63] x $(12 \times 5^1/_4)$ [63].

353. Upstairs.

The missing letters are U and A.

354. B.

Reading across columns and down rows, unique elements in the first two circles are transferred to the third (bottom or right). Common elements disappear.

355. C (beef stew).

356. Humbug.

357. A (covey).

358. C (necessity).

359. C.

At each stage the triangle rotates 180°, the large circle rotates 90° clockwise, the small white circle rotates 45° anti- (counter) clockwise, and the small black circle rotates 90° anti- (counter) clockwise.

360. C.

Differently positioned circles in adjoining pentagons on the same row are carried into the pentagon between them in the row above. Similarly positioned circles in the same place are dropped.

361. B (universal).

362. A (5916 : 7734 : 9552).

At each stage add 1818.

363. Periscope.

364. Botanical.

The missing letters are B and T.

365. F.

The others all have identical pairs in different rotations, A and G, B and E, and C and D.

366. Ill at ease.

367. C (teal, which is a shade of blue). The others are all brownish shades.

368. B (sore) and D (raw).

369. C (precise).

370. D (courgette).

It is another name for the vegetable.

371. Pale and pail.

372. B (ABD).

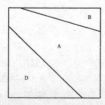

373. D.

The second dot appears in the link between the triangle and the square.

374. B (row).

The words can all be prefixed by SPAR, to make sparrow, sparred, sparking, spartan.

375. Voodoo.

376. –6.

There are alternate sequences, – 4 and + 2.

The series are: 6, 2, –2, and –6, and 7, 9, and 11.

377. Stake.

378. Anywhere. The missing letters are Y and H.

379. Annoying and worrying. The missing letters are N and G (annoying) and W and Y (worrying).

380. C.

381. B (arictooraoy) and E (proletariat).

382. Can.

383. Creche.

384. A.

At each stage the short-lined black circle rotates 180°, the small white circle rotates 120° clockwise, the long-lined black circle rotates 60° clockwise, the large circle rotates 120° anti- (counter) clockwise, and the cross rotates 60° anti- (counter) clockwise.

385. C (flabby).

386. Cudgel.

387. E (observance).

388. C (loquacious).

389. 2A.

390. Opulence (outer ring) and richness (inner). the missing letters are P, L, and E (opulence) and S and H (richness).

391. Disbelief and messenger.

392. 365. At each stage multiply the previous number by three, then subtract one.

1 x 3 - 1 = 2;
2 x 3 - 1 = 5;
5 x 3 - 1 = 14;
14 x 3 - 1 = 41;
41 x 3 - 1 = 122;
122 x 3 - 1 = 365.

393. D (authentic).

394. E.

The others are the same figure in different rotations.

395. C (chicken).

The others are all astrological signs (Capricorn – goat, Taurus – bull, Leo – lion, and Aries – ram).

396. Reindeer. The words are:

he**R**, fo**E**, le**I**, si**N**, ha**D**, ar**E**, wo**E**, ba**R**.

397. A (2516). The first and third digits and second and fourth digits are made into two, two-digit numbers and multiplied together.

96 x 78 = 7488;
78 x 48 = 3744;
34 x 74 = 2516.

398. A. Impartial.

399. Signature. The missing letters are G and R.

400. B. The circles in the two boxes are transferred to the third one only if they are not in similar positions. Similarly-placed circles disappear.

401. D (epithet : name).

402. C (theme).

The initial letters of the words are the same as the days of the week.

403. Fine and dandy.

404. E.

405. Evolve.

406. Down.

407. Overhaul and overtake. The missing letters are V and H (overhaul) and V and K (overtake).

408. A (spiritual) and D (corporeal).

409. C (pedlar).

410. 64. In each case the sum is

(top left – bottom right) x (bottom left – top right). (26 – 18) [8] x (21 – 13) [8] = 64.

The others are:
(14 – 7) [7] x (16 – 8) [8] = 56;
(7 – 1) [6] x (11 – 2) [9] = 54;
(14 – 11) [3] x (17 – 8) [9] = 27.

411. 2C.

412. Cutter.

413. Harp.

414. Meteor.

415. D.

Different symbols in adjoining circles on the same row are carried into the circle between them in the row above. Similar symbols in the same place are dropped.

416. Piquancy.

The missing letters are Q and C.

417. D (siskin, a bird).

The others are trees.

418. A (bashful).

419. A.

At each stage the large circles both rotate 120° clockwise, the dot rotates 60° clockwise, and the cross rotates 60° anti- (counter) clockwise.

420. Native and ethnic.

421. D (fist).

All words have letters in the correct alphabetical order without repeating.

422. 1595.

Reverse the digits and add it to the original to make the next number.

31 + 13 = 44; 44 + 44 = 88; 88 + 88 = 176; 671 + 176 = 847; 748 + 847 = 1595.

423. B (soft, which is quiet in tone).

The others are all specifically tuneful or pleasant.

424. Manipulative.

The missing letters are, reading from top to bottom, P, T, and V.

425. Improvidence.

426. D.

427. D. The others are exactly the same figure rotated.

428. 148.

Reverse the digits in the outer numbers and add them together.

74 + 13 + 61 = 148.

The others are
12 + 23 + 41 = 76;
51 + 26 + 42 = 119.

429. Heroic.

The letters are: stout**H**earted, f**E**arless, int**R**epid, d**O**ughty, val**I**ant, **C**ourageous.

430. A (large, which is big).

The others mean "general".

431. B (drum).

A tambour is a type of drum as a clavier is a type of piano.

432. 5.5.

The sequence is: ÷ 3, + 3, x 3, – 3.

1.5 ÷ 3 = 0.5; 0.5 + 3 = 3.5; 3.5 x 3 = 10.5; 10.5 – 3 = 7.5; 7.5 ÷ 3 = 2.5; 2.5 + 3 = 5.5.

433. End, to make offend and endanger.

434. 40 mph.

180 miles at 40 mph = 4 hours, 30 min; 180 miles at 45 mph = 4 hours.

435. G.

Reading across columns and down rows, unique elements in the first two are transferred to the third (bottom or right). Common elements disappear.

436. B (pious) and D (irreverent).

437. Flotsam and jetsam.

438. Frequent.

439. 6.

(6 x 5 = 30; 6 – 2 = 4; 6 x 2 = 12; 6 + 5 = 11; 6 ÷ 2 =3).

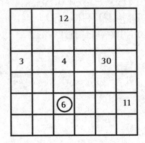

440. C, a circle is outside and a triangle is in the middle. The others all have the same figure on the outside and in the middle.

441. B (gauche).

442. A**L**mo**ST**, **ST**ri**DE**, **DE**si**RE**, **RE**vi**LE**, **LE**th**AL**.

443. B (request).

444. Jamboree and carnival.

The missing letters are J and B (jamboree) and N and V (carnival).

445. A (a mountain nymph).

446. 0.625. The lowest common multiple of 8, 12, and 6 is 24, so redo the sum as

$$\frac{21 + 14 - 20}{24}$$

15/24 = 5/8, which is 0.625

447. F (GONEDUD or dudgeon, a fish). The others are LIGWATA (wagtail), KYSRLAK (skylark), RAWSOPR (sparrow), and KITRALT (titlark).

448. Consummate.

449. B (maunder) and D (meander).

450. C.

At each stage the black circle rotates 135° clockwise, the white circles both rotate 90° clockwise, and the dot with a line rotates 45° clockwise.

451. 60.

The sums are

(top left x top right x bottom left) ÷ bottom right = middle.

(9 x 5 x 4) [180] ÷ 3 = 60.

The others are:
(6 x 3 x 7) [126] ÷ 2 = 63;
(8 x 4 x 9) [288] ÷ 4 = 72.

452. C (rayful).

453. B (flummery, a sweet dessert or porridge).

454. 8.

The sum of all diagonally opposite segments is 19.

455. A.

456. Brazil.

457. A (a Turkish dish).

458. B (percaline, a cloth).

459. 1A.

460. B (vituperative) and F (malignant).

461. Fortitude.

462. C (a fan).

463. 10.

Reading across each line, the sums are (first column x third column) – second column = fourth column.

(6 x 5) [30] – 20 = 10.

The others are:
(7 x 3) [21] – 14 = 7;
(8 x 5) [40] – 23 = 17;
(9 x 3) [27] – 21 = 6.

464. 1.

Start at 11 and read alternate segments clockwise, the sums are – 1, – 2, – 3, and – 4, respectively.

465. 2B.

466. B (drugget, a type of cloth).

467. 51.

At each stage add 3^2, 4^2, 5^2, 6^2, and 7^2.

$1 + 3^2 [9] = 10$;

$10 + 4^2 [16] = 26$;
$26 + 5^2 [25] = 51$;
$51 + 6^2 [36] = 87$;
$87 + 7^2 [49] = 136$.

468. A (a slice of meat).

469. A.

Brainstorm

• •

Now for a change of pace. These are not quick-fire problems but bigger, more detailed puzzles that will require some lengthy consideration and much scribbling on the backs of envelopes. One of these puzzles might take you an hour or so to work out. Since there are a couple of hundred of them you're going to be busy.

1.   In Ordered Succession

One of the easiest forms of puzzles to set, but not to solve, is the series puzzle. You know, the type that asks you to find the missing number from a row of numbers. I know only too well that when new ideas seem to elude the puzzle setter's mind, the temptation to resort to composing yet another series puzzle can be overwhelming.

In order to discipline myself not to write a book full of such conundrums but yet cater for those people who happen to like solving them, I have begun this compendium of mind-teasers with 10 such puzzles. I make no apologies for this, and I cannot promise not to include any more within these pages, but I thought it would be better to get these out of the way before embarking on the more adventurous types of puzzle.

Each term given below is related to its neighbour in some way, no matter how obscure that relationship may seem. You are asked to find the missing term in each case.

1.	1	3	6	11	18	29	?
2.	4	5	9	18	34	59	?
3.	1	2	5	11	21	36	?
4.	2	8	24	64	160	384	?
5.	0.5	0.75	0.8333'	0.875	0.9	0.91666'	?
6.	2	6	18	54	162	486	?
7.	7	?	63	189	?	1701	
8.	2	12	30	56	90	132	?
9.	1	5	15	34	65	111	?
10.	1	3	7	15	31	63	?

See answer page 442

2. The Four Jays

Four friends, Jane, June, Jean and Jenny discovered that, if a different number was designated to each letter of their names and added together, it produced their ages.

June is 17, Jenny is two years older, while Jane and Jean are both sweet 16. All the girls agree that June is in her prime.

Can you find the numbers the girls assigned to each letter of their names?

See answer page 442

3. The Woodcutter's Conundrum

A cutting blade for a woodworking machine, shown in the diagram below, had to be manufactured from a blank piece of steel. He needed to know the radius of the curved section in order to form his grinding wheel to the correct shape. This was not given on his drawing and needed to be calculated. His mathematical abilities were limited, so he asked his boss and his workmates to help, but he could find no one with enough knowledge to assist him. His boss, being an impatient sort of person, insisted that the cutter be made without further delay. In desperation the man tried to make the blade by trial and error. After many attempts, and several grinding wheels later, he was dismissed for not being able to do his job properly.

If you had been there, could you have solved the problem for him?

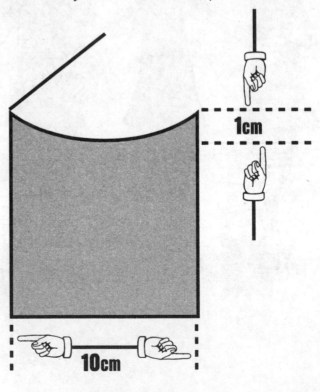

1cm

10cm

See answer page 442

4.   The Farmer's Fields

A farmer owned two pieces of land. The first was eight times larger in area than the other, and the two were separated by an access road. He grazed cattle on the first, while he grew vegetables in the other.

As time went by, it became necessary to replace the fencing that surrounded the two fields. When the farmer measured the perimeters of both sections of land, he was surprised to find that it was going to take twice as much fencing to surround the smaller area than it was to surround the larger.

Both sections of land were rectangular in shape and the fences were continuous. The gates of the fields were to be a removable section of fence.

How much fencing did he need to buy?

See answer page 442

5. Three Little Boys

Three little boys who were comparing their allowance money found that each of them had only one type of coin in his pocket.

The first had his money all in five-cent coins, the second had all ten-cent coins, and the third had only fifty-cent coins.

The boys thought that it would only be fair if they had equal amounts of money. Mental arithmetic was not their strongest subject, so they started exchanging coins, recounting after each exchange.

After some time they eventually ended up with $1.80 each, and found that each boy had given two of his original coins to each of the other two boys.

How many of each type of coin did each of the boys have to begin with?

See answer page 442

6. Letters to Numbers

A popular form of code is to assign numbers to letters so that a sentence becomes a sequence of seemingly unrelated numbers.

In the next puzzle I have reversed the process and given each number a letter. In this code, however, there is a mathematical relationship between the letters. I could make the puzzle easier by saying what that relationship is, but I'm sure you can solve the puzzle without any help, can't you?

$$\textbf{CAB} = \textbf{CGHGF}$$

$$\textbf{DAB} = \textbf{HGGGFH}$$

$$\textbf{GIB} = \textbf{GB}$$

$$\textbf{CACH} = \textbf{GCCD}$$

Can you find which numbers have been assigned to each of the letters?

See answer page 442

7. The Engineer

An engineer of international reputation was assigned the job of constructing a foundation for the siting of a large piece of machinery. The machine was very heavy and the reinforced concrete foundation, 1 m thick, had to be a high specification both in strength and in flatness. This part of the job was not a problem for the engineer as he had organized such a construction many times before. The problem arose from the way the machine was to be fastened to the foundation.

Due to the high vibrations the machine was subject to when fully working, the normal method of drilling the concrete and fastening the machine to its foundation with anchor bolts after final positioning was not acceptable.

The manufacturers of the machine gave instructions that pockets would be cast into the concrete at specific locations as the foundation was being laid, the idea being that after final positioning a special compound would be poured into the cavities and the holding down bolts dropped into it. The compound would then harden within 24 hours and provide a permanent, vibration-resistant location for the machine.

The pockets were to be in the shape of an inverted 'T'. The cavity had to be 200mm below the surface of the concrete and in the shape of a 150mm cube. A hole of 30mm diameter would connect the cavity to the surface to allow access for the compound and for the bolt.

No wooden or other type of shuttering could be used, as these could not be removed after the concrete had set. Neither could they be left in situ, because they would eventually rot and allow the hardened compound to become loose in the cavities.

The engineer tried long and hard to think of a way of forming the cavities. He thought of using blocks of ice supported from below – he could then cast the concrete and the ice would melt, leaving the necessary pockets. He dismissed the thought almost at once. The ice would freeze the water in the concrete mix and cause it to crumble around the place where strength was most needed.

Eventually he hit on an idea which he put into action immediately. The idea worked, and the foundation was cast to everyone's satisfaction.

How did he do it?

See answer page 443

8. Training the Trainee Train Driver

The goods yard at the railway company's depot was fitted with an oval track and two branch lines. This track was normally used by apprentice engine drivers to gain experience of handling locomotives, but occasionally it was used to store goods before dispatch if all the sidings were occupied. At the far end of the oval track was a narrow tunnel, which was just wide enough to allow the engine to pass through it.

On this occasion two freight carriers, situated at either side of the oval, had been loaded with cargo that was wider than the tracks. A mistake had been made and the wrong cargo had been loaded on to the wrong carriage. The cargo on the first carriage should have been put on to the second carriage and vice versa.

As there was no access road around the track, the simplest solution to the problem seemed to be to move the carriages into their correct locations using a locomotive. The manager of the depot asked one of the apprentices to do this.

'But the loads are too wide to pass through the tunnel,' protested the apprentice as he studied the task.

'That's right,' replied the manager, 'but to someone of your intelligence that shouldn't be a problem. By the way, the engine is on one of the branch lines. I want it back in its place when you've finished.'

So the problem is: move carriage A into the position of carriage B, carriage B into the position of carriage A and put the engine back into the siding. Remember the engine can pass through the tunnel, but the carriages cannot.

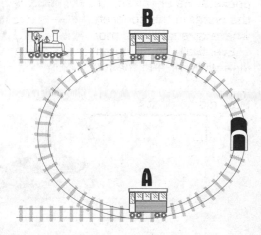

See answer page 443

9. Serving the Wine

The manager of a small restaurant buys his house wine in bulk from the local cash-and-carry. The wine comes in plastic containers of two different sizes. One holds five units and the other holds three.

The wine is included in the price of the meal and the manager allows $1/4$ of a unit of wine per person. This is normally served by placing a jug of wine in the center of the table for the customers to help themselves as and when they require it.

On a particular busy evening with a party of 16 people arriving in 10 minutes' time, he finds that he has only one of each size container of wine left in stock. For 16 people, all seated together, two jugs would be required, each holding two units of wine. He has two identical glass jugs, but no method of measuring exactly two units, all other jugs and containers being in use at this time.

As he is a fair-minded businessman, the manager refuses to give the customers short measure, but by the same token he will not give them more wine than they have paid for. He devises a way, by using only the jugs and the containers, of serving precisely two units of wine in each jug and leaving exactly two units of wine in each of the containers for future use.

How does he do it?

See answer page 443

10. Little Tommy Tomkins

A teacher at a local school decides to improve the young children's arithmetic by teaching them how to measure. He explains that most things are measurable, and demonstrates with a number of different measuring instruments. He sets the pupils a number of tasks involving measurement, and asks them to calculate such things as area, change in temperature, weight of different objects, etc. For homework he asks them to use measuring instruments that they have in their homes to measure and calculate whatever they choose. The next day, as he is marking the homework, he opens the book belonging to little Tommy Tomkins and is dismayed to see:

$$7 + 10 = 5$$
$$8 + 5 = 1$$
$$4 + 11 = 3$$
$$9 + 7 = 4$$
$$6 + 8 = 2$$
$$5 + 7 = 12$$

Angered by what he sees, he immediately sends for little Tommy. 'This work is a disgrace,' he cries, 'only one right out of six simple additions, you ought to be ashamed.'

'But they are all the right answers,' protests Tommy. 'I checked them carefully, every one of the sums is correct.'

The teacher, his patience a little strained, allows Tommy to explain why he thinks the answers are correct.

After hearing Tommy's explanation the teacher agrees that the sums all have the right answers.

What did Tommy say to the teacher?

See answer page 444

11. Get It Out!

Mechanical engineers are often faced with this type of problem: how to successfully remove a worn bearing from its location without damaging the housing or surrounding parts of the machinery.

There are many different types of bearing extractors or pullers on the market to assist the engineer in most situations. However, there are some situations in which even the most sophisticated of tools are of little help. This occurs when the bearing has been pressed into a blind hole and there is no room to locate any kind of extractor behind the offending part.

One trick of the trade is to heat up the housing, expanding the surrounding metal, thus making the hole larger and allowing the bearing to become free in its location and be removed easily. But there are times when for practical reasons this is not possible.

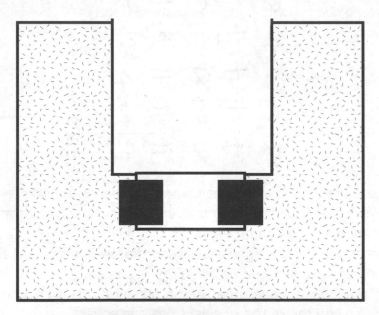

In the diagram above I've shown such a situation. How does the engineer remove the bearing without damage to himself or to the housing, without special tools and without heating up the surrounding metal?

See answer page 444

12. Chasing the Girls

Alex and Phillip were good friends who lived in a large apartment building. Alex lived at number 60, while Phillip lived at number 102. Alex wanted to become friendly with a girl from the ground floor. He knew she lived at number 12, as he had often seen her entering that apartment on the way home from school. He wanted to know her name but was too shy to ask.

Phillip was infatuated, too, but with a girl who lived on the top floor. Her name was Diana, but she refused to tell him her apartment number, saying something about not wanting him hanging around outside her door.

The boys had known for some time that there was a link between their names and their apartment numbers. They wondered if they could use the same link to discover the name of the girl from number 12 and the number of the apartment where Diana lived. They tried the system and found that it worked.

What was the name of the girl from number 12, and in which apartment did Diana live?

See answer page 444

13. More MPG

Mr Stingy lives at the bottom of a very steep hill. His son and his family live exactly one mile away at the top of the hill. The son does not own a car, and there is no public transport between the two houses. Mr Stingy, much to his displeasure, has to drive to the son's house every week in order to see his grandchildren.

He calculates that because of the steepness of the hill and the constant use of low gears, his car only produces 10 miles to a gallon of fuel on the upward journey. This is compensated for by the fact that on the downward journey, he can almost free-wheel, and the car produces 100 miles to the gallon for that one mile.

Assuming that he uses his car for no other purpose than to visit his grandchildren, what is his average mileage per gallon?

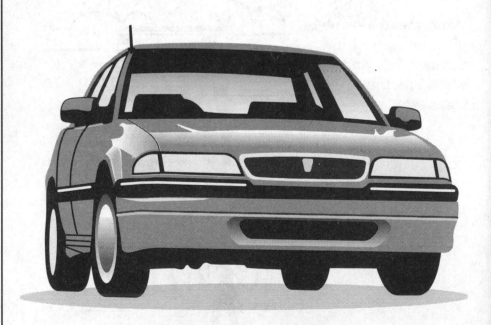

See answer page 444

14.   The Flight of the Pigeons

The pigeon fanciers' club wanted to transport their pigeons for the start of a championship race. They were against the traditional form of transport, that of keeping the birds in individual cages, for such a long journey, so they hired a special container vehicle. This was fully air conditioned, warm, well lit, large enough for the birds to fly around in and rigged out with nest boxes and perches.

The birds looked quite content as they were individually loaded into the container, quietly sitting in rows, side by side along the perches. Over 100 birds were on board when the truck set off on its journey

As it pulled away, one club member asked a question that puzzled everyone concerned. If the truck drove over a pothole in the road and frightened the birds to the extent that they all took flight at the same time, would the total weight of the truck and the cargo be less than when all the birds sat on their perches?

See answer page 444

15. The Klondike

A prospector arrived in the Klondike to stake his claim. He brought with him half a mile of rope with which to form the boundaries of the claim. Being an educated man, he knew that he could enclose the greatest area by forming the rope into a circle. This he did, but he soon ran into trouble with the authorities. The land he had claimed was larger than the maximum allowed, and he was ordered to reduce the area by half. Not wishing to fall foul of the authorities again but still wanting the maximum area he was allowed, he formed the claim into a different shape, but still used the full half mile of rope.

What shape did the prospector's claim finally take, and how many acres did it cover?

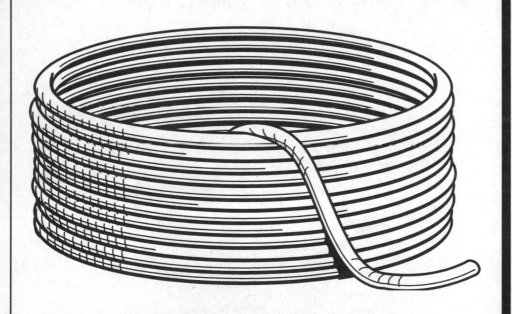

See answer page 444

16. Walking the Plank

The greatest weight or mass that can be supported by a wooden plank of a given thickness varies directly with the variation in width and inversely with the variation in length.

A plank which is 20cm wide and 15m long can support 200kg.

What weight will a plank which is 30cm wide and 20m long support?

See answer page 445

17. Digital Crossword

This little game is, as the title suggests, a crossword with a difference. Rather than use words to complete the grid we use numbers. The rules are simple. Each clue, either across or down gives a total of the addition of the numbers on the grid in that particular row or column. You must find the numbers that add up to that total. All the numbers must be integers. Numbers may only be used once anywhere on the grid. Negative numbers are not allowed, nor is the number 0.

Clues Across

c)............37
f).............64
h)...........47
i)............32

Clues Down

a).............26
b)............64
d)............31
e)............15
g)............55

See answer page 445

18. Playing on the Swings

When my son was a little boy it was one of my pleasures to take him to the local park and let him have a ride on the swings. One day after such a ride, when I had been pushing him ever higher, he asked:

'When I was at the highest point, how far did the swing travel to the highest point at the other side.'

This I thought would be a useful conundrum to include in this collection so . . . If the ropes of the swing were 3.6 m long, and the seat when stationary was 60 cm above the ground, the highest point of the arc of the swing was just above my head, say 1.8 m.

How far did the swing travel to the highest point at the other side?

See answer page 445

19. The Infinite Stadium

Imagine, if you can, a stadium with an infinite number of seats. Such a place can be full and still accommodate more spectators. The manager simply moves the person in Seat 1 into Seat 2, the person in Seat 2 into Seat 3, and so on. Each spectator occupies a seat with a higher number than before, and Seat 1 remains vacant for the next late arrival.

On one particular day, as the game is about to start, a coach arrives with an infinite number of passengers all wanting seats in the shortest possible time.

How does the manager deal with this situation?

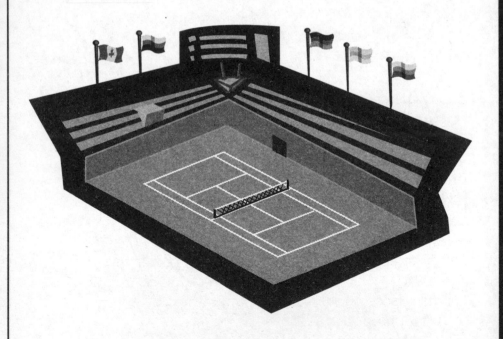

See answer page 445

20. The Witch's Polyhedron

The number five was regarded as very unlucky during the Middle Ages, as it was thought to represent the five wounds inflicted at the Crucifixion and the five points of the pentacle, believed to be a symbol used by witches in 'black magic'. Even the sight of a pentacle or pentagram was enough to fill people with fear and foreboding. The crystal ball was another of the witches' instruments of magic, and the combination of the crystal ball with the five-pointed figure was the ultimate in mystical power.

One particular witch had such an instrument, a crystal ball that had been fashioned into a polyhedron, each face of the polyhedron taking the shape of a regular pentagon. The local people believed this witch could foretell not only the future but many other things simply by looking into the different faces of the magical implement. Indeed, it was widely believed that she could capture the souls of unsuspecting victims, who would be entombed forever within the confines of the crystal.

Now we live in more enlightened and possibly more mundane times, and such an instrument would be to us merely an interesting geometrical shape. But please bear in mind, if you ever come across a crystal polyhedron with faces in the shape of the pentagon, treat it with respect, for it may contain the soul of one of your ancestors.

How many faces would the crystal have, and what is its geometrical name?

See answer page 445

21. Numerical Code

Many types of code have been developed over the years for the passing of messages. The obvious purpose of these codes is to protect the message from being intercepted by anyone other than the intended recipient. The most common form of code is one that allocates numbers to letters of the alphabet so that the sender simply writes words as a series of numbers. The only problem with this method is that the receiver must have the correct number to the letter sequence in order to decipher the message.

There is one numerical code that does not need the recipient to memorize any special sequence. It does, however, require the use of a numerical instrument. I have written a sentence below with the last word in code. It is a nine-letter word, and each integer represents a letter.

Can you decipher the word?

'You may say the last word of this sentence is 378163771.'

See answer page 445

22. Noughts and Crosses (Tic Tac Toe)

The game of noughts and crosses has been played for centuries. This game is different. Instead of the players trying in turn to complete a line of either all noughts or all crosses, the winner is the person who can fill the bottom line of the matrix with a combination of noughts and crosses that logically completes the array.

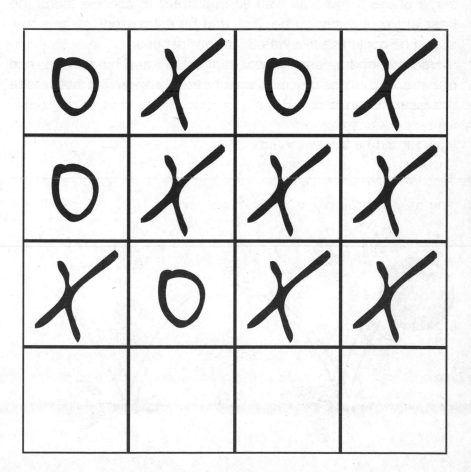

See answer page 445

23. Stone-Throwing

Many small boys enjoy throwing stones into water. Indeed, when a group of boys are near a lake or the ocean, it is unusual not to find at least one of them throwing pebbles into the water. One such boy took his pebble-throwing very seriously and practiced daily to improve his technique. He found that it was not only the speed of the stone that gained maximum distance but that the angle of the throw was also an important factor. He found the best angle of throw to be 45°, and he estimated the greatest speed he could achieve was 30 m per second.

He arranged a contest between himself and his friends, and putting all his theory into practice he threw his stone the greatest distance.

How far did he throw the stone?

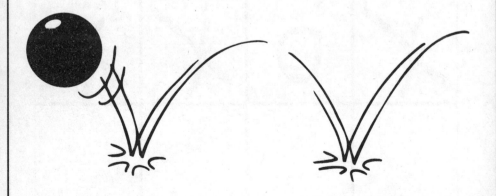

See answer page 445

24. Musket Balls

Ammunition for muskets and flintlock pistols was usually made of lead. The making of lead shot was a simple matter. Each soldier was issued with a ladle and a mold, and they would make their own ammunition from lead obtained by collecting spent shot from the battlefield or scrounged from the local population. They would melt the lead over the campfire and pour it into the mold with the use of the ladle. Each mold could make three musket balls at once.

One resourceful soldier had the idea of making his own ladle from a section of the barrel of an old musket the same caliber as his own. By cutting a small section of the barrel, blocking one end with clay and using a length of wire for the handle, the new ladle was made. By trial and error the soldier fashioned the length of the cylindrical bowl of the ladle so that it was able to hold the exact amount of molten lead needed to make the three musket balls. This saved time and reduced the risk of spillage. Obviously, the diameter of the bowl of the ladle was the same as the diameter of the musket ball, but what length did the soldier make it?

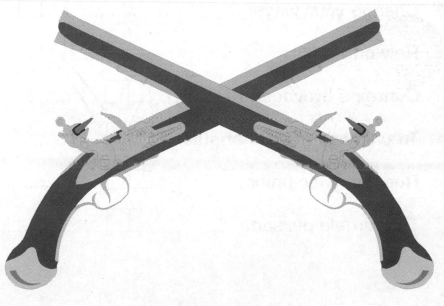

See answer page 446

25. Missing Word

Many word puzzles are based on letters that end one word and start another, and many puzzles have been written in which the solver is asked to find the missing derivative. I've decided to include such a puzzle in this collection of conundrums to provide an interlude between the number puzzles.

In order to make it more interesting I have given you the privilege of first finding the words and then finding the connection. The rules are simple. Below are eight clues from which eight separate words can be found. When this has been done, find a three-letter word, which, when added to the end of the first four words and to the beginning of the last four, combines to form eight new words. The clues are:

1. **To protect.** .... ☐☐☐

2. **Respond to stimulus.** .... ☐☐☐

3. **Change your ways.** .... ☐☐☐

4. **Rely on.** .... ☐☐☐

5. **Contains hydrogen (usually).** ☐☐☐ ....

6. **To undergo mental anguish.** ☐☐☐ ....

7. **Run away for union.** ☐☐☐ ....

8. **The female person.** ☐☐☐ ....

See answer page 446

26. Numbers for Letters

This puzzle asks you to give a value to each of four letters. The letters are P, Q, R and S. They have been put into a matrix and the sum of each row and each column has been calculated. Your job is to find the number assigned to each of the given letters.

P	Q	R	S	119
P	P	S	S	90
Q	R	R	P	143
S	S	Q	R	112
102	119	136	107	

See answer page 446

27. Elementary Series

Do you, as I sometimes do, grow weary of puzzles involving a series of numbers? 'Not another series problem!' I can almost hear the cries of dismay from here. Wait, don't turn the page just yet; read on. This is a series you can really get to grips with – not one of the mundane prime-number variations or the arithmetic or geometric progression type. This is different.

Below is a series of letters written in a particular order. Each letter follows the last for a unique, logical reason. All you have to do is to find that reason and so find the next letter(s) in the listing. The letters are:

B C N O F ?

See answer page 446

28. Changing Signs

Mental arithmetic is always a good way of exercising the little grey cells. With the constant use of the electronic calculator, people are becoming less and less skilful in this department. What used to be regarded as an easy calculation is today becoming a major problem if a calculator is not available. This next puzzle – and I ask you to solve it without the use of a calculator – is very straightforward. Below is a row of numbers. Using the signs for addition, subtraction, multiplication and division once each in the spaces between the numbers, complete the operation. Work from left to right.

$$2 \ldots 3 \ldots 4 \ldots 5 \ldots 6 = 1 \, 0$$

See answer page 446

29. The Inaccessible Object

In school we are taught how to calculate the height of objects by using the well-proven methods of Pythagoras or by trigonometry. Both methods, as we know, make use of right-angled triangles. This is all very well in the classroom, but out in the real world things are not always that straightforward. There is almost never a clear line from the base of the object to a suitable distance for accurate measurement. The object to be measured is very rarely at 90° to the ground, and sometimes we cannot even reach the object to begin to collect the required data. The next conundrum involves such a problem and puts all those many hours of schoolwork into practice.

A surveyor needs to find the height of a rock formation, which is located at the other side of a river. He has no method of crossing the river and no way of measuring its width at that point. All he has with him is an instrument for measuring angles and a 50 m tape measure.

How does the surveyor calculate the height of the rocks?

See answer page 446

30. Extra Letter

Many people prefer word games to number puzzles, so I have tried to cater for all tastes by including a few in this collection of conundrums. My next mind- twister uses a quotation, and is very apt to the dedicated puzzle solver who is constantly having his concentration interrupted.

Below is a six by six matrix containing the quotation. It starts at one corner and moves from letter to letter in any direction except diagonally. To make the puzzle more interesting I have inserted an extra letter at the end of the quotation (so there are 36 letters given, but the quote only contains 35). Sneaky? Well, you don't want it to be too easy, do you?

Which is the letter that does not form part of the sentence?

I	D	A	N	D	L
A	E	E	W	T	E
M	T	W	H	A	N
O	D	S	O	C	B
O	G	H	V	E	E
B	E	R	E	L	C

See answer page 447

31. Triangles

We are taught that all triangles have angles that add together to give 180°. No exceptions, we are told. But I am thinking of a triangle that exists in the real world, that has two base angles of 90° each, all of whose three sides are straight lines, and yet two of the sides meet at the apex to form a third angle.

What or where is this triangle?

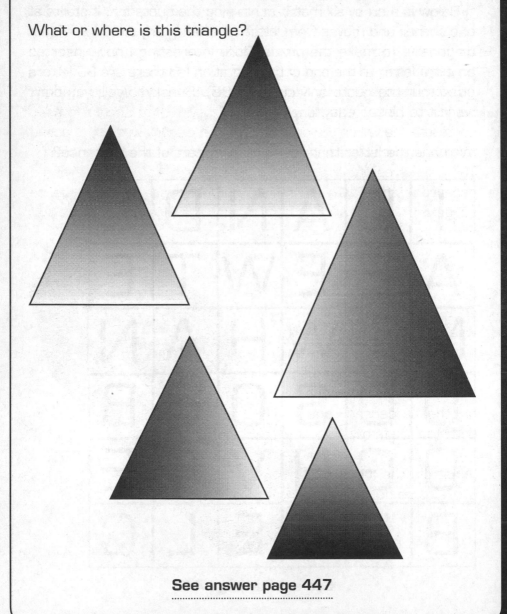

See answer page 447

32. You Can't Take It With You

Mrs Avarice was a very rich and very miserable old lady. She refused to accept the fact that she could not take her riches with her when she threw off her mortal coil and passed over to the next world. She hated all her relatives and was too mean to give anything to charity, so she devised a plan of campaign. She instructed the executor of her will that in the event of her death all her assets were to be liquidated and the money placed in her coffin alongside her body. Her wish was for the coffin and its contents then to be cremated.

Eventually the old lady died and the executor proceeded to follow her instructions. The family, who believed they were to inherit a fortune, contested the will on the grounds that the old lady was not of sound mind when the will was made. The matter was referred to the courts. The judge presiding over the case asked for further evidence of the deceased's state of mind when the will was made. All the evidence suggested that the old lady knew exactly what she was doing at that time. After hearing the evidence the judge retired to his chambers to consider the matter.

After much deliberation, the judge ruled that the last wishes of the deceased must be paramount. He was, however, also sympathetic to the heirs of the estate and finally passed a judgement that satisfied the wishes of the deceased and delighted the family.

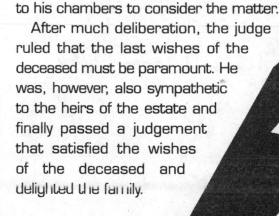

What did the judge order to be done?

See answer page 447

33. The Haunted Hotel

The manager of a remote hotel in the mountains had reports of strange figures appearing in certain rooms at certain times of year — good for business, as guests would arrive hoping for a visitation. On the other hand, it was bad for business, as the guests fled in terror after a figure had reportedly been seen floating through walls and generally causing a nuisance.

The manager had an idea. If he could predict which room was to have a visitation he could warn the guests in that room beforehand. This gave the guests the opportunity to leave or stay without a mass exodus from the hotel.

He monitored the sightings and found that from January to March Room 3 was haunted every other night. April through to June Room 4 was haunted every third night. July, August and September Room 9 became the target for the ghostly apparition, but only every fourth night. He was puzzled by this sudden jump from Room 4 to Room 9 and tried throughout the summer to figure out which room the specter would visit next and on which nights it would appear. Can you help?

See answer page 447

34. The Used Car

Fast Buck Joe, the used car salesman, bought a well-used car and then sold it for 30% profit. The poor unsuspecting person who bought the car was happy with the vehicle until it started breaking down three months later. The disgruntled customer went back to Fast Buck Joe and demanded his money back. Joe refused because of the the length of time the car had been out of his possession, but he offered to buy back the car at 20% less than the customer had paid for it. The customer reluctantly agreed.

What percentage of profit did Joe make on the overall deal?

See answer page 447

35. The Shepherd and his Sheep

A shepherd is planning to build a rectangular enclosure for his sheep, using an existing wall for one side of it. He uses pieces of pre-made fencing, each 2 m in length, and will not allow any overlap of the sections. The width of the enclosure must be greater than 20 m and the length greater than 40 m. He has only 45 sections of fence.

What size should he build the structure to enclose the greatest possible area?

See answer page 447

36. The Gambler

Mr Mensaman was attending a convention in Las Vegas when he thought he would try his luck at the tables. The convention took place over four days, and he visited the casino every evening. Each time he arrived at the casino he had to pay an entrance fee of $100, and each time he left he gave the cloakroom attendant a $10 tip. Every evening, unlucky Mr Mensaman lost exactly half of what he started with, and went home after four days with only $10 in his pocket.

How much did Mr Mensaman have at the start of the four days?

See answer page 447

37. The Bus Driver

Two young men boarded the city bus and approached the driver. 'One to the city centre, please,' the first man said.

The driver duly gave him the ticket, and the next man approached.

'A short back and sides, please,' said the second man.

'What?' said the puzzled bus driver.

'A crew cut, then,' the man said, unperturbed by the bus driver's apparent lack of comprehension.

'Sorry,' replied the driver.

'Well just a little off the top with a few highlights if you think that is better.'

The driver was lost for words. The first man, on seeing the driver's lack of understanding, spoke up.

'I must apologize for my friend,' he said; 'he only speaks Hairdo.'

The problem over, the bus driver continued on his way.

In the bus driver's cash tin was a certain sum of money made up of 10-cent coins and twice as many five-cent coins. If the number of 10-cent coins were doubled and the number of five-cent coins decreased by 10, the sum of money would be increased by $1.10.

What was the original number of five-cent coins?

See answer page 447

38. Touching Circles

There has been a lot of publicity in recent years about the appearance of corn circles. Having seen one of these circles for myself, I am convinced that most of them are not man-made. Some of the designs and the precision with which the circles are formed make it difficult to believe that anyone using crude instruments and working in complete darkness could form these patterns in one night. But then again I am a believer in the supernatural.

My next conundrum does not, unfortunately, involve the supernatural, but it does involve circles. Three circles of different diameters touch externally. Their centers form a triangle whose sides are 5 cm, 6 cm and 9 cm respectively.

Can you find the radii of the three circles?

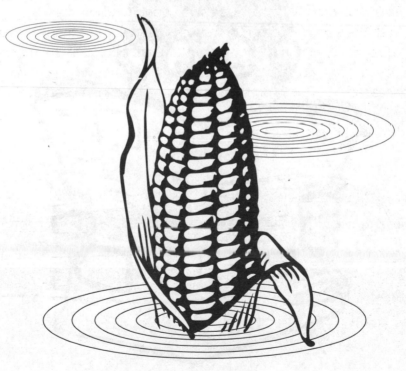

See answer page 447

39. The News Vendor

This next puzzle involves newspapers and could be something to think about as you take your daily constitutional. A newsagent sells three newspapers, the Echo, the Moon and the Advertizer. He sells 70 copies of the Echo, 60 of the Moon and 50 of the Advertizer.

17 customers buy both the Echo and the Moon, 15 buy both the Moon and the Advertizer and 16 buy both the Echo and the Advertizer. Three customers buy all three papers.

How many customers does the news vendor have?

See answer page 447

40. Weather changes

When we look back at the summers of our childhood we only remember the good days and forget the dull, dismal, rainy days when we sat in our rooms, bored out of our minds, and stared endlessly out of the rain-splattered window. We probably remember only half a dozen sunny days from each summer, which merge together to form one long, hot, sunny memory.

I have recently collected data on the changes in the weather where I live, and have arrived at the following possibilities for the month of June. If it is fine today, the probability that it will be fine tomorrow is 3/4. If it is wet today, the probability that it will be fine tomorrow is 1/3. Today is Thursday, and the weather is warm and sunny. I plan to go walking on Sunday.

What is the probability that Sunday will be a fine day?

See answer page 448

41. The Sum of the Parts

It has been stated that a person's personality is often shaped by their name. I'm not sure that I agree with this. I think it is far more probable that a person's choice of occupation or profession has been suggested by a link with their lifelong handle. I have known personally a Mr Burns the Fireman, a Mrs Sheen the cleaner and a Mr Hedges the gardener. I am sure that somewhere in the world there will be a Mr B. Troot the greengrocer and Phil McCavity the dentist. The point is that everything and everybody is the result of the combination of many different components.

The next puzzle is a variation on the sum of two parts. The cost of making a table is calculated by adding two variables. One is proportional to the area and the other to the square of the length. If the cost of a table 2 m by 3 m is $50 and the cost of a table 1.5 m by 4 m is $64, what is the cost of a table that is 2.5 m square?

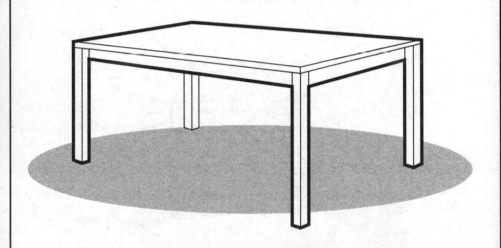

See answer page 448

42. One Man and His Dog

A farmer took his dog with him everywhere he went; they were great friends and almost inseparable. One day the farmer had to check on his flock of sheep, which was grazing on pastures three miles from the farmhouse. He set off on the three-mile walk across the open moorland with the faithful old hound close at his heels. On arrival at the pasture he checked and rechecked the sheep. Convincing himself that all was well, he eventually started his journey home. The dog knew instinctively where they were going and ran on ahead all the way back to the farmhouse. Finding the farmhouse door closed, the dog ran back to meet the farmer. When the dog reached the farmer it immediately turned and ran back to the farmhouse. The dog continued running backward and forward between the farmer and the farmhouse until they both reached home together.

Assuming the farmer walks at a speed of two miles per hour, and the dog can run at six miles per hour,

How far did the dog run on its journey home?

See answer page 448

43. The Prince and the Princess

Many years ago in adjacent kingdoms lived a prince and a princess who were ideally suited. They planned to marry one day, but their plans of happiness together came to a sudden end when the two kingdoms declared war on each other. From that day on they were forbidden to see or communicate with each other. To ensure the king's command was obeyed they were each locked in a secure tower and guarded night and day.

One day the prince persuaded the guard to deliver and collect written messages from himself and the princess. For this service he would be paid handsomely provided he did not tell anyone about the arrangement. The guard agreed. The prince, however, did not trust the guard not to read the letters, which were for the princess's eyes only. Even if he were to seal the letters, the guard could open, read and reseal them without the princess knowing. This problem was overcome when the prince devised a way of securing the letters that made it impossible for the guard to read them before they were delivered.

How did he do it?

See answer page 448

44. Chickens and Ducks

Old Farmer Giles finds that there is a demand for free-range eggs in the local village. To fill this demand he decides to start keeping poultry in his farmyard. He estimates the maximum number of birds he can accommodate is 25, and he is willing to invest $80 in livestock.

Off he goes to market with the $80 tucked safely in his pocket. On arrival he finds chickens are selling at $4 each and ducks are on offer at $2 each. Speaking to more experienced poultry farmers, he finds he can expect at least five eggs per week from each chicken but only four eggs per week from each duck.

How many of each bird should he buy to obtain as many eggs per week as possible?

See answer page 448

45. The Open Box Question

A sheet-metal worker has a piece of metal that is 80 cm square. He needs to make an open box that has the greatest possible volume. He cuts equal square pieces from each corner of the sheet and the remaining piece is bent to form an open box.

What size would the box need to be to obtain the maximum possible volume and how much would it hold?

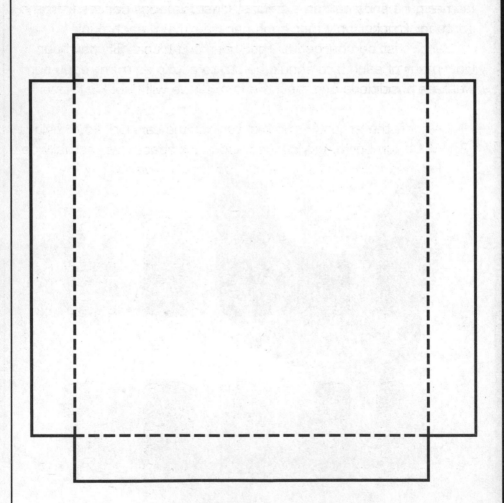

See answer page 448

46. The Car Park

Up to 6,000 m² of land is available to build a car park for cars and small trucks. The local government has stipulated five conditions that must be met before the project can be put before the planning committee for approval:

ⓐ. There must be at least 50 spaces for trucks.
ⓑ. Each car must be allocated a minimum space of 15 m².
ⓒ. Each truck must be allocated a minimum space of 30 m².
ⓓ. The car park must have at least twice as many spaces for cars as for trucks.
ⓔ. Cars must be charged $2 per hour and trucks $5 per hour.

If these conditions are met, the committee will need to know:

1. What is the largest number of vehicles the car park could hold?
2. What number of car spaces and truck spaces will actually be provided in order to generate maximum revenue?

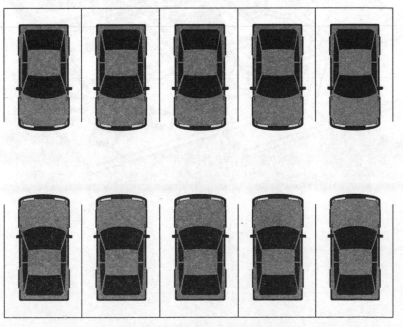

See answer page 448

47. The Tiler's Dilemma

Mr Fixit needed to tile a small section of his kitchen. When he visited the local do-it-yourself store, he found there were two sizes of tiles that suited his needs. Both sizes of tile were perfectly square, but the first tile was 2 cm smaller in length and width than the other.

He calculated that he would need only 63 of the larger tiles to cover the area he required, but he would need another 49 if he were to choose the smaller tile.

What are the sizes of the two tiles?

See answer page 448

48. The Lost Consonants

This little problem is for the less mathematically minded readers among you and is a pleasant change from the number-crunching exercises that have dominated most of the last few pages. There have been many word puzzles that give a famous phrase or saying, leaving out the vowels and asking the puzzle solver to find the sentence. This puzzle is slightly different. This time you are given the vowels and are asked to fill in the consonants.

Below is a famous Shakespearean quotation with only the vowels in place. What is the complete quotation and from which famous play is it taken?

I _ _ U _ I _ _ E _ _ E _ OO _ O _ _ O _ E, _ _ A _ O _ .

See answer page 449

49. A Pile of Bricks

Have you ever wondered about the mysteries of arithmetic? Does 1 + 1 always = 2? Suppose I dig a hole in the ground and then dig a second hole immediately alongside it. If I then add the two holes together by removing the dividing wall, I end up with only one hole, bigger I admit, but still only one hole.

Say I have a pile of bricks in one corner of my yard and another pile of bricks in the opposite corner of my yard. If I add the two piles together, I end up, again, with only one pile of bricks. So it must be true that in a lot of cases 1 + 1 = 1. All this has absolutely nothing to do with the next problem except it has brought bricks into the conversation.

A young lad started work on the local building site. His first job was to stack a pile of bricks, which had been tipped, randomly, from the back of a truck. He was told that each stack must contain the same number of bricks and must be no more than eight bricks high. He tried stacking them in equal piles of two high, then three, then four, then five, then six, but each time he found he had one brick left over. He finally found that by stacking them in equal piles of seven he had no bricks remaining.

What is the smallest number of bricks in the original pile?

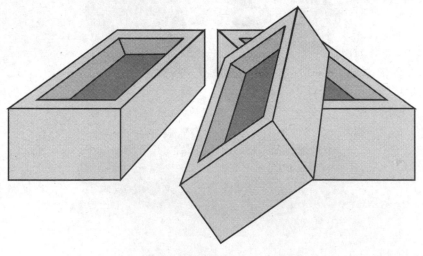

See answer page 449

50. The Lion, the Donkey and the Carrots

Once upon a time there was a lion traveling south for the winter. On his journey he met a traveler leading a donkey with a sack of carrots tied to its neck.

'Greetings,' said the lion; 'are you going far?'

'Just to the other side of the river,' replied the traveller.

'Do you mind if I walk with you?' asked the lion. 'I'm going that way myself, and I will need some help to cross the river. I cannot steer the boat by myself you see.'

'You can walk with us by all means, but please don't stare at my donkey with that hungry look in your eyes.'

The three continued on their way without incident until they came to the river. They walked along the bank a little way until they found a small boat. This was the only means of transport across the river; but the boat was very small, only large enough to take two of them across at a time (and not the load of carrots), and the traveler was the only one who could steer it.

'Take me across first,' said the lion.

'I can't leave the donkey alone with those carrots,' replied the traveler. 'There will be none left by the time I return.'

'Then take the carrots first,' said the lion with a gleam in his eye.

'Then I would have no donkey left when I returned, would I?'

How did they all cross the river safely, without the lion harming the donkey or the donkey eating the carrots?

See answer page 449

51. Counting Sheep

One of the many problems facing farmers who rear grazing animals is keeping them fed at all times. You may think that during the summer months when the grass is growing this should not be a problem. The food supply replenishes itself. However, this is a problem in itself. How quickly will the grass grow? Will the animals eat the grass more quickly than it grows? How many animals will a field of pasture feed and for how long? These are some of the many problems that are a constant worry to the farmer. He has to assess continually the pastures, the weather, the growth rate of the grass, etc., in order to keep a constant food supply for his animals.

Here is a typical problem that sheep farmers face: 15 sheep eat 10 acres of grass in 18 weeks. Provided that the grass grows at a uniform rate, how many sheep can an area of 36 acres support for 18 weeks?

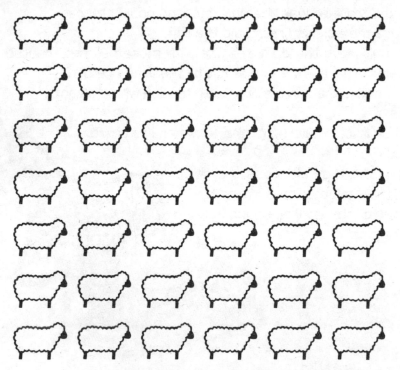

See answer page 449

52. The Merciless Captain

The two principalities of Catania and Dognia had been at war with each other off and on for centuries. At the time of this incident an uneasy peace existed between them. In order to promote harmony between the two peoples, the leaders passed a law that all merchant shipping must be manned by equal numbers from each nationality.

One fateful day such a ship set sail. The crew consisted of 30 men: 15 Catanians and 15 Dognians. The captain, a cruel and heartless man, was a strong Dognian patriot. Before very long the ship ran into a dreadful storm and suffered considerable damage. The captain decided that the only way to save the ship was to lighten the load by throwing half the crew into the sea. In order for the choice to be seen to be fair the unfortunate crew members would be chosen by lots. The method agreed upon was that all the crew members would stand in line and the captain would count along the lines in nines. Every ninth crew member would be thrown into the sea.

How did the captain organize the line-up so that it was always a Catanian and never a Dognian who was in the ninth place?

See answer page 449

53. Feeding the Needy

The relief truck arrived at the village to distribute much-needed food. The small village had a population of exactly 100 people. The truck contained 100 loaves of bread, and the food was about to be distributed evenly when the proceedings were suddenly stopped by the village chieftain.

'The elders of the village will make the decision on how the food will be divided,' he said in a loud booming voice.

The relief workers stopped, not wanting a confrontation, and waited for the decision from the council of elders. After a short while, the chieftain approached the truck. 'Each child will receive half a loaf of bread, each woman two loaves and each man three,' bellowed the chieftain.

'But we may not have enough to go round in those proportions,' argued a relief worker.

'You have 100 loaves?' asked the chief.

'Yes,' replied the worker.

'Then that is enough.'

How many men, women and children lived in the village?

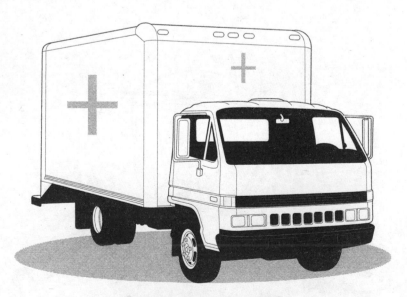

See answer page 449

54. What, No Pi?

Have you ever wondered if the advancement of knowledge would ever have been inhibited if Pi (3.142), the ratio of the circumference of a circle to its diameter, had never been discovered? Would we still be unable to find the area of a circle without it? To this end I offer you this challenge.

Imagine, if you will, that you are a native villager, living in the remotest region on earth. You have had no contact with civilization, but you have developed basic arithmetic skills. You also have a crude measuring stick, but the value of Pi or even its existence is unknown to you. You need, for whatever reason, to find the area of a wheel on the ground in front of you. You can measure quite accurately the diameter of the wheel. You can even find its circumference by rolling it one complete revolution and measuring the distance travelled, but can you calculate the area of the wheel?

See answer page 449

55. Catch Me If You Can

John Pedlar, a keen cyclist, sets off on his bike one day on a prearranged journey. His head is full of the important things in life for a teenager, such as girls, pop music, football and clothes. Forty minutes later his father finds John has forgotten something crucial for the journey. Father decides to follow John in his car and catch him before he arrives at his destination.

Now John can ride his bike at an average speed of 23 km per hour and his father drives his car at an average speed of 50 km per hour.

How far will John have travelled before his father catches him?

See answer page 449

56. Slow Down George!

George Docile had just started driving down the highway with his wife, on the way to a vacation in France. His wife sat nervously in the rear seat, one hand on the back of the seat in front of her.

'You're going too fast,' she snapped, her knuckles turning ever whiter as she gripped the upholstery.

'If I slow down we'll miss the ferry,' replied George humbly.

'Nonsense,' his wife snapped again, 'we have plenty of time.'

'But I've calculated the speed exactly,' snivelled George. 'It's a 140 km journey, and I'm going at the exact speed for us to arrive at the terminal exactly on time.'

'Don't you argue with me,' his wife cried as she swung her handbag at the back of George's head. 'Now slow down.'

'Yes dear, anything you say dear, you know best.'

George sighed as he slowed the car down by 14 km per hour.

All was quiet for a time as his wife dropped off to sleep. George kept the car at the lower speed for the rest of the journey, not daring to increase it in case his wife woke up. Eventually they arrived at the terminal just in time to see the ferry leaving the dock and moving slowly out to sea.

'You stupid man,' cried his wife as her handbag made contact with the back of George's head once again.

'You've made us 20 minutes late; I can't trust you to do anything right.'

How fast was George driving before he reduced speed?

See answer page 449

57. The Conference

Five major powers are to hold a meeting to discuss matters of international importance. The organizers of the meeting are faced with the task of formulating the seating arrangements. No party must be made to feel inferior to any other. There have been no objections or instructions as to who sits next to whom. Each delegation will consist of three members who must sit together. The leader of each will sit in the middle with a secretary at either side of him. The decision is made for the discussions to take place at a round table.

In how many different ways can the members be arranged around the table?

See answer page 449

58. Connections

There are many words that can be connected to other words to form a completely different meaning. The word in this puzzle has only four letters, but it has at least two different meanings in its own right. It can act as a prefix to at least 12 others to form new and varied words. The meanings of these 12 words range from 'supposition' to 'the rate of breathing' and from 'insincerity' to 'part of a triangle'. The word itself can mean 'slightly' or can be a nickname for a particular chemical.

Can you name the word?

1 ☐☐☐☐ ....

2 ☐☐☐☐ ....

3 ☐☐☐☐ ....

4 ☐☐☐☐ ....

5 ☐☐☐☐ ....

6 ☐☐☐☐ ....

7 ☐☐☐☐ ....

8 ☐☐☐☐ ....

9 ☐☐☐☐ ....

10 ☐☐☐☐ ....

11 ☐☐☐☐ ....

12 ☐☐☐☐ ....

See answer page 449

59. The Hockey Team

The manager of the local hockey team has the unenviable task of selecting the players. The team is always made up of five men and six women. The club has seven male members and nine female members all of equal ability. As usual everybody wants to be in the first team. He tries his best to be impartial in his selection, but is always accused of favouritism by the people left out.

Throughout the season the manager tries to make sure everyone plays at least once in the first team and also endeavors to try all the combinations of players in order to find the most effective winning team.

How many games will the team have to play to ensure every club member plays in the first team at least once and all team combinations have been tried?

See answer page 450

60. The Astronaut

One of the problems that an astronaut has to deal with is weightlessness, which I imagine might not be unpleasant. What I do believe might be unpleasant is gaining weight again on return to earth: having to feel your limbs becoming heavier and heavier as you approach the earth.

The weight of an astronaut varies inversely as the square of his distance from the center of the earth. If we take the radius of the earth as 6370 km, at what height above the surface of the earth will the astronaut's weight be 1/10 of his weight on earth?

See answer page 450

61. Take a hike

A group of walkers hiked from Town A to Town B at an average speed of four miles an hour, and then back from Town B to Town A at a speed of one mile an hour. The outward journey took one hour less than the return.

How far did they walk on the round trip?

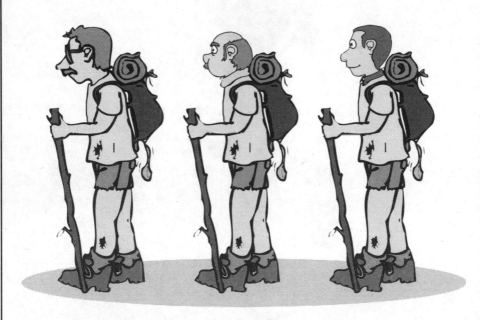

See answer page 450

62. A Drive to the Med

Mr White felt he needed a holiday in the sun, so he took his family on a motoring trip to the south of France. The distance from the English Channel to the Mediterranean is 1,200 km. His car will travel an average distance of 9 km per litre of fuel and 600 km to a litre of oil. He calculated the cost of the journey to be $85.

On the way his fuel consumption was as he expected, but he had to buy an extra litre of oil, which he paid for, as he did for his fuel, in French francs. On his arrival, at the Mediterranean coast, he found he had spent the equivalent of $87.60 on fuel and oil.

What was the average price per litre of the fuel he used?

See answer page 450

63. The Fish Pond

Mr Brown is building himself a fishpond in his back garden. He has dug a circular hole 3 m in diameter and 1 m deep. The sides of the hole are as vertical as he can make them, and the bottom of the hole is perfectly level. He now needs a sheet of waterproof material in order to line the pond, allowing half a meter of overlap all the way around the top.

On his visit to the local aquatic center he finds the lining material is sold only by the square meter. He calculates the area to be covered and asks the sales assistant for 22 m² of material.

The assistant, who is familiar with what Mr Brown is building, says, 'That's not enough to cover the bottom of the pond, the walls and the overlap.'

'Yes it is,' replies Mr Brown. 'I've calculated it carefully.'

'Look,' says the assistant, 'Your pond is 3 m diameter, plus two walls 1 m each, plus 1/2m each side for overlap, which makes a circle of 6 m in diameter. The area of such a circle is $\pi \times 3 \times 3$, which equals 28.27 m², so you need 29 m.'

'No, no,' cried Mr Brown, 'Looking at it from above you will see a circle of 3 m for the pond plus 1/2 m each side for overlap, making a 4 m diameter circle. Find the area of that and add it to the area of the walls you get: $(\pi \times 2 \times 2) + (2 \times \pi \times 1.5 \times 1)$ equals 21.99 m², so I only need 22 m.'

Who is correct?

See answer page 450

64. The Prisoner

Once upon a time there was a ruthless landowner who treated his servants as slaves. One such unfortunate soul was a young man named John. He was given the task of repairing the flat roof of a stone-built out-building set in a remote area of the grounds. He worked night and day on the task in order to please his temperamental master, all to no avail. The landowner was angered by what he called the outrageous cost of the materials. He accused John of stealing and ordered him to be imprisoned in the building until he confessed to his crime.

The weeks passed as John, innocent of any wrongdoing, lay in the single roomed building. There were no windows, and the only entrance was a thick wooden door. The building was unheated, and the floor was made of solid rock. Fearing he would be entombed forever John planned his escape. His only chance was to tunnel through the stone walls. He paced his cell, in the darkness and found it measured 5 m by 4 m. He remembered the area of the roof to be 34 m² and he assumed all the walls would be of the same thickness.

How thick are they?

See answer page 450

65. The Airliner

In planning the layout of a new airliner, it is proposed to install a certain number of complete rows of first-class seats and a certain number of economy-class seats. The conditions governing the installation are:

i. Each row of first-class seats occupies 1.6 m of the length of the cabin, and each row of economy-class seats occupies 1 m; the total length of cabin available is 40 m.

ii. Each row of first-class seats holds 6 passengers, whereas each row of economy-class seats holds 8 passengers; the airline requires that the cabin can seat at least 192 passengers altogether.

iii. Each first-class passenger is entitled to 20 kg of baggage, and each economy-class passenger is entitled to 15 kg of baggage; the total baggage carried must not exceed 3,840 kg.

What is the minimum permissible number of economy-class passengers under these conditions?

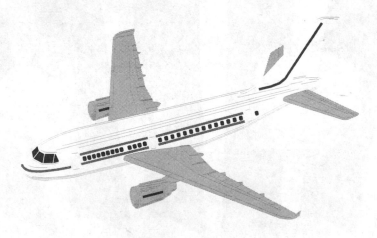

See answer page 450

66. Hieroglyphics

It has always amazed me how experts such as Egyptologists and archaeologists can decipher the strange picture-like writing that is found on many ancient tombs. Where do they begin? How do they know for certain that their interpretation of what is written is correct? I imagine it is purely by mutual agreement between experts in the same subject that any interpretation is accepted.

For my next conundrum I ask you to test your skills in the interpretation of what appear to be hieroglyphics. Below is a series of shapes. Each one follows the last for a particular logical reason. I ask you to find the next shape in the series and explain why the symbols are the shape they are?

See answer page 450

67. The School Teacher

Mr Jones, the school teacher, had an obsession for fine ball-point pens. He had many in his collection, but he only used four of them for work. Each of these pens contained a different coloured ink. Sometimes he only took one pen to work, sometimes two, sometimes three and occasionally all four. He tried to take a different combination of pens to school with him each day.

For how many consecutive days can he take a different selection of pens to work?

See answer page 450

68. Share and Share Alike

Five tramps agreed to meet one evening and share evenly the amount of food and cash each of them had managed to acquire during the day. The first had three loaves of bread, but no cash. The second had two loaves of bread and $1.50. The third had one loaf and $3. The fourth had half a loaf and $3.75. The fifth had no bread but $4.50. Rather than simply pool their spoils and divide it between them, the men with the bread sold it to the men without bread until each man had equal amounts of bread and money.

What was their price for a loaf of bread?

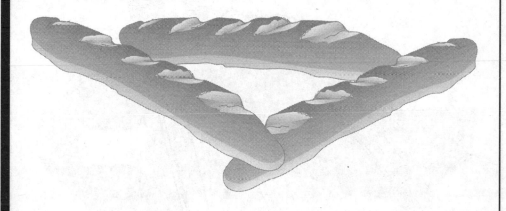

See answer page 450

69. The Sheep Ranch

Lucky Mr Thrifty inherited a sheep ranch in Australia. The documents sent to him by the local attorney described the land as a triangular section, bounded by straight lines joining three small towns. Town B was directly west of town A, while town C lay somewhere between the two, but several miles to the north. The distance between A and B was 12 miles, between A and C 17 miles and between B and C 14 miles.

Having no wish to emigrate to Australia Mr Thrifty instructed the solicitor to sell the land at a price of $1,000 per square mile.

How much money can he expect to receive from the sale of the land?

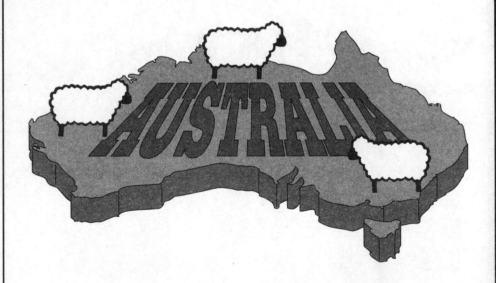

See answer page 450

70. Fuel Prices

In a world of ever-increasing prices we all have to make economies from time to time. Mr Thrifty was more eager than most to do this. He decided that every time the price of fuel was increased by a certain percentage, he would decrease his annual mileage by the same amount, and he would keep careful records of his mileage and the amount he spent. When the last increase of five cents in the dollar came into effect, Mr Thrifty decreased his annual mileage by the same percentage and took a note of his mileage and expenditure.

After a year he compared his expenditure on fuel to the previous year and to his surprise found that he had saved $2.

What was his annual fuel bill before the increase?

See answer page 450

71. Take the Train

Modernization of the transport systems is a continuous process, with the main emphasis on decreasing journey time. Trains are now probably the fastest form of travel for medium-length journeys, although getting to the nearest station is still a time-consuming business.

On average, trains can now cover the same distance in 3/4 of the original time.

How much faster do trains now travel as a fraction of their original speed?

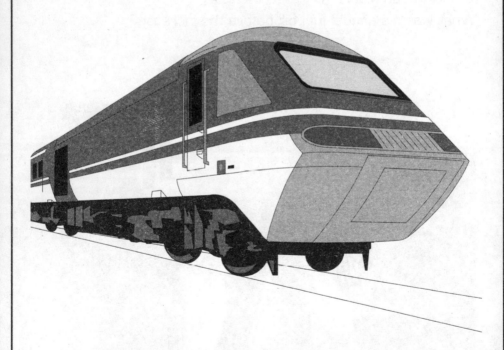

See answer page 450

72. The Jogger

Mr Smith's place of employment is nine miles from his home. One day he decides to jog to work in order to increase his fitness. He estimates the journey time to be a little over 1 hour 45 minutes.

At first he feels fine, but before long his energy begins to fade and he realizes he will not be able to run the whole distance. A passing cab is the answer to his prayer. Mr Smith hails the cab and completes his journey, arriving at work one hour 10 minutes earlier than he had anticipated.

Assuming Mr Smith could run at 1/6 the speed of the cab, how far did he run before he hailed the taxi?

See answer page 450

73. In The Bar

'I am three times as old as my son,' the bartender sighed as he pulled a pint of draught beer.

'Well, none of us is getting any younger,' the man across the bar replied with a degree of sympathy.

'No,' agreed the bartender, 'but it makes me feel better knowing that in 12 years' time I'll only be twice his age.'

'Really!' exclaimed the customer. 'How old are you now then?'

'Ah, that would be telling,' grinned the bartender. 'Work it out for yourself.'

Another customer, overhearing the conversation between the bartender and the first customer, butted in. 'When you've solved that problem, see if you can figure out my age. Eight years ago I was eight times the age of my daughter. Now if you add our ages together they come to 52 years. If you can figure that one out, I'll buy you your next drink.'

See answer page 451

74. Still In The Bar

Some time later, as the bar was closing and the bartender was collecting the empty bottles, he complained to his wife, 'Why do we have to return all these bottles to the brewery? Why can't we just throw them away?'

'Each bottle with its top costs eight cents to make,' replied his wife. 'That's why we have to return them.'

'But we throw the tops away. How much do they cost to make?'

'I don't know, but the bottle costs six cents more than the top. You figure it out.'

See answer page 451

75. Digits, Digits and more Digits

A number containing two digits is increased by 54 when the digits are reversed. If the sum of the digits is 12, what is the number?

A number containing two digits is such that twice the 10 digit is greater than the unit digit by six. When the digits are reversed the number is increased by nine. What is the number?

A number with three digits has the hundred digits three times the unit digit, and the sum of the digits is 19. If the digits are written in reverse order the value of the number is decreased by 594. What is the number?

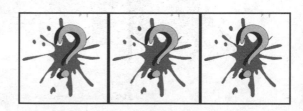

See answer page 451

76. Working his Way through College

A struggling university student, Ivor Nodosh, needs to earn extra cash to subsidize his scholarship. During the summer vacation he manages to obtain temporary work as a shelf-stacker in the local supermarket. His employer, having experience of poor attendance from students he has hired in the past, employs him under certain conditions. Ivor must work for five days a week over a four-week period. He will be paid $25 for every day he works, but will have $10 deducted for every day he fails to attend. He will be paid in a lump sum at the end of the period, provided he attends work on that day.

Ivor works hard for most of the time, but as the days pass his enthusiasm begins to fade and he fails to attend work on several occasions. He does, however, manage to attend on the last day and receives a payment of $395 before deductions.

How many days did he fail to turn up for work?

See answer page 451

77. Student Life

The apartment where Ivor Nodosh lives while at university consists of two rooms. Both rooms are perfectly square, and one room is 1 ft larger in its internal dimensions than the other. The rent Ivor is charged is $1.20 per ft² of floor area per term.

If the rent Ivor pays is $375.60 per term, what are the internal dimensions of the rooms?

See answer page 451

78. Think of a Number

I'm thinking of a number. I double that number, add six and multiply the result by 10. I now divide the result by 20 and take away the number I first thought of.

What is the result?

See answer page 451

79. Think of a Number (Again)

I am now thinking of a two-digit number. I find that if I add the two digits together and divide them into the original number, I obtain the answer seven.

What was the number I was thinking of?

(There are four possible answers.)

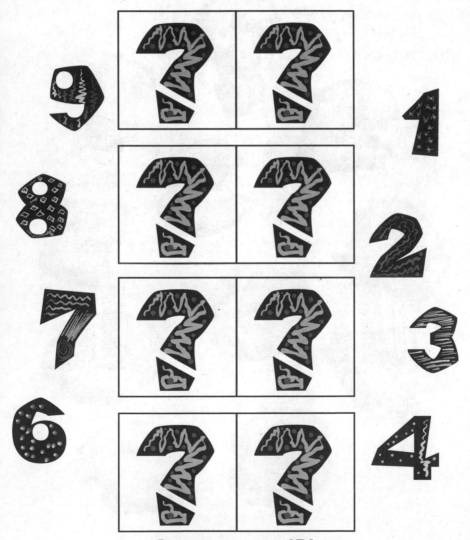

See answer page 451

80. Party Time

We invited 10 married couples to our last New Year's Eve party. When they had all arrived I found all the ladies preferred to drink spirits while the men wanted cans of beer. Having only a limited supply of drinks, I decided it would be only fair to share the cans equally between the men before the party got fully underway. To my surprise, I found that if I had invited one more couple, each man would have received one drink less and I would have been able to have the extra can myself.

How many cans were shared at the party?

See answer page 451

81. The Boatman

A boatman whose craft can travel at 6 mph in still water finds that whenever he travels upstream the journey takes twice as long as the return trip. This happens every time, regardless of the length of journey. The current of the river on which he travels is always at a constant speed.

What is the speed of the current?

See answer page 451

82. The Round Trip

Mr Mensaman, who resides in Southtown, has to travel to Northtown to visit his brother. He catches the 11.20am train and arrives in Northtown in time for lunch. Looking at the station clock as he disembarks, his razor-sharp brain calculates the average speed of the train to have been 72 km/h.

After spending two hours taking lunch and visiting his brother he decides to return home by bus. The route the bus takes is 2 km longer than the train journey, but it stops directly outside Southtown railway station. As Mr Mensaman steps down from the bus he confirms his time of arrival as 3.15 p.m. He calculates the speed at which the bus has been travelling and finds it to have been 40 km/h.

What is the distance between Southtown and Northtown by train?

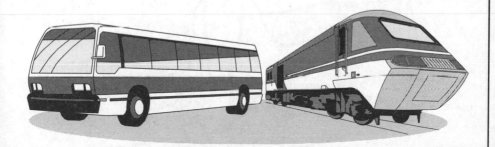

See answer page 451

83. Vacation by the Sea

Mr Mensaman always goes to the same place for his vacation. This year, money is a little tight, so he takes with him only $420 to cover his hotel bill and spending money. He budgets his expenditure very carefully and tries to make the vacation last for as long as possible. As the money runs out and the vacation inevitably draws to a close, Mr Mensaman recalculates his finances. He finds that if he had spent $7 a day less he could have extended the vacation for another five days.

How long a vacation did he have?

See answer page 451

84. A Day in the Life of a Greengrocer

Mr B. Troot, the greengrocer, bought a certain number of pineapples for $72, but found he could not sell the last 10% and they were wasted. The rest he sold at a profit of 8 cents per pineapple. Mr Troot found he had made a profit of $14.40 on the deal.

How many pineapples did he buy?

Mr B. Troot next bought a number of pounds of apples for $4. If they been 4 cents per pound cheaper, he could have bought 5 lb more for the same money.

How much did he pay, per pound, for the apples?

After carrying sacks of potatoes each day Mr B. Troot becomes tired and has to take a rest. On these occasions he uses the time to work out his finances. He stocks two types of potatoes, one type he buys for $1.50 per sack and the other for $1.70. He calculates that if he had bought half as many at $1.50 and twice as many at $1.70, his bill would have been $196 instead of the $188 he actually paid.

How many sacks of each type of potato did he buy?

See answer page 451

85. More and More Moores

Old Mrs Moore was having a party to celebrate her 90th birthday and needed to hire a reception hall in order to accommodate all her descendants. She invited her children and their spouses, her grandchildren and their spouses and all her great-grandchildren.

She had three times as many grandchildren as she had children and three times as many great-grandchildren as grandchildren. 86 people in all attended the party.

How many children did Mrs Moore have?

See answer page 451

86. Are You Sitting Comfortably?

Sitting uneasily in the doctor's waiting room one day, a prospective patient stared at the clock on the wall. She had been waiting for what seemed an age.

To take her mind off the reason for her visit she started to invent little puzzles to solve.

Estimating the length of the minute hand of the clock to be 4 in, she calculated the distance the hand had travelled around the clock since she had first arrived to be 15 in.

How long had she been waiting?

See answer page 451

87. Coffee Break Quiz

This brief interlude from the more studious conundrums is to provide the dedicated puzzle solver with a little relaxation before embarking on the next section of mind-straining problems. Each statement is a cryptic clue to a well-known phrase or saying. Your job, obviously, is to find the correct interpretation.

1. Sewing the herb stops one over the eight.
2. Soft pencil or hard pencil.
3. A quick leaf through his astronomy magazine cheers up the sheep herder no end.
4. A quick swig won't make the sun shine.
5. Peter and Thomas hope the Captain doesn't appear and ruin the appetizer.

The next five statements are cryptic clues to the titles of Bond films.

1. The mean physician.
2. The satellite gardener.
3. Au. I.
4. The eight legged cat.
5. Stormy dance.

And finally, in case there is a tie :

What well-known event is hidden in this statement: 'the subscription to the candle-makers' union'?

See answer page 451

88. Take the Train 2

From Ammington to Cadfield is 375 miles by rail. Brotherton is on the line between them and is 150 miles from Ammington. At 12.00 a train sets out from Ammington and travels to Brotherton, arriving at 13.15. It waits there for 15 minutes and then travels on to Cadfield, arriving at 15.00. Another train leaves Cadfield at 12.30 and travels non-stop to Ammington at an average speed of 100 miles per hour.

How far from Brotherton do the two trains pass each other and at what time?

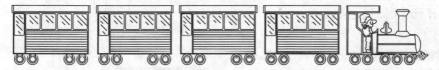

See answer page 451

89. How High is the Mountain?

The Canary Islands are known for a particular landscape feature, the Peak of Tenerife. Mountaineers who have climbed the peak are said to be able to see the coast of Africa on a clear day.

One such adventurous person took with him an instrument for measuring angles with the intention of calculating the height of the mountain for himself. On reaching the summit he accurately measured the angle of depression to the horizon and found it to be 1.97°. Taking the diameter of the earth to be 7,914 miles,

How high is the mountain?

See answer page 452

90. What Time is it Over There?

Have you ever considered how time is calculated when travelling? We have to put our clocks and watches forward if we travel west and back if we travel east. For convenience we use multiples of one hour, but this is not absolutely correct. As we travel, time must change at a uniform rate in either direction.

From this we can form a little problem, which may keep us occupied on those long boring journeys.

Today is June 21 and it is 12 noon.

What is the absolute time at a place exactly 75° west?

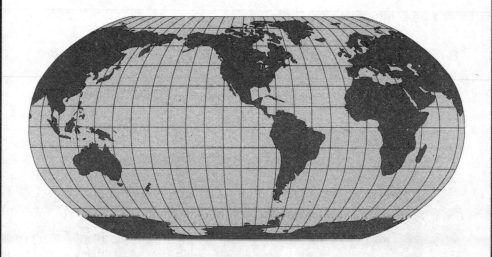

See answer page 452

91. Over a Barrel

Barrels and casks have been made and used for centuries for the storing of many different types of liquid. Barrel-making is a highly skilled job, and the art is more or less declining as metal casks become more common. Have you ever wondered how the coopers of old knew how large to make a barrel to hold a specified amount of liquid? Nowadays with the help of calculus and modern computers there is no problem, but calculus was not developed until the late 17th century, and barrels had been in use for a long time by then. My next conundrum asks you to calculate the capacity of a barrel. Unfortunately you do not have the advantage or the opportunity to use trial and error, and neither are you allowed to use calculus or a computer. A barrel has a diameter of 24 in at its base and its head, a diameter of 32 in at the center and a height of 40 in.

How much liquid will it hold?

By the way, just to add to your vexation, I need the answer in gallons.

See answer page 452

92. Bubbles in the Bath

When sitting in the bath tub as a child, did you ever wonder why bubbles are round?

The scientific explanation is that a sphere holds the maximum volume for the smallest surface area. The gas inside a bubble tries to expand while the surface tension tries to contract, thus forming a sphere. Checking the theory for myself I found that if I took the volume of a sphere 2 in in diameter and divided it by the surface area, I arrived at the ratio of 1:3.

If I did the same thing, but with a 2 in cube, I arrived at the same ratio.

Was this coincidence or is the scientific explanation in doubt?

See answer page 452

93. Cannon Balls

The complexity of mathematics used by our ancestors long before such things as calculators or computers were invented never ceases to amaze me. One such formula I came across recently while browsing through my collection of old books was for the calculation of the initial velocity of a projectile as it was fired from a cannon. It appears that the velocity of a cannon ball is directly proportional to the square root of the weight of the charge of gun powder and inversely proportional to the weight of the cannon ball. It is given by this formula:

V = 1600 x the square root of 3C/B where C is the weight of the charge and B is the weight of the cannon ball.

Given that the velocity of a cannon ball weighing 24 lb is 800 ft per second, what would be the velocity of an 18 lb ball fired with the same charge?

See answer page 452

94. The Playing Field

The local school was holding a sports day in the nearby playing field. This field was perfectly square and the ground reasonably flat. A race between the school's fastest runners was arranged. The coach wanted the race to be staged on the longest and straightest course possible, so he marked out a track along the diagonal of the field. The race was won by little Billy Wiz in a time of 28.28 seconds. The coach, pleased with the result, calculated that Billy had run at a speed of 5 m per second.

What is the area of the field to the nearest square metre?

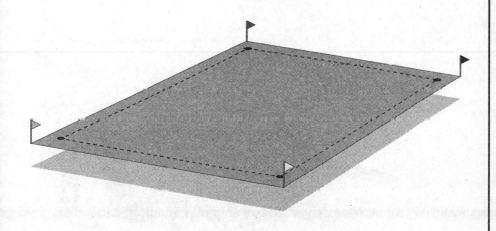

See answer page 452

95. The Inscribed Circle

A triangular field which has one side 10 m in length is the pasture for Nanny the goat. She is tethered to a rope which is tied to a stake set into the ground. The position of the stake and the length of the rope is such that Nanny can just reach each of the boundaries of the field. Two sides of the field, which are equal in length, both form angles of 70° with the 10 m side.

What is the area of pasture available for Nanny to feed from?

See answer page 452

96. The Circumscribed Circle

The cutting tool that bores large circular holes into wood is often in the shape of an equilateral triangle with a cutting edge on each vertex. This shape of cutter is often preferred because it allows more clearance between the work piece and the tool, and yet provides perfect balance when run at high speeds. The only problem with this type of cutter is choosing the correct size tool for a particular size of hole. Being triangular in shape it cannot be measured directly across the diameter and so the size of hole it will produce has to be calculated. Such a cutter is selected and when measured between the vertices is found to be exactly 5 cm.

What is the diameter of the hole it will produce?

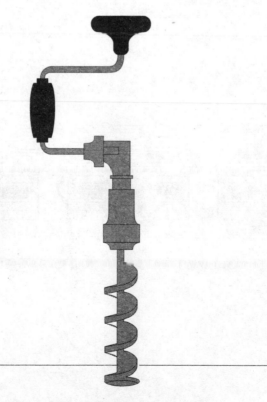

See answer page 452

97. The Builder's Conundrum

A builder builds three identical detached houses beside each other. Each one requires a connection to gas, water and electricity. The local utility companies are renowned for non-cooperation with each other. All three companies agree to supply the service required for each of the houses, but only under certain conditions: the route chosen for the supply cable or pipe-work must be such that it does not cross over, at any point, either of the other two services, and the supplies must be laid below ground level. The supplies cannot pass beneath any buildings.

Can you find such a route?

See answer page 453

98. There's a Hole in my Bucket

In my garden there is an old metal bucket in which I collect rain water to irrigate my plants. The bucket measures 20 cm at the base, 30 cm at the brim and is 25 cm deep. During a recent downpour the bucket was filled to overflowing with rainwater, but unfortunately it suddenly sprang a leak right at the bottom. It now loses water at a rate of one millilitre per second.

How long will it take for the bucket to empty, provided that it doesn't rain in the meantime?

See answer page 453

99. Stop the Leak

In order to conserve as much rainwater as I could, I tilted the bucket at an angle. (This is the same bucket as in 98.) The hole was located where the bottom joined the side, right in the corner. Turning it so that the hole was uppermost, I secured the bucket in such a position that the upper rim and the hole were on the same level. Last night it rained, filling my tilted bucket with as much water as it can hold in its present position.

How much water will it now hold?

(Answers in litres, please.)

See answer page 453

100. Going into Orbit

Have you ever wondered what the earth looks like from outer space? The view must be fantastic. I know we have all seen photographs, but I imagine these cannot compare in the slightest with the real thing. If we travelled far enough away from the earth we could see half of its surface at once, but how far must we travel away from the earth in order to see just 1/3 of its surface?

See answer page 453

101. The Wicked Queen

Once upon a time in a land far away lived a wicked queen with an insatiable appetite for strong young men. She would take them into her palace, make use of them and then draft them into the army when she grew tired of them.

One such young man, named Sam, came to the attention of the queen. He lived on a farm with his widowed mother. The queen ordered him report to the palace the very next day. Sam's mother pleaded with the queen not to take her son. She could not run the farm alone; without him she would starve. The queen, unmoved by the mother's appeal but not wishing to seem unfair in the eyes of her courtiers, struck a bargain with her.

'Meet me, with your son, in the courtyard tomorrow,' she demanded. 'There we will put two pebbles in a bag, one black and one white, and your son will pick out one of them. If he chooses the black pebble then he is mine. If he chooses the white pebble he is yours. If he refuses to pick a pebble then you will both be charged with treason and thrown into prison.'

Next day Sam and his mother waited in the courtyard of the palace. Eventually the queen arrived with one of her attendants. Sam watched as the attendant bent down and picked up two pebbles from the gravel pathway. His keen eye noticed that the attendant placed two black pebbles into the bag. The queen then asked Sam to pick out the pebble that would determine his fate and that of his mother.

How did Sam resolve the situation?

See answer page 453

102. The Pentagon

Anyone who watches American television will be familiar with the headquarters of the American Department of Defense. Their offices are situated in a five-sided building in Washington D.C. known as The Pentagon.

Now a pentagon is one of the more difficult of the geometrical shapes to draw accurately. There are several ways to construct one inside a circle, but they are all quite complex and difficult to remember. There is a way of calculating the length of the side of a pentagon given the radius of the circle that encloses it. The formula is quite straightforward if you can find it. Once you have done that, find the length of the side of a pentagon which is enclosed in a circle 12 cm in diameter.

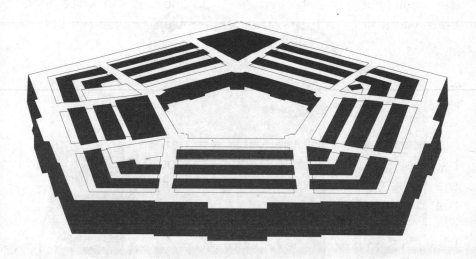

See answer page 453

103. Squares and Circles

A well-known trick for a surprise present at a birthday party is to buy a small item and place it in a cardboard box. The box is placed in a larger box, and that box into one which is larger still, and so on until the small present looks like a much larger one. My next conundrum involves boxes within boxes, but with a slight difference.

A box in the shape of a perfect cube with a volume of 1 litre is placed inside a globe. The diameter of the globe is such that the box fits exactly inside it. The globe is then, in turn, placed in a larger cubical box. Again it is a perfect fit.

What is the volume of the larger box?

(Ignore the thickness of the walls of the smaller box and the globe.)

See answer page 453

104. The Wine Glass and the Crystal Ball

This next conundrum is a particularly evil one. Like all good conundrums it has the appearance of simplicity, but there is a nasty sting in the tail (or tale).

A large conical wine glass is filled to the brim with fine red wine. A perfectly spherical crystal ball is placed, gently, into the glass, causing the wine to spill over. If the diameter of the glass at the mouth is 5 in and the depth is 6 in, while the diameter of the ball is 4 in,

How much wine is spilled?

See answer page 454

105. Wire It Up

One cubic foot of copper is to be made into one continuous length of wire. This is done by heating the copper to a point where the metal is pliable and then drawing it through a series of rollers. Each pair of rollers has a circular groove around its circumference. The diameter of the groove decreases slightly with each pair of rollers so that the copper is forced through the grooves until it reaches the required diameter. Obviously the formed wire increases in length with every pair of rollers it passes through. The speed of the wire passing from roller to roller also increases as the copper is forced to become ever smaller in cross-sectional area.

For my next conundrum I ask you to find the length of wire produced from one cubic foot of copper when its diameter is reduced to 0.025 in.

(I would like the answer in miles please.)

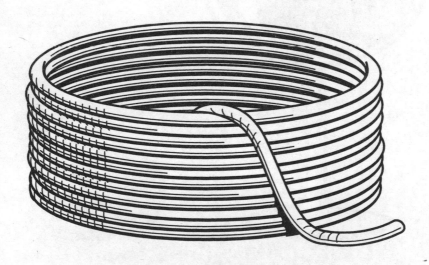

See answer page 454

106. Belt Up

Most people who drive a car or ride a bicycle are familiar with transference of momentum via a belt or chain from one pulley or gear to another. One pulley is driven by the engine or by muscle power, and the movement is transferred to the belt, which in turn drives the second pulley. The size difference of the two pulleys determines the final speed of the second pulley.

To calculate the length of the belt between two pulleys of equal diameters we must add together the two halves of the circumferences of the pulleys and twice the center distance between them. For example, if two pulleys 15 cm in diameter are fixed 45 cm apart, then the length of belt required to connect them is found by:

$$\tfrac{1}{2} (2 \times 3.142 \times 15) + (2 \times 45) = 137.1$$

But can you find the length of belt required if the speed is to be increased by a ratio of 1:4? A pulley 30 cm in diameter is connected by a belt to a second pulley 7.5 cm in diameter. The centers of the two pulleys are fixed at a distance of 45 cm apart.

What is the length of the belt which connects them?

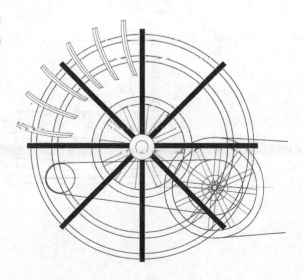

See answer page 454

107. Bridge over Troubled Water

The little village of Soggyfoot in the mountains is famous for its picturesque village green and its large circular duck pond. The pond is 140 m in diameter and is the centerpiece of the village. The village pub and the local shops are on one side of the pond while most of the residential buildings are on the other. The residents have complained to the council about the distance the elderly have to walk around the pond to reach the shops and have campaigned for a bridge. Reluctantly the local government has agreed, but to save costs the bridge is not to pass over the centre of the pond. It will be built to one side, as this is a shorter span. The proposed bridge will be positioned 1/4 of the way along the diameter of the pond, splitting the pond in a ratio of 3:1. The cost of the bridge is estimated at $100 per metre.

How much money will be saved by building the bridge in this position rather than straight across the centre?

See answer page 454

108. The Legacy

When an old man died he left his 10 grandchildren a large sum of money to be divided between them. The old man had one failing in his life: he showed blatant favouritism among his descendants. This continued after his death.

The will was read and the conditions of the legacy were disclosed. A list was provided with the names of the 10 grandchildren written in order of preference. The money, $100,000 in all, was to be distributed in this order, the name at the top of the list receiving the most and the name at the bottom of the list receiving the least. There were to be even increments between the 10 so that the difference between the amounts of money each of them received was constant.

If number eight on the list received $6,000 how much did each of the other nine receive?

See answer page 454

109. Fields of Corn

A farmer owns two fields of different sizes, in which he grows corn. Together they cover an area of 30 acres. From the first field he can reap 40 kg of corn per acre but from the second only 30 kg per acre. At harvest time he weighs the total yield from each field and finds that he has produced 500 kg more from the larger field than from the smaller.

What are the sizes of the two fields?

See answer page 454

110. The Three Wise Women

Three fashion-conscious young women were downtown shopping one day. They stopped and looked in the window of a shop selling hats. There in the window was a hat that each of them liked, priced at $170, but none of them had enough money left to buy it. They each examined the contents of their purses.

The first said to the other two, 'If you lend me 1/2 of what you have I can buy the hat.'

The second said to the other two, 'If you lend me a 1/3 of what you have I can buy the hat.'

'But,' the third said to the other two, 'if you loan me a 1/4 of what you have I could buy the hat.'

How much money did each of them have in their purses?

See answer page 455

111. Fit for a King

For his coronation the King of Catania commissioned a crown to be made. It was to be embedded with diamonds, rubies and other precious stones, but his main cause of concern was the weight of it. He gave special instructions that its weight before the stones were positioned on it was to be no more than 60 oz. It was to be made from gold, platinum, silver and copper. The gold and silver together would make up 66.66 per cent of the weight, the gold and the copper 75 per cent of the weight and the gold and the platinum 60 per cent.

How much of each metal was used to make the crown?

See answer page 455

112. Pipes and Tanks

A large water tank is fed from four different supplies. Each supply has a different sized pipe. The largest pipe, when running at full bore, can fill the tank in one day. The next largest can fill the tank in two days, the next in three days and the smallest in four.

How long will it take to fill the tank with all four pipes running at their maximum flow?

(Answer in hours and minutes, please)

See answer page 455

113. The Charity Walk

A group of five people of various ages and fitness agreed to organize a sponsored walk for charity. The walk was to be in the form of a relay over a distance of 100 miles. It was agreed that each person would cover a different distance according to their ability. The oldest person would be the first to go and would walk a given distance. The next person would walk the same as the last plus a measured amount, and so on. This allowed the youngest and fittest to be the last walker and cover the greatest distance. A list of the names and distances to be covered was prepared. This was scrutinized by the group, and they discovered that the last three walkers were covering seven times the distance of the first two.

How far was each member asked to walk?

See answer page 455

114. The Owl and the Weasel

A wise old owl was sitting high in a treetop one moonlit night waiting for his supper to arrive. He knew that a weasel lived in a hole at the base of the tree, and he was determined that the weasel would become his evening meal. Eventually the weasel arrived at a spot which was three times the height of the tree away from the hole. The owl and the weasel's eyes met at the same instant!

The weasel made a dash for the hole. The wise old owl instantly assessed the speed at which the rodent was running and swooped down to a point of interception. When the owl grabbed the weasel they had both travelled equal distances in straight lines.

How far was the weasel from the hole when he met his fate?

See answer page 455

115. Unit Fractions

The ancient Egyptians regarded fractions differently than we do today. To them general fractions such as 3/4 were part of an incomplete process. They believed that all fractions, with the possible exception of 2/3, were the sum of a series of unit fractions – that is, fractions with the number 1 as the numerator, such as 1/2, 1/4, 1/3, etc. For example 2/5 can be expressed as 1/3 + 1/15, or 2/11 can be written as 1/6 + 1/66.

My next conundrum asks you to express a fraction in the terms of two unit fractions, if you can.

If 1/x + 1/y = 2/103, find x and y when x and y are whole numbers and x does not equal y.

See answer page 456

116. The Six Brothers

There once was a farmer who had six sons. Each one was born exactly a year after the last. As the years went by the farmer thought it was time for the boys to learn the rudiments of crop growing, so he allocated each boy a piece of land which was proportional to their ages. He did this by dividing one of his rectangular fields with a fence which ran along the diagonal, thus forming a triangle. He then sub-divided the triangle with six fences equal distances apart, parallel to the side, which formed a right-angle with the length. The length of the triangular field was 120 m, and it covered an area of 3,000 square metres. Now each section of land was allocated to one of the brothers, the oldest receiving the largest, the next oldest receiving the next largest and so on with the youngest receiving the smallest.

Each piece of land was smaller than the one next to it by the same proportion; that is to say, the pieces of land decreased in area by a constant increment.

By how much did each section of land decrease in area?

See answer page 456

117. In the Heat of the Sun

It was high noon when the truck broke down, traveling east to west on the main road that runs exactly along the equator across Africa. The red ignition light on the dashboard had been showing for some time; now the battery was completely dead, and the truck came to a standstill. Luckily the driver had his mobile phone with him, and he telephoned for help, but it was going to be several hours before anyone could reach him.

The sun blazed down making the cab as hot as an oven. The driver could sit in it no longer; he had to find some shade. He looked around. The landscape was completely flat; the only thing standing was a line of telegraph poles that ran parallel with the road. Even these did not create shade as the sun was directly overhead. The only place to hide from the sun's rays was under the truck. The driver crawled under there, and lying on his back on the hot tarmac he waited.

Eventually the rescue truck arrived. As the driver emerged from beneath his own vehicle he noticed that the telegraph poles now had shadows. These seemed to be equal in length to the height of the poles.

What time was it when help arrived?

See answer page 456

118. Busy Bees

A colony of bees lives in a square-shaped beehive, the corners of which face north, south, east and west. The entrance to the beehive is on the south-facing corner. Bertie Bee is flying home, in a southerly direction, fully laden with pollen. On reaching his home he flies past the western corner at a distance of 2.5 m away and level with the entrance. Unable to negotiate a sharp left-hand turn, because of the weight he is carrying, he flies in a spiral around the hive and lands safely at the entrance. If the beehive is 50 cm² on each side, how far did Bertie fly from when he started his spiral to when he landed?

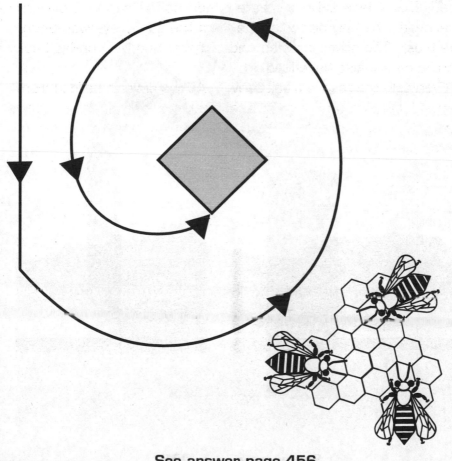

See answer page 456

119. A Roll of Ribbon

My wife has a small roll of white ribbon with which she wishes to decorate a present for a wedding. The ribbon is 0.01 cm thick and is wound around a centre core 1 cm in diameter. The overall diameter of the roll is exactly 3 cm. Just before starting the decoration she asked, 'Can you tell me how much ribbon there is on this roll without me going to the trouble of unwinding it?'

'Of course my dear,' I replied, and set about the calculation.

How much ribbon was on the roll?

See answer page 456

120. A Pack of Candles

A candle manufacturer needed to pack his candles in such a way as to prevent them moving about within the packaging and damaging each other. The best and cheapest packaging he could find was hexagonal tubing. Into cardboard tubing in the shape of a hexagon he could fit seven candles snugly, with six of the candles touching three others and the side of the tube, and the seventh candle held firmly by the other six. This method of packaging prevented movement and subsequent damage. If the candles are 3.5 cm in diameter, what is the length of one of the sides of the hexagon?

See answer page 457

121. To Catch the Train

Mr Commuter lives in a apartment in the centre of town, but works in London. He garages his car some distance away from his home and uses it each morning to drive to the station where he catches the train to London. The garage is en route to the station. Mr Commuter walks the distance at a speed of 8 km/h and then motors the rest of the way at a speed of 40 km/h. The normal journey time is 21 minutes.

One morning he is late and runs to the garage at 16 km/h and motors to the station at 60 km/h. He completes the journey in 11 1/2 minutes.

How far is it from Mr Commuter's home to the station?

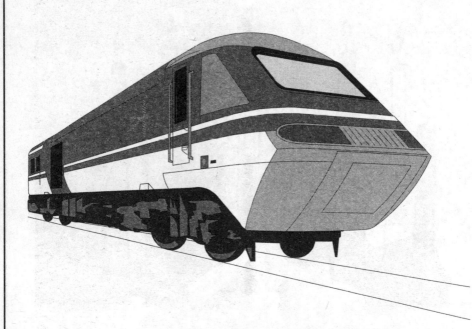

See answer page 457

122. The Travellers

A survey was recently carried out at a busy airport to find just where all those travellers had been to. Of those interviewed 55 said that in the past year they had been to Spain, 53 had been to France and 79 to Germany. 18 had been to Spain and France, 17 to Spain and Germany, and 25 to France and Germany. 10 travelers said they had visited all three countries.

How many people took part in the survey?

See answer page 457

123. The Pine Tree

In a forest grew a pine tree. The magnificent tree grew tall and perfectly straight. Its height reached a full 25 m. All was quiet and peaceful in the forest. The wild flowers grew, and the rabbits and squirrels played on the forest floor. The grass was speckled with sunlight, which peered through the branches of the pine tree. Slowly the sunlight was blocked by heavy rain clouds which blackened the sky, filling the forest with darkness. The small animals scurried back into the holes for protection. A storm was brewing.

Suddenly, and without warning, the forest was lit by a bolt of lightning. It struck the pine tree at a point some way up the trunk. The pine tree swayed as smoke rose from the wound. It swayed once more before it came crashing down, the noise almost drowned by the crash of thunder that followed the lightning bolt. The tree-top hit the forest floor some 5 m away from its base. The ground shook slightly with the impact.

As quickly as they had come the storm clouds cleared, and once again the sunlight beckoned the creatures out of their hiding places. They looked at the poor tree, standing with the fallen top part still attached to the trunk like some giant triangular monument, a lasting reminder of the power of nature.

How far up the trunk did the lightning strike?

See answer page 457

124. Sinking a well

Calculating the cost of sinking a well is quite a complicated procedure. The cost is directly proportional to the time it takes to sink the well. The time taken varies, as the depth varies, in two different ways: partly as the square of the depth and partly as the cube of the depth.

A well needs to be sunk to a depth of 20 m. The cost has been estimated at $50 per hour. The manager of the drilling rig knows that it took 60 hours to sink a well which was 10 m deep, and it took 146 1/4 hours to sink a well 15 m deep. He now needs to calculate the cost of sinking the new well 20 m deep.

Can you help?

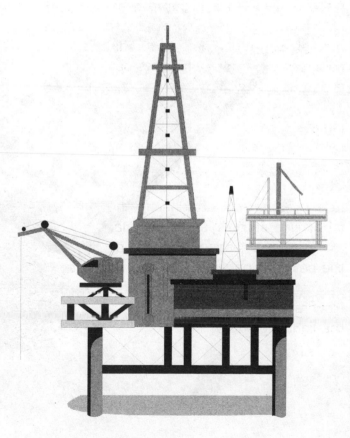

See answer page 458

125. Find the Fraction

With the popularity of the pocket calculator, standard fractions are becoming used less and less. This next little conundrum will help to exercise those skills that are in danger of being forgotten.

If seven is added to both the numerator and the denominator of a fraction, it becomes equal to 5/6. If instead five is added to the numerator and seven to the denominator, it becomes equal to 3/4.

Find the original fraction.

See answer page 458

126. The Bowling Green

The members of the local bowling club hold a meeting to discuss the condition of the green. In recent times the green has been ruined by local children playing on it when the club is closed. It is proposed that a trench be dug all around the green to try to prevent children gaining access and the soil from the trench be used to raise the surface of the green by 1 ft in height. The green is 300 ft long and 200 ft wide, and it is agreed that the trench needs to be 8 ft in width to prevent easy access.

How deep does the trench need to be to provide the necessary amount of soil?

See answer page 458

127. An Old Babylonian Conundrum

The Babylonians, who lived some 4,000 years ago, were the occupants of the area of land between the Tigris and Euphrates rivers, a land known as Mesopotamia. The ancient people of Babylon were quite remarkable. They had mastered the rudiments of algebra, and the relationship between the sides of a right-angled triangle was known to them many hundreds of years before it was attributed to Pythagoras.

An old Babylonian tablet unearthed at Susa asks for the radius of a circle circumscribing a triangle whose sides are 50, 50 and 60. Now these people did not, as far as we know, have access to tables of trigonomical values such as sine, cosine and tangents. They were able to solve the problem by use of algebra and the relationship between the sides of triangles.

Can you solve the problem without resorting to the use of trigonometry?

See answer page 458

128. De Morgan's Conundrum

Augustus De Morgan, an eminent mathematician of the 19th century, helped to found the British Association for the Advancement of Science in 1831. De Morgan was appointed a professor of mathematics at the newly established London University at the age of 22, where he continued to teach for many more years. He was a lover of conundrums, many of which are listed in his BUDGET OF PARADOXES edited by his widow after his death.

At one time he proposed the following conundrum concerning his age: 'I was x years old in the year x squared.'

Can you figure out in what year Augustus De Morgan was born?

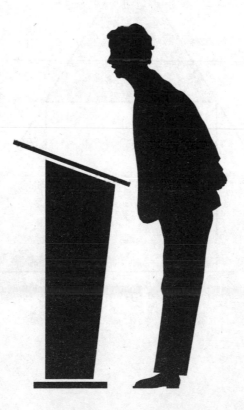

See answer page 458

129. A Square in a Triangle

In the garden of a stately home, there is a pathway that forms an isosceles triangle. It surrounds three triangular flower beds and a square of lawn. The pathway measures 12 m by 10 m by 10 m. The lawn forms a perfect square and touches the pathway along the 12 m length. It also touches the two 10 m lengths of path at two points.

What is the length of the side of the lawn?

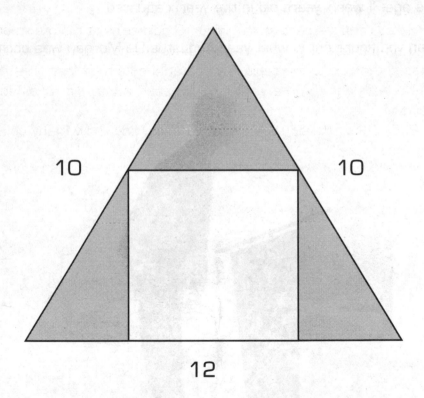

See answer page 458

130. Buried Treasure

Many years ago a group of six pirates uncovered a hoard of gold coins buried in the sand on a remote desert island. The captain of the group, being a mean and bloodthirsty cut-throat, demanded a third share of the booty for himself. No one argued except the first mate, who claimed that if the captain had a third share then the mate should have a quarter and the boatswain a fifth. The captain agreed but said that because the cook had to be kept sweet he could have an eighth share.

'What about us?' cried the last two pirates, one a scurvy crewman and the other the cabin boy.

'Here,' cried the captain, throwing 10 gold coins at the crewman, 'and as for little Jim here, he can have a single gold piece.' He passed the coin to the cabin boy and grinned a toothless grin, his foul breath choking the lad as he pressed it into his small soft hand.

'But . . .' stuttered the frightened cabin boy, 'how many coins have we found?'

See answer page 459

131. The Farmer's Fields

A farmer owns two plots of land. They are both perfectly square and together cover an area of 1,000 m². The length of the side of the smaller field is 10 m less than 2/3 the length of the side of the other field.

What are the dimensions of the two fields?

See answer page 459

132. Sharing the Winnings

Six men together win $180 at the races. The winnings are to be divided between them, but not in equal proportions. The sum is divided in such a way as to ensure the difference between the amounts is always constant, and the sum of the four largest shares is 5 3/7 times the sum of the two smaller shares.

How much did each man receive?

See answer page 459

133. Washing the Blanket

One day Mrs D. Tergent decides to wash her favorite blanket. Placing it in the washing machine and setting the program on hot wash, she stands back and watches as the machine does its job.

On completion of the wash Mrs D. Tergent starts to remove the blanket from the machine and stares in horror. It has shrunk. The blanket is now 7/8 of its original length and 9/10 of the original width.

By what percentage of its original area has the blanket decreased in size?

See answer page 459

134. Stacking the Shelves

A supermarket manager was designing a new display for breakfast cereals. He wished to display four different types of cereal in the ratio of 1:2:3:4. The display shelf held 10 packets less than his minimum requirements so he increased the length of the shelf by 50 per cent. The new shelf held all he required plus another 10 packets. Assuming all the packets were of equal thickness, how many of each type of cereal did he finally have on display when the new shelf was full?

See answer page 459

135. The Three Drunks

Fred, Stan and Bill foolishly embark on a drinking campaign to see just how much beer each one of them can consume before passing out. The rules are that each man will drink as much as he can and continue drinking until every one of them is completely paralytic.

Bill is the first to collapse in a drunken stupor, much to the amusement of the other two. Four pints later Stan follows him under the table, but Fred carries on drinking. Fred manages to force down yet another four pints before he can no longer stand upright. The landlord reckons that together they drank 15 litres of beer.

How many pints of beer did each man consume?

See answer page 459

136. A Cubic Calendar

Two perfect cubes have numbers painted on the sides to enable them to be used as a calendar. By arranging the cubes, placed side by side, the number combination of the two faces on display can be made to show the date of each day in the month. There are 12 faces in total and each face has only one number painted on it.

What are the numbers on each face of the two cubes?

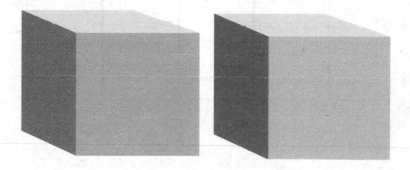

See answer page 460

137. A Five-Letter Word

There is a five-letter word that contains three consonants and two vowels. Although the word has five letters, three of them are the same. The two vowels are different letters, but the three consonants are all alike.

What is the word?

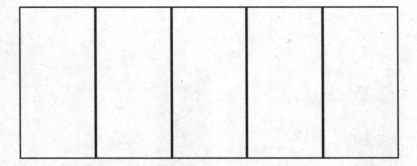

See answer page 460

138. An Angle in Time

The old long-case clock in the corner of the room ticks away as it has done for over a hundred years. Time and constant cleaning has removed all the numbers and decoration from the clock face. Now all that is left are the hour and minute hands slowly revolving across a white background.

As I look at the clock it is a quarter past the hour, and the angle between the center lines of the hour and minute hands is 37.5°. In 20 minutes' time I will look at the clock again and find the angle between the two hands has changed to 72.5°. My stomach tells me it must be about time to eat.

Will someone please tell me what the time is now?

See answer page 460

139. From an Ellipse to a circle

If a circular cylinder is cut by an inclined plane that does not intersect the base, the resultant shape is an ellipse. It must follow from this that if an elliptical cylinder is cut by an inclined plane that does not intersect the base, it can form either another ellipse; or, if it is cut in the correct plane at the correct angle, the result can be a perfect circle.

An elliptical cylinder whose major axis is twice its minor axis is cut by an inclined plane with the resulting shape being a perfect circle.

At what angle and in what plane must this cut be made to give the desired result?

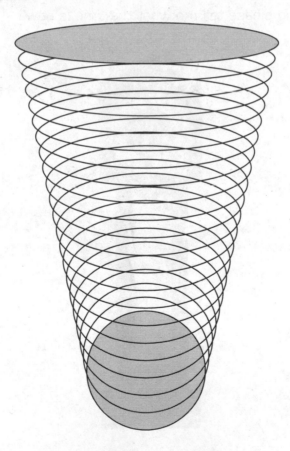

See answer page 460

140. The More You Buy the More You Get

On a Saturday morning in the market place there are many bargains to be had, particularly among perishable goods. On one particular day a flower-seller had a large amount of stock left that had to be sold. At 3 p.m. he offered flowers at a price of 10 for $4. By 3.30 he had increased the offer to 17 for $5. He continued to increase the offer during the afternoon until by close of trading he was practically giving them away at 37 for $7.

How many flowers did he offer for sale at the price of $6?

See answer page 460

141. Changing the Patio

At the rear of Mr Mason's house there was a rectangular patio made from flagstones each 2 ft x 2 ft. The patio fitted nicely across the rear of his lounge on the north side and the wall of his extension on the west. Mrs Mason wanted the patio made smaller in order to create a flower bed. It was decided that the best way to do this was to cut along the diagonal of the patio from the south-west corner to the northeast corner with a stone saw and take up half of the flagstones leaving a triangular patio. Mr Mason could then use the uncut flagstones that he had removed to build a sun terrace at the bottom of the garden.

If the original patio measured 26 ft on the north side and 22 ft on the west, how many uncut flagstones did Mr Mason recover from the alteration?

See answer page 460

142. Cowboy Joe

Out riding one day Cowboy Joe finds himself 6 miles north and 2 miles west of his log cabin. He wishes to water his horse before starting the journey home. There is a long straight river 5 miles west of his present position which runs directly north to south.

What is the shortest route he can take to reach the river and then his home, and how far will he have to travel?

See answer page 460

143. The Pool Player

A player wishes to hit the white ball so that it bounces off the cushion (assumed perfectly elastic) and strikes the other ball without first hitting the black.

Which of the positions marked on the cushion should the pool player hit the white ball towards to ensure hitting the red?

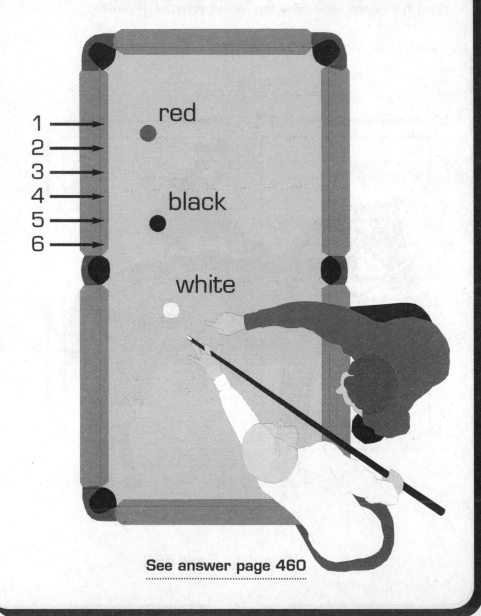

See answer page 460

144. The Case of the Different Areas

Study carefully the diagram below. You will see a rectangle measuring 11 cm by 13 cm which has been divided into two parts by a diagonal line. Each section has been sub-divided into two triangles and a rectangle. But there is a problem. If you calculate the areas of the sub-sections on one side of the diagonal line and compare them with the areas of the other side you will find one side of the diagonal is 1 cm² larger in area than the other. Why?

What is wrong with the diagram?

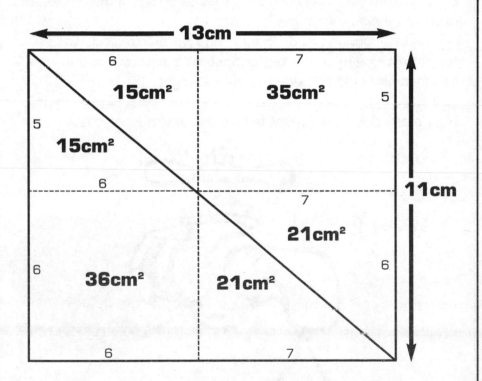

See answer page 460

145. The Dripping Tap

On my many business trips away from home I often find it difficult to sleep in a strange hotel bed. On one such occasion, lying awake in the early hours, I became aware of the sound of a tap dripping in the en suite bathroom. The sound appeared to become louder and louder in the silence of the room until it became almost deafening. All my attempts to stop the tap dripping failed. Even plugging my ears with cotton wool failed to stop the endless drumming of the drops of water hitting the base of the shower. It was then that I decided to count the drips to see if it would have the same effect as counting sheep and eventually send me to sleep. It didn't. The only good thing that came out of that unpleasant experience was this puzzle.

I started counting at 3.36 a.m. and my alarm clock was set to ring at 7.00 a.m. If the tap dripped at a rate of once every 17 seconds and I did not sleep at all that night,

How many drips did I count before the alarm went off?

See answer page 461

146. The Edges of a Polyhedron

A regular polyhedron that has 20 faces is called an icosahedron. This is the largest number of faces that can be formed on a regular polyhedron. Each face forms the shape of an equilateral triangle, which means it will have 12 points or vertices. If an icosahedron has 20 faces and 12 vertices,

How many edges does it have?

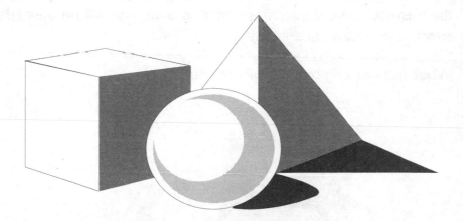

See answer page 461

147. The Kingdom of Truth

A long time ago in a far distant land there lived a king who decreed that it was a crime to tell a lie – a crime so serious that it was punishable by death. He discovered that one of his wives had been telling untruths for a long time, and she had to be put on trial, if only to prove to his subjects that no one was above the law. The court found her guilty as charged, but it was left to the king to sentence her.

Not wanting to see his wife killed, the king spoke privately with her before he passed sentence in open court. The court assembled to hear sentence passed.

The king said, 'You have been found guilty by this court, and the sentence is death, but you must say one last thing before you die. If your last statement is true, you will be given poison and you will die painlessly, but if your statement is a lie, you will be burned alive.

What had the king told his wife to reply?

See answer page 461

148. Missing Number

If I subtract six from a particular number, the result is divisible by seven. If I subtract seven from it, the result is divisible by eight, and if I subtract eight from it, the result is divisible by nine. In fact, whatever number I subtract from it, the result is divisible by one more than the number I subtracted.

What is the number?

See answer page 461

149. How Old is Grandma?

'How old are you, Grandma?' the young boy asked one day.

'Don't you know it's rude to ask a lady's age?' replied Grandma to the curious little boy.

'Sorry,' replied the boy, 'I didn't know, but I still want to know your age.'

'Well, see if you can solve this puzzle,' smiled the old lady. 'It may help you with your sums.'

The little boy listened as his grandma spoke.

'Next year,' said the old lady, 'I will be six times as old as I am now, less six times as old as I was 10 years ago.'

How old is Grandma?

See answer page 461

150. Come into my Parlour

'Come into my parlour,' said the spider to the fly. 'That's very kind of you,' replied the fly. 'I will take a break. All this flying around does tend to tire one so.'

Without further ado the fly walked into the spider's den. The spider quickly slammed and locked the door behind him. Suddenly there were spiders everywhere. They pounced on the fly, dragging him to the floor. He felt a sharp pain in his side, and his head began to spin as the poison from the spider's bite slowly reached his tiny brain. From that point on the fly offered no resistance. The spiders wrapped him in silk and carried him into the store cupboard.

Shortly, the fly regained consciousness and opened his eyes. He struggled, but there was no escape. Lying face down he looked through the gap under the store cupboard door. He could see the remains of many of his fellow creatures scattered around the floor of the kitchen. The spiders were walking over them, busy laying the table for their next meal. The fly counted 166 legs altogether and, counting both the spiders and the remains of the dead flies, 25 bodies.

How many spiders were in the kitchen?

See answer page 461

151. The Cowboy Plumber

A miserly factory owner needed a length of pipe-work installed in his factory. The pipe was to be 3 in in diameter and 120 ft long. It was to be used to carry steam from the boiler house to a heating unit attached to the far end wall of the factory. Instead of using a qualified plumber the factory owner asked an inexperienced pipe-fitter to do the job. The steel pipe was to carry steam at 165° C. The pipe-fitter did the best job he could, sealing the joints and securing the pipe as tight and as close to the wall as possible. The job over, the steam was allowed into the pipe. Within seconds the pipe began to twist and bend as it ripped itself out of its mountings. He had forgotten to take the expansion of the length of pipe into consideration.

If the ambient temperature of the factory is 20° C, by how much will a 120 ft long steel pipe increase in length when the temperature is raised by 145° C? (N.B. the coefficient of expansion of steel is 0.000012.)

See answer page 461

152. The Speed Boat

A motor boat travelling at a constant speed is timed over a distance of 4 km and an average speed is calculated. The speed is then increased by 3 km per hour, and it is found that the journey time has decreased by four minutes over the same distance.

What was the original speed of the boat?

See answer page 461

153. Changing the Fraction

If the fraction 7/17 has the same number added to both the numerator and the denominator, the fraction is changed to 3/5.

What number is added?

See answer page 461

154. Consecutive Numbers

The difference between the squares of two consecutive numbers is 53.

What are the two numbers?

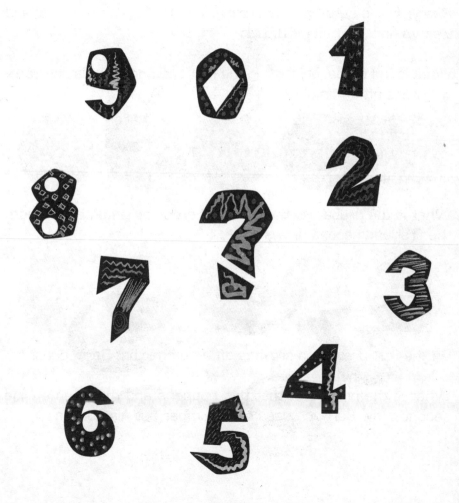

See answer page 461

155. Bingo

In a simplified game of Bingo for children, there are 30 similar balls numbered one to 30 in a box. These are drawn out at random one by one and not replaced. Each child has a card with five numbers on it, and whenever a ball with one of those numbers is drawn out the child crosses off that number. The first child to cross off all five numbers on his card wins.

On this occasion there are only two children playing, Alan and Barry; Alan's card has the numbers 1, 8, 18, 19, 27 on it and Barry's has 1, 8, 10, 13, 29.

What is the probability that on the first draw neither Alan or Barry will cross off a number?

What is the probability that Alan will cross off a number on both the first and second draws?

On the first draw Alan crosses off a number but Barry doesn't.

What is the probability that this happens and that then on the second draw Barry crosses off a number but Alan doesn't?

See answer page 462

156. The Cost of a Call

Some years ago the cost of a telephone call was 1 cent for so many seconds. Later it was changed to 1 1/2 cents for six seconds more. As a result of the change the cost of a three-minute phone call was increased by 1 1/2 cents (a steeper price difference would accrue if the call was a second longer than three minutes).

How many seconds were we allowed for 1 cent before the change?

See answer page 462

157. The Seating Arrangement

The local amateur dramatic society is putting on its latest production. The audience can be seated partly in easy chairs and partly in upright chairs, for which the tickets will be cheaper. The hall has a floor area of 90 m²; easy chairs require 1 m² of space, and upright chairs require 0.6 m². The organizers must allow for an audience of at least 100, but there are only 50 easy chairs available.

Assume that easy chairs are put in rows of 10 and tickets cost $4 each, upright chairs are put in rows of 12 and tickets cost $3.50 each, and the rows must alternate to maintain satisfactory sight lines to the stage.

Which layout will be the most profitable to the company, assuming all seats are sold?

See answer page 462

158. From the Mouths of Babes

As every parent knows, young children ask an enormous amount of questions – questions that show the inquisitiveness of a healthy young mind eager to learn. Sometimes the questions concern things we have never thought about before, things we have taken for granted and never questioned ourselves. These are the gems of learning, proof that things can be looked upon from a different angle, even by a young child. Here is one such typical conversation between a father and his small son.

'Dad, why do big balloons float up into the sky?'

'Because they are full of hot air and heat rises.'

'Do all hot things rise?'

'Heat makes anything that is fluid, such as gas or liquid, rise upwards.'

'So in a room the hottest place is next to the ceiling and the coldest place is next to the floor?'

'That's right.'

'So in the bath the hottest place is the top of the water, and the coldest place is on the bottom.'

'You've got it.' There then followed a short pause.

'Dad?' asked the boy after much deliberation.

'Is ice colder than water?'

'Yes, of course it is.'

'Why then does the fish pond freeze on the top and not on the bottom, if that is the coldest place?'

'Ask your mother.'

See answer page 462

159. Pythagoras Revisited

As all 15- and 16-year-old pupils studying for their mathematics exams will know, the Pythagorean theorem states that the area of the square drawn on the hypotenuse of a right-angled triangle is equal to the sum of the areas of the squares drawn on the other two sides.

This is the most proved theorem in mathematics and is all very well, but what about other shapes drawn on the sides of a right-angled triangle?

Is it true that the area of a regular pentagon drawn on the hypotenuse is equal to the sum of the areas of similar pentagons drawn on the other two sides?

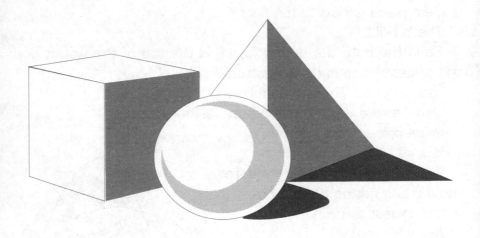

See answer page 462

160. A Game of Marbles

Six boys organize a marble competition between them. They start the game with 20 marbles each, and the competition is fierce. At the end of the game the winner has six times as many marbles as the boy who has lost the most. The other four boys have consecutive numbers of marbles left, and one of them has half as many as the winner.

How many marbles did the boy who lost the most have at the end of the game?

See answer page 462

161. A Tale of Two Ladders

Two ladders, one 20 ft long and one 30 ft long, are placed against opposite walls of an alley, which is 11 ft wide. The foot of each ladder is placed firmly against the base of the wall opposite. The two ladders cross each other a certain vertical distance from the ground.

How far above the ground do the two ladders cross?

See answer page 462

162. The Three-Number Problem

I have chosen three numbers. The second is twice the first, and the third is three times the second. The sum of the first two when multiplied by the sum of the last two happens to be the same as the first number multiplied by the square of the second number.

What are the three numbers?

See answer page 462

163. The Genius of Hipparchus

In the second century B.C. Hipparchus, the greatest astronomer of the ancient worlds, created a branch of mathematics that was ingeniously applied to the charting of the heavens and the earth. He had already instituted the system of locating points on the earth's surface by means of latitude and longitude, and he had calculated the radius of the earth by means of the ratios of the sides of a right-angled triangle – the method we now know as trigonometry. Hipparchus calculated the distance from the earth to the moon, or rather the distance from the centre of the earth to the centre of the moon.

How did he do it?

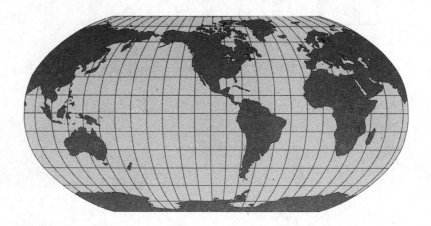

See answer page 462

164. We Are Sailing

A sailing ship is fitted with three sails of different sizes. When the largest sail is used, the ship can make a certain voyage in two days. When the next largest sail only is used, the voyage takes three days, and when the smallest sail only is used, the voyage takes four days.

How long will the voyage take when all three sails are used, assuming a constant wind speed?

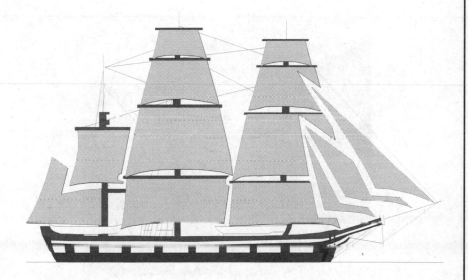

See answer page 462

165. Reducing the Cube

A cube of a certain volume has its height reduced by 1/2. Its width is reduced by 2/3, but its length is trebled. The volume of the resultant cuboid is 864 cm³.

What were the original lengths of the sides of the cube?

See answer page 463

166. Disks in a Rectangle

Two circular disks, one of radius 2 cm and the other unknown, can just be fitted into a rectangle whose sides are 6 cm and 5 cm. The two disks each touch two sides of the rectangle and the other disk.

What is the radius of the second disk?

See answer page 463

167. Plane for Hire

A travel agency charted a plane for $1,200 to fly a party of people abroad. It was agreed that each member of the party should pay an equal share of the cost. It was later discovered that four members of the party would be unable to travel. The agency calculated that if it contributed $30, the fare of the remaining passengers would have to be increased by $5 in order to cover the cost of $1,200.

What was the original number of people in the party, and how much did each passenger finally pay?

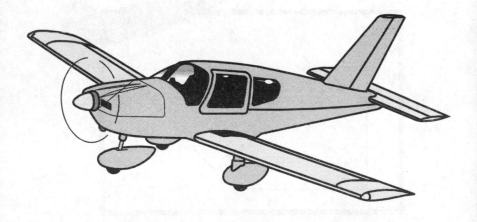

See answer page 463

168. In the Foundry

In a foundry a solid circular cylinder 7 cm long is to be melted down and reshaped into a solid rod 25 cm long. The cross-section of the rod is a regular hexagon whose sides are 2 cm.

What was the radius of the original cylinder?

After remolding, the rod is dipped into a protective fluid contained in a cylindrical tank of diameter 10 cm in such a way that the axes of the tank and the rod are both vertical.

If the rod is just immersed when it touches the bottom of the tank, what was the depth of the fluid before the rod was inserted?

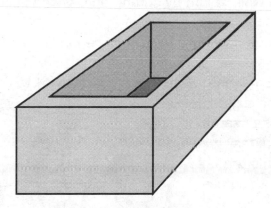

See answer page 463

169. The Hikers

Three keen hikers, Brown, Smith and Jones, were out walking one day when they had a disagreement and decided to go on their separate ways. They were standing at the junction of two long straight roads which were inclined to each other at an angle of 60°. The three men leave the junction at the same time and walk at a constant speed of three miles an hour. Brown walks along the right hand fork and Jones along the left hand fork, while Smith walks across the fields between the two roads so that he is always an equal distance from each road. After walking for exactly an hour all three men stop, regretting the harsh words they have spoken to each other. They contact each other by mobile phone, and Smith suggests that he stays in his present position and the other two walk to where he is.

How far will Brown and Jones each have to walk to reach him?

Brown disagrees with the suggestion, turns around and walks back the way he came. After half an hour Jones, who is still at his original position, phones Brown and tells him to stay where he is and that he will walk to him by cutting across the fields.

How far will Jones now have to walk to reach Brown?

Jones contacts Smith and tells him he is going to walk to where Brown is now waiting and suggests Smith does the same. Smith, who realizes it is getting late and is tired of arguing, reluctantly agrees.

How far does Smith have to walk to meet up with the other two at Brown's position?

See answer page 463

170. Working with Sheet Metal

A square sheet of metal whose sides measure 8 cm has two identical rectangles cut from the bottom left and the bottom right of the square. The removal of the rectangles produces a T-shaped piece with horizontal and vertical members which are the same width.

If the two rectangles that have been cut from the square are equal to half the original area, what is the width of the horizontal and vertical members of the T-shaped piece?

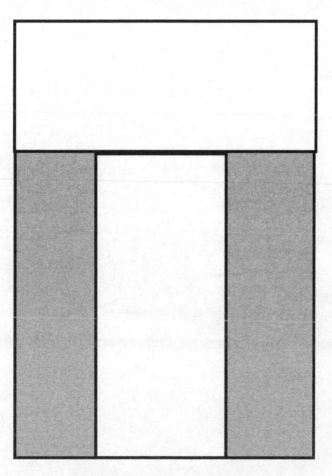

See answer page 463

171. In the Hotel Dining Room

A large rectangular block of cheese whose edges measure 6 in, 4 in and 3 in is placed on a flat cheese board in the hotel dining room. In order to keep it fresh the head waiter places a large silver cover in the shape of a hemisphere over it. The cover rests on the cheese board and is such that the four top corners of the block of cheese are in contact with the inner surface of the hemisphere.

What is the radius of the inside of the hemisphere?

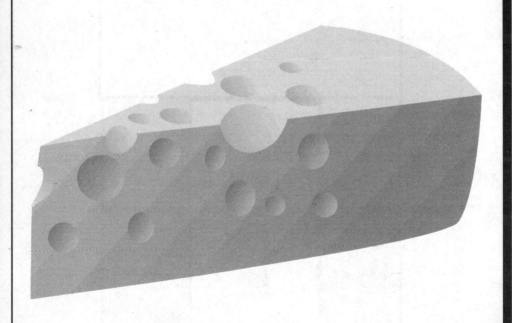

See answer page 464

172. From Town to Town

A party of 11 people need to get to the next town, 40 miles away, as quickly as possible. The only transport available is a car, which can take a maximum of six people (including the driver) and can only travel at an average speed of 30 miles an hour. The 11 people set off at noon, six travelling by car and five walking at an average speed of 4 miles per hour.

The driver takes his passengers to the next town and immediately returns to meet the five walkers. He then takes them to meet with the original six at the next town. Ignore the time taken to set down and pick up passengers.

What time did the last five people reach the next town?

See answer page 464

173. The Tetrahedron

Four equilateral triangles, each of which has an area equal to the square root of 3 cm2, are joined together to form a regular tetrahedron.

What is the volume of this tetrahedron?

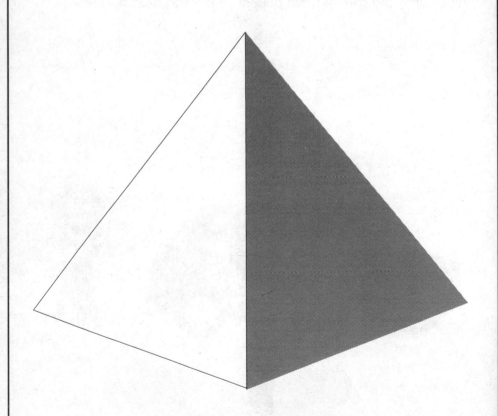

See answer page 464

174. The Sum of the Fractions

When a particular number is divided into quarters, thirds, fifths and eighths, I find that one-third plus one-eighth is one more than one-fifth plus one-fourth, but one-eighth plus one-fifth is 31 less than one-third plus one-fourth. Also one-fourth plus one-third plus one-fifth plus one-eighth is 11 less than the number itself.

What is the number?

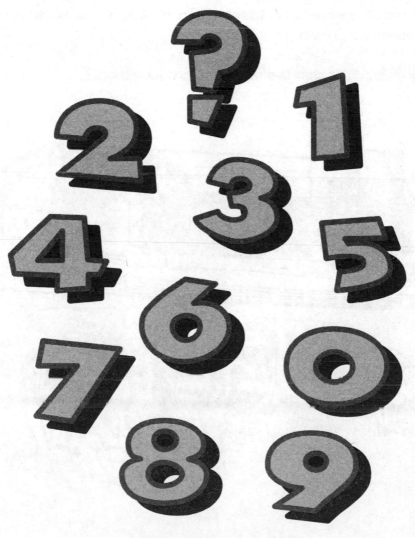

See answer page 464

175. Percentage Increase

A farmer's produce is harvested and dispatched to the processing plant. The farmer, in order to stay in business, sells the produce for 15 per cent more than it costs him to grow it. The processing plant sells the goods to the wholesaler for 25 per cent more than it paid the farmer for them. The wholesaler adds 15 per cent to the price and sells them on to the retailer. The retailer, whose turnover is small in comparison, adds 50 per cent to the price he paid and then value-added-tax at 17.5 per cent. The shopper buys the goods for $1.75 per kilogram.

How much did it cost the farmer to produce them?

See answer page 464

176. A Six-shaded Problem

If green plus blue makes 89, and red plus black makes 56,

What does yellow plus brown make?

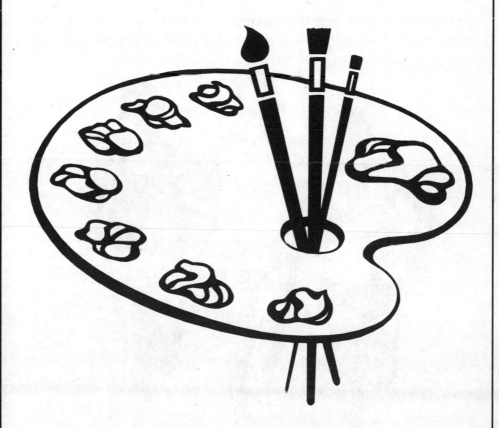

See answer page 464

177. The Fun Run

Three unfit middle-aged men agree to test each other's fitness by competing in a charity fun run. The course is over rough country, and although the three set off full of energy and a keen competitive spirit, none of them manages to complete the course. Bill soon drops out, but Alan manages to run five times as far as him before he collapses with exhaustion. Charlie keeps going but gives up 1 km short of the finishing line.

If Charlie ran 3 km less than twice the distance Alan ran, and the three ran 21 km between them, how long was the course?

See answer page 464

178. Murder at the Manor House

Romeo and Juliet lived happily in the old manor house. They kept themselves to themselves and had no enemies as far as anyone knew. One day a hysterical maid ran to tell the butler that she had found them both dead on the living room floor. The butler went with the maid to the living room, and there, just as the maid had said, the bodies of the two were laying motionless on the floor. There was no sign of violence, and the bodies were unmarked. There was no evidence of forced entry, and nothing untoward except for some broken glass on the floor. The butler ruled out suicide, as they were not the type. Poison was also out of the question, as he had prepared and served their food himself. On examination of the bodies he could find no evidence as to the cause of death, but he did notice that the carpet on which they were lying was wet.

How did they die, and who killed them?

See answer page 464

179. The Cost of Silver Plating

The cost of silver-plating a tray varies as the square of its length. If the cost of silver plating a tray 8 cm x 8 cm is $15,

What is the cost of plating a round tray 12 cm in diameter?

See answer page 465

180. The Diet

Two foods, A and B, contain respectively 4 and 6 units of protein and 5 and 3 units of fiber. The cost of A is 40 cents per kilo, while B is 50 cents per kilo. The minimum daily intake is at least 16 units of protein and 11 units of fiber.

What is the cheapest way of meeting those requirements?

See answer page 465

181. The School Concert

At the school concert the price of the first three rows of chairs was $1 each, and the other seats cost 60 cents each. The takings were $204. On the second night of the concert the price of the fourth row of chairs was increased to $1, and the takings were $212.

Assuming the hall was full on both occasions and that there were the same number of chairs in each row, how many chairs were in the hall?

See answer page 465

182. Investments in Shares

A man holds 200 shares in one company paying a dividend of 3 1/2 percent, the $1 shares in the company standing at $0.80. He also holds 400 shares in another company paying a dividend of 6 per cent whose $1 shares stand at $1.25. He sells both holdings and reinvests all the money in 5 per cent shares of nominal value $1 standing at $1.10.

What is his decrease in annual income?

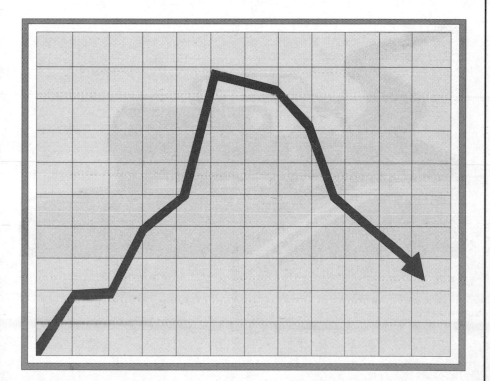

See answer page 465

183. Across the Desert

The roads that cross the desert wastelands of the world are usually perfectly straight. On one such road there were four villages set at different distances apart. The third village was 60 miles from the first village; the fourth village was 40 miles from the second village, and the third village was 10 miles nearer to the fourth village than it was to the second village.

How far was it from the first village to the fourth village?

See answer page 465

184. A Tale of Two Trees

Two trees, an oak and an ash, grew together side by side in the forest. Over the years the ash grew to be 1 1/4 times as high as the oak. One day the woodcutter came along and lopped 3 m off the height of both trees. Now the ash is 1 1/3 times as high as the oak.

How high was the ash originally?

See answer page 465

185. Barrels of Beer

Two barrels of beer were both part full. One was 1/3 full and the other 9/14 full. If half the contents of the second barrel were emptied into the first and 2 1/2 liters were poured from the first barrel back into the second both would be half full.

How much would the barrels hold if they were both full?

See answer page 465

186. The Stronghold

Baron von Kinklehoffen built himself a castle to protect his ill-gotten gains from the hands of his enemies. He chose a flat piece of land high above the surrounding countryside on which to build it, and made every effort to make the building secure. The castle covered a section of land that was 50 yd on a side. His advisors told him that a good method of keeping out his enemies was to surround the castle with a moat. The baron agreed, and a moat was dug all the way around the outer walls of the castle.

Now the baron had to pay taxes based on the total area of land that the castle and moat occupied. When the final demand for his tax payment arrived, the baron studied it carefully. To his surprise he found that the area of land taken up by the moat was only 100 yd2 less than the area of land on which the castle stood.

How wide was the moat?

See answer page 465

187. The Swimmer

A boy wishes to swim across a river that is flowing at a rate of 1m every five seconds. He wishes to land on the opposite bank 10 m below the point at which he enters the water. The river is 50 m wide, and he can swim at a speed of 0.5 m per second.

At what angle to the bank should he head, and how long will it take him to swim across?

See answer page 465

188. Going Shopping

Mrs Spendalot likes to go shopping and also likes to exercise. She combines the two several times a week by walking to the shops, which are some distance from her home. The trouble with this arrangement is that Mrs Spendalot usually buys more goods than she can carry home and has to phone her husband to ask him to collect her in the car. Now, Mrs Spendalot walks at a speed of 5 km per hour, and her husband drives at an average speed of 30 km per hour. On a particular day Mrs Spendalot leaves home at 10 a.m., walks to the shops and spends two hours shopping. Phoning and waiting for her husband to bring the car takes a further 20 minutes, and she arrives back home at 12.55 p.m.

How far are the shops from her home?

See answer page 465

189. Three Fat Ladies

Once upon a time there were three sisters who lived together at Corpulent Lodge in the village of Blubberville, set in the countryside of Tubbyshire. The three sisters, Annie, Betty and Cally, were what one might call large ladies. Their total weight was 900 lb. Annie was the largest of the three, weighing twice as much as Betty, while Cally was only 100 lb heavier than Betty.

What was the weight of each of the three sisters?

See answer page 465

190. Changing Dimensions

Mr Hedges the gardener was building a vegetable garden. He selected a site which covered an area of 288 m2 .He found that if he increased the length by 6 m and decreased the width by 4 m the area was unchanged.

What was the length and width of the original piece of land?

See answer page 466

191. The Farmer's Daughters

Farmer Giles had three daughters of whom he was very proud. He was surprised at how quickly they were growing up. Time was passing faster than he had expected, and already the eldest was talking about leaving home. This he strongly objected to until his wife made him realize that this time next year the eldest daughter would be one and a half times the age of the middle daughter, and the middle daughter would be twice as old as the youngest.

If the sum of their ages is now 33 years, what are the ages of the three girls?

See answer page 466

192. The Ramblers

A group of keen walkers set off one day to climb a steep hill. They parked their car at the foot of the hill and began the four-mile journey to the summit. The hill was rocky, and the going was slow. It took them exactly two hours and 20 minutes to reach the top, including a 20-minute break half-way up. They rested at the summit for an hour, enjoying the view and their packed lunches, before setting off back. The downhill journey was much easier, and they ran most of the way down. They arrived back at their starting point feeling tired but happy that they had achieved their objective. The round trip had taken them exactly four hours.

Having covered a total of eight miles in four hours, the ramblers calculated that their average speed for the total journey was 2 mph.

But what was their average walking speed?

See answer page 466

193. Dirty Pool

As most people know, pool consists of 15 colored balls and one white ball. At the start of the game, the colored balls are arranged in a triangular formation with the black ball at the center of the arrangement. The balls are placed in a triangular frame and positioned near the bottom center of the table, and the frame is then removed.

This next conundrum does not concentrate on the game of pool or even the balls but on the triangular frame. If, on this particular table, the balls are each 2 in in diameter, and 15 balls fit exactly into the frame,

What is the area of the triangle into which the balls are placed?

See answer page 466

194. The Ballad of Shamus Magee

One day in the Forest of Dee
Crept a hunter named Shamus Magee
With his trusty arrow
Aimed strait at a sparrow
Way up at the top of a tree.

Now a sparrow is not a fierce prey,
Just not worth the time, some would say,
But the man in our ballad
Said, "twill go well with a salad,'
And was the first game he'd spotted all day.

As Shamus now pulled back his bow,
He imagined the sparrow was crow;
He let loose the dart,
Aimed straight at the heart
Of the poor bird now fully on show.

At an angle of sixty degrees
The arrow flew into the trees.
Fifty meters per second
Was its speed, Shamus reckoned,
Unaided by wind or by breeze.

But the arrow flew harmlessly past
The bird perched high up on that mast.
With a chirping of fright
The sparrow took flight.
The word Shamus uttered was 'blast'.

In no time the sparrow had flown,
And Shamus was left there alone.
He now had to seek
For that arrow so sleek,
For it fell where the brambles had grown.

The arrow had made a full arc
And landed somewhere in the park.
It marked the ground
With a dull thumping sound,
But how far from our man was that mark?

See answer page 466

1. In Ordered Succession

1) 42. The interval between each term is a prime number in sequence.

2) 95. The interval between the terms is a square number in sequence.

3) The answer is 57. The interval between each term is a triangular number in sequence.

4) Each term = N x N**2 where N = 1, 2, 3, 4, 5, 6; hence the last term is 7 x 2**7 = 896.

5) The numbers are 1/2, 3/4, 5/6, 7/8, 9/10 and 11/12 when written in decimals; therefore the last term is 13/14, which is 0.9286.

6) The answer is 1,458. Each term is three times the last.

7) The missing numbers are 21 and 567, each number being three times the last.

8) The numbers are 1 x 2, 3 x 4, 5 x 6, 7 x 8, 9 x 10, 11 x 12, so the next number in the series must be 13 x 14 = 182.

9) The terms in the series are (1), (2 + 3), (4 + 5 + 6), (7 + 8 + 9 + 10), (11 + 12 + 13 + 14 + 15) and (16 + 17 + 18 + 19 + 20 + 21), so the missing term is (22 + 23 + 24 + 25 + 26 + 27 + 28), which equals 175.

10) The interval between each term is double the interval between the previous two terms, so the last number in this series is 127.

2. The Four Jays

The little clue 'June is in her prime' should have helped, as it suggests that all the numbers in her name are prime numbers. As the total is 17 all the numbers must be less than 10, so:

J = 2

U = 7

N = 5

E = 3

Setting these numbers in the word Jane or Jean we can conclude that 16 = 2 + A + 5 + 3 so A = 6.

Putting these numbers in the word Jenny in the same way we find Y = 4.

3. The Woodcutter's Conundrum

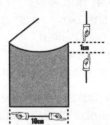

Referring to the diagram we see we have a right-angled triangle with R as the hypotenuse, (R - 1) the second side and 5 cm the third side. Now:

R**2 = (R - 1)**2 + 5**2

So R**2 = R**2 - 2**R + 1 + 25

0 = 26 - 2R

2R = 26. So R = 13. Hence the radius of the curved section is 13 cm.

4. The Farmer's Fields

The first piece of land measured 63 m by 64 m and the second 252 m by 2 m giving areas of 4,032 m^2 and 504 m^2 respectively. Therefore the total length of fencing he needed to buy was:

2(63 + 64) + 2 (252 + 2) = 254 + 508 = 762 m.

5. Three Little Boys

The first boy had 16 five-cent coins; the second had 11 ten-cent coins; and the third had seven fifty-cent coins.

6. Letters to Numbers

A =9, B = 8, C = 7, D = 6, E = 5, F = 4, G = 3, H = 2, I = 1, J = 0, and the operation is multiplication so:

CAB = CGHGF becomes 7 x 9 x 8 = 7 x 3 x 2 x 3 x 4

DAB = HGGGFH becomes 6 x 9 x 8 = 2 x 3 x 3 x 3 x 4 x 2

GIB = GB becomes 3 x 1 x 8 = 3 x 8

CACH = GCCD becomes 7 x 9 x 7 x 2 = 3 x 7 x 7 x 6

7. The Engineer

The engineer formed the cavities by using expanded polystyrene blocks suspended from the metal reinforcing with wire and accurately positioned. The concrete was gently poured around them and allowed to set. When the concrete was partly cured a solvent was poured onto the polystyrene which dissolved it totally. As concrete does not fully cure for 28 days, there was enough time for the solvent to evaporate and not to interfere with the chemicals in the compound. All that was left in the cavities was a sticky residue which lay harmlessly at the bottom of the pocket.

8. Training the Trainee Train Driver

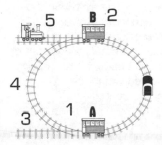

On the diagram, each number represents a position on the track. First move the engine down and connect to carriage B. Now move carriage B and leave it at position 3. Move down the track and connect to carriage A. Change the switches, move this carriage a short way back up the track and leave it at position 4. Let the engine travel all the way around the track, passing through the tunnel and re-connecting to carriage B. Back up a short way and change the switches again so that we can move both engine and carriage B to re-connect to carriage A. Now move the engine and both carriages around to position 2. Disconnect the engine and travel all the way around the track so that the engine arrives at the other side of the two carriages. Push both carriages into the siding and disconnect carriage B at position 5. Move back down the track and disconnect carriage A at position 1. Leaving carriage A in its new position we can now travel all the way around through the tunnel once again to arrive back at the other side of carriage A. Reverse up the siding and re-connect to carriage B. Reverse down the siding, and move carriage B around to its new location at position 1. Now drive the engine back to its original position 5.

9. Serving the Wine

The manager has two identical glass jugs and two containers, one holding three units and the other five.

0   0   3   5

First he empties the three units into one of the glass jugs.

0   3   0   5

He then fills the three-unit container from the five-unit container,

0   3   3   2

putting the two units remaining into the empty jug.

2   3   3   0

He then pours the three units into the five

2   3   0   3

and tops up the five from the first jug.

2   1   0   5

Now he again fills the three unit container from the five.

2 1 3 2

Placing the two jugs together he pours wine from the three units into the jug holding one unit until the levels of the two jugs are the same,

2 2 2 2

leaving two units in each of the jugs and the containers.

10. Little Tommy Tomkins

Little Tommy Tomkins explained that he had been measuring time from the family's 12-hour clock, so he insisted quite correctly that all the additions were accurate:

7 o'clock plus 10 hours is 5 o'clock.

8 o'clock plus 17 hours is 1 o'clock.

4 o'clock plus 11 hours is 3 o'clock.

9 o'clock plus 7 hours is 4 o'clock.

6 o'clock plus 8 hours is 2 o'clock.

5 o'clock plus 7 hours is 12 o'clock.

The teacher had to agree.

11. Get It Out!

The engineer would pack the centre of the bearing as tightly as possible with thick grease. Then, after making sure that the grease did not hold any air pockets, he would place a shaft of the correct size into the hole in the centre of the bearing. He would then strike the shaft sharply with a soft hammer. The force of the hammer blow would be transmitted to the grease, which, with nowhere else to go, would be pushed into the small gap behind the bearing. The grease would transmit the pressure to the housing and to the bearing, which would move upward.

12. Chasing the Girls

The boys had found that their apartment numbers were the sum of the Roman numerals in their names:

Alex = L + X = 60

Phillip = I + L + L + I = 102

Using the same system they found that Diana would live at number 501:D + I = 501. Thus the girl who lived at number 12 must have a name whose letters add up to that number. The only combinations they could find were:

X + I + I = 12 and V + V + I + I = 12

They convinced themselves her name must be Vivian or Trixie.

13. More MPG

For the upward journey, at the rate of 10 miles to the gallon, Mr Stingy would use 1/10 of a gallon of fuel. The downward journey would use only 1/100 of a gallon, so the round trip would use 0.11 gallons . Average fuel usage is calculated by distance divided by consumption so 2 miles divided by 0.11 gives an average of 18.18 miles per gallon.

14. The Flight of the Pigeons

The answer to this conundrum is largely theoretical, but I believe that the overall weight of the vehicle and cargo would not change whether the birds were in flight or not. When a bird flies its weight is supported by the air beneath its wings. The air within the container is supported by the container, so the total weight of the cargo would be constant, the weight of the birds being transferred to the air and the combined weight being supported by the container.

15. The Klondike

Although there are infinitely many ways of solving his problem, the prospector chose the simplest and quickest: he knew that reducing a circle's circumference by half reduces its area by a quarter. By using half the rope he formed a circle 1/4 the size, so he formed two circles using the whole length of rope and in doing so retained half the original area. His claim formed a shape like a "figure 8", each circle has a diameter of 440/Pi or 140.06

yards and encloses 15406.2 sq yds.

16. Walking the Plank

The way to solve this kind of problem is to put the width over the length, multiply this by a constant 'K', and make it equal to the known weight. Then we need to find a value for K from this, and put it into a second equation using the new dimension. With all our measurements in the same units:

20/1,500 x K = 200

20K/1,500 = 200

20K = 300 000

K = 15,000

Using the value of K we can work out the weight the new plank will hold.

30/2,000 x 15,000 = 225, so the new plank will hold 225 kg.

17. Digital Crossword

There is probably more than one solution to this puzzle, but mine is shown below:

a. 6 + 2 + 18 = 26

b. 20 + 25 + 13 + 1 + 5 = 64

c. 25 + 4 + 8 = 37

d. 4 + 3 + 24 = 31

e. 8 + 7 = 15

f. 18 + 23 + 13 + 3 + 7 = 64

g. 23 + 22 + 10 = 55

h. 22 + 1 + 24 = 47

i. 17 + 10 + 5 = 32

18. Playing on the Swings

Make a sketch of the path of the swing, then form two right-angled triangles with a hypotenuse of 3.6 m and an adjacent side of 2.4 m. Find the angle which the swing passes through by using trigonometry.

Cos x = 2.4/3.6; x = 48.1896°, say 48.2°

Multiply this by two and we have the angle 96.4°. 96.4° divided by 360 will give us the fraction of the full circle that the swing traveled: 0.2677˙.

Now calculate the circumference of the full circle and multiply it by this number to find the length of the arc of the swing:

2 x 3.142 x 3.6 x 0.26777˙ = 6.057 m

19. The Infinite Stadium

Instead of moving the spectators as before, the manager moves the person in Seat 2 into Seat 3, the person in Seat 3 into Seat 5, the person in Seat 4 into Seat 7, and so on. The infinite number of seats with even numbers are now vacant for the infinite number of latecomers.

20. The Witch's Polyhedron

The crystal ball, with each face shaped like a pentagon, would have 12 sides, and is called a dodecahedron.

21. Numerical Code

This code needs the use of a nine-digit display pocket calculator. Type in the numbers 378163771 and read the display upside down. You should see the word ILLEGIBLE.

22. Noughts and Crosses (Tic Tac Toe)

By substituting the digit 1 for each X the lines of the matrix can be read as binary numbers. The lines have the value 5, 7 and 11. These are all prime numbers, so logically the next number in the array will have the value 13, which would be:

X X O X

23. Stone-Throwing

The range of a projectile on a horizontal plane is found by squaring the velocity, multiplying it by the Sine of twice the angle and dividing by gravitational acceleration. This gives a distance of 91.83 m.

24. Musket Balls

The volume of a sphere is 4/3 multiplied by Pi (π, or 3.142) times the radius cubed. The volume of a cylinder is Pi times the radius squared multiplied by the height. If we express the height of the cylinder as:

H = 3 x $4/3\pi r3$ divided by $\pi r2$, we have the height equal to 4r, which is twice the diameter of the cylinder.

25. Missing Word

The answer to the eight clues are:

1. Defend

2. React

3. Repent

4. Depend

5. Acid

6. Agonize

7. Elope

8. Her

The three-letter word that can be added to the end of the first four words and to the beginning of the last four is ANT.

26. Numbers for Letters

The full analysis of the puzzle is as follows.

Taking Column 1 and Row 2, we have:

2P + S + Q = 102

2P + 2S = 90

Subtraction gives - S + Q = 12 so Q = S + 12

Taking Row 3 and Row 1 we have:

2R + Q +P = 143

R + Q + P + S = 119

Subtraction gives R - S = 24

So S = R - 24, therefore R = Q + 12

Taking Column 3 (substituting for S and Q):

2R + R - 24 + R - 12 = 136

4R - 36 = 136

4R = 172 so R = 43

Taking Row 3 and substituting for Q:

R - 12 + 2R + P = 143

3R - 12 + P = 143

3R + P = 155

P = 155 - 3R but R = 43

P = 155 - 129   then P = 26

As S = R - 24   then S = 19

As Q = R - 12   then Q = 31

27. Elementary Series

The clue was in the title. Each letter is the chemical symbol of an element written in the order of their atomic numbers.

B is boron, atomic number 5

C is carbon, atomic number 6

N is nitrogen, atomic number 7

O is oxygen, atomic number 8

F is fluorine, atomic number 9

So the missing letter(s) are Ne. Ne is neon, which has the atomic number 10.

28. Changing Signs

There is only one way to arrange the signs to complete the sum:

$2 \div 3 - 4 + 5 \times 6 = 10$

29. The Inaccessible Object

The surveyor measures the angle of elevation of the rock formation from two points 50 m apart. From this he can calculate the height by multiplying the distance between the two points by the product of the tangent of the two angles, and dividing by the difference between the tangents of the two angles:

Let the first angle be called angle A and the second angle B, the unknown distance to the rocks X and the height H, then:

$H/X = \text{Tan } A$ and so $X = H/\text{Tan } A$

$H/X + 50 = \text{Tan } B$; $H = \text{Tan } B$
$(X + 50)$

Substituting for X we have

$H = \text{Tan } B [(H/\text{Tan } A) + 50]$

So $H = [H \text{ Tan } B/\text{Tan } A] + 50 \text{ Tan } B$

It follows that H Tan A = H Tan B + 50 Tan B Tan A

So H Tan A - H Tan B = 50 Tan B Tan A

H(Tan A - Tan B) = 50 Tan B Tan A

Thus H = 50 Tan B Tan A/Tan A - Tan B

30.   Extra Letter

The quote is from 'The Farewell' by Charles Kingsley. From the bottom left, the words can be traced: 'Be good sweet maid and let who can be clever.' The letter H at the end is not part of the sentence.

31.   Triangles

The triangle is formed on the surface of a sphere. Imagine, if you can, two travellers standing exactly on the equator, one in Africa and the other in South America. Both men head north. Their direction of travel makes a 90° angle with the equator in each case. They will eventually meet at the north pole, making the third angle. The only triangles that have angles of 180° are those constructed on a flat surface.

32.   You Can't Take It With You

The judge ordered the attorney to put all the money into a separate bank account. He was then to write a check for the full amount to Mrs Avarice, sign it, and place it in the coffin. The cremation would then go ahead as planned. If the check had not been cashed within 30 days, the money would be evenly divided between the immediate descendants.

33.   The Haunted Hotel

Take the room number where the sightings are at present, multiply that by number of days between the sightings, then subtract the number of days between the sightings. The number of days between sightings increases by one for each period, so room 3 x 2 - 2 = room 4; 4 x 3 - 3 = 9. So the next sighting is calculated by 9 x 4 - 4 = 32. The next room to be visited by the restless spirit would be Room 32, and the sightings would occur every fifth night.

34.   The Used Car

The answer is 26%.

35.   The Shepherd and his Sheep

The structure would enclose the largest area if it was built 22 m wide and 46 m long, giving an area of $1,012 \text{ m}^2$.

36.   The Gambler

The answer is $1,960.00

37.   The Bus Driver

The answer is 32 five-cent pieces.

38.   Touching Circles

The radii of the three circles are 5 cm, 4 cm and 1 cm.

39.   The News Vendor

Since three people buy all three papers, 14 buy the Echo and the Moon, 12 buy the Moon and the Advertizer and 13 buy the Echo and the Advertizer. Since 70 buy the Echo, the number who buy the Echo only must be 70 - 14 - 13 - 3 = 40. 60 buy the Moon, so the number who buy the Moon only is 60 - 12 - 14 - 3 = 31. 50 buy the Advertizer, so the number who buy the Advertizer only is 50 - 12 - 13 - 3 = 22. Thus the newsagent has 40 + 14 + 31 + 12 + 3 + 13 + 22 customers, that is 135.

40.   Weather Changes

The probability that it will be fine on

Sunday is found by working out the total number of combinations of weather changes for the next three days. They are:

Fine, fine, fine.

Wet, fine, fine.

Fine, wet, fine.

Wet, wet, fine.

The probability for each combination and add them together:

$(3/4 \times 3/4 \times 3/4) + (1/4 \times 1/3 \times 3/4) + (3/4 \times 1/4 \times 1/3) + (1/4 \times 2/3 \times 1/3)$, which equals 347/576 – so I think I'll risk walking on Sunday.

41.   The Sum of the Parts

Let the length of the table = L, the area = A and the cost = C, so C = aA + bL**2

When A = 6 and L = 3, C = 50, so 50 = 6a + 9b

When A = 6 and L = 4, C = 64. so 64 = 6a + 16b

Subtraction gives 14 = 7b so b = 2

Substitution gives 50 = 6a + 18 so a = 5 1/3

Therefore the connection between C, A and L is C = 5 1/3A + 2L**2

When A = 6.25 and L = 2.5

C = (5 1/3 x 6.25. + (2 x 6.25)

The cost of a table 2.5 m square is $45.83.

42.   One Man and his Dog

The best way to solve this puzzle is to forget about the dog for a moment and concentrate on the farmer. If the farmer walks at a constant speed of two miles per hour for a journey of three miles, then the walk will take him 1 1/2 hours. Assuming the dog runs constantly for that period of time at a speed of six miles per hour, the dog will cover a total distance of nine miles.

43.   The Prince and the Princess

The prince knew that the princess was highly intelligent and would instinctively know what part she had to play in the plan. First he bought a casket and a padlock. He then wrote a letter, placed it in the casket, and sealed it with the padlock. The guard took the casket to the princess. On receiving the casket the princess fastened a padlock of her own onto the casket and told the guard to return it to the prince with both padlocks intact. When the casket reached the prince he removed his own padlock and told the guard to take it back to the princess. She then removed her padlock, opened the casket and read the letter. This mode of communication continued until the war was over.

44.   Chickens and Ducks

The maximum number of eggs per week, given the constraints of an $80 investment and a maximum number of 25 birds, will come from 15 chickens and 10 ducks:

15 + 10 = 25 birds

15 x $4 + 10 x $2 = $64 investment

16 x 5 + 8 x 4 = 115 eggs per week.

45.   The Open Box Question

The box would measure 53.4 cm by 53.4 cm by 13.3 cm and would have a volume of 37,925.7 cm^3.

46.   The Car Park

The maximum number of vehicles that the car park could hold is 350: 300 cars and 50 trucks. To maximize revenue, the car park would provide spaces for 200 cars and 100 trucks, giving an hourly income $900.

47.   The Tiler's Dilemma

The larger of the two tiles would be 8 cm square and the smaller 6 cm square.

48. The Lost Consonants

The quotation is from Shakespeare's Twelfth Night I, i: IF MUSIC BE THE FOOD OF LOVE, PLAY ON.

49. A Pile of Bricks

The smallest number, which when divided by two, three, four, five and six leaves remainder one but divides exactly by seven, is 301. There were 301 bricks in the original pile.

50. The Lion, the Donkey and the Carrots

The traveler would have to remove the carrots from the donkey's back and take the donkey across the river first. He would then return, take the lion across, then bring the donkey back with him. He would then leave the donkey and take the carrots across. Finally he would return for the donkey.

51. Counting Sheep

If 10 acres are sufficient to pasture 15 sheep for a period of 18 weeks, then proportionately 36 acres would be sufficient to pasture 54 sheep over the same period.

52. The Merciless Captain

The captain issues all crew members with a number and orders them to form a circle standing in single file in numerical order. He then counts in nines, starting with number one and throwing every ninth crew member into the sea. The Dognians are issued with the numbers 1, 2, 3, 4, 10, 11, 13, 14, 15, 17, 20, 21, 25, 28, 29. The unfortunate Catanians have the numbers 5, 6, 7, 8, 9, 12, 16, 18, 19, 22, 23, 24, 26, 27, 30.

53. Feeding the Needy

There are six possible solutions to this problem, seven if we include the one where there are no women in the village. The most popular answer is 11 men, 15 women and 74 children.

54. What, No Pi?

You may or may not know that the area of a circle can be found by multiplying the radius of the circle by the circumference and then dividing by two. In other words, the area of a circle is exactly the same as the area of a triangle whose base is the radius of the circle and whose height is the circumference.

55. Catch Me If You Can

The car would catch up with the bike after traveling for 34.07 minutes. The car travels at a speed of 50/60 km per minute, so 50/60 x 34.07 = 28.39 km. Thus Father catches John when he is 28.39 km away from home.

56. Slow Down George!

Poor old George had timed his journey exactly to try to prevent his nagging wife from complaining about having to wait at the terminal. His original speed would have been 84 km per hour, giving them a journey time of 1 hour 40 mins. Reducing his speed by 14 km per hour to 70 km per hour meant that the journey would take two hours, making them 20 minutes late.

57. The Conference

The number of ways in which the members can be arranged in groups of three with the leader of each group always placed in the middle is 768.

58. Connections

The word I'm thinking of is 'hypo', which means 'under,' 'below normal' or 'slightly'. It is also the nickname for sodium thiosulphate, a photographic fixer. Some of the 12 new words prefixed by 'hypo' are: hypochondria, hypocrisy, hypodermic, hypotenuse and hypoventilation. I'll leave you to find the rest.

59. The Hockey Team

A mixed hockey team containing five men and six women chosen from seven men and nine women can be formed in 1,764 different ways, so the team would have to play that number of matches before all possible combinations had been tried.

60. The Astronaut

The height above the surface of the earth, where the astronaut's weight would be 1/10 of that on earth is calculated by:

$1/10 = 637**2/d^2$

That is, $d^2 = 10 \times 6370**2$

$d = \sqrt{10} \times 6,370$

$d = 20,143.7$ km

Therefore his height would be 20,143.7 - 6,370 = 13,773.7 km

61. Take A Hike

The answer is 2.666 miles.

62. A Drive to the Med

Mr White had to buy an extra liter of oil, so we can take it that the $2.60 he spent over his estimated amount was the cost of this oil. He bought 3 liters of oil on the journey, so the amount spent on fuel was $87.60 less 3 x $2.60 = $79.80.

1,200 km at a rate of 9 km per liter would mean a total fuel usage of 1,200/9 - 133 1/3 liters. Cost per liter is found by Total cost/Total used, so $79.80/133 1/3 = $0.5985. So his average price per liter was $0.60.

63. The Fish Pond

Mr Brown's calculations found the precise surface area of the pond's foundations; however, unless Mr Brown has some method of making a flat sheet into the exact shape of his pond – that is, an inverted top hat shape – then 22m^2 will be too small. If he lays the flat sheet over the site and then pushes the sheet into the hole, the sheet will inevitably fold over on to itself around the walls. This will take up the extra 6 m^2 of material. In reality, waterproof material is almost always sold from a roll. So Mr Brown would need material from a roll 6 m wide, and he would have to buy a length 6 m long. This means he would have to buy 36 m^2 in order to cover a precise area of only 22 m^2.

64. The Prisoner.

The best method of solving this problem is by the use of quadratic equations, but to save you the trouble the walls are 0.676 m or 67.6 cm thick.

65. The Airliner

The minimum number of economy-class passengers allowed under these conditions is 88.

66. Hieroglyphics

Cover the right-hand half of each of the symbols: you'll see the numbers 1, 3, 5 and 7. The next symbol in the series will obviously be 9 – but it will appear as one number attached to a reversed 9.

67. The Schoolteacher

The number of consecutive days is 15.

68. Share and Share a like

The price per loaf was $1.50.

69. The Sheep Ranch

Lucky Mr Thrifty can expect to receive $83,026.73 from the sale of the land.

70. Fuel Prices

Mr Thrifty used to spend $800 per year on fuel before the increase in price.

71. Take the Train

Trains now run 1 1/3 times as fast.

72. The Jogger

Poor Mr Smith could only manage to run 1.8 miles before he had to hail the taxi.

73. In the Bar

The bartender was 36 years old.

The customer's age was 40 years.

74. Still in the Bar

If the total of the price of the bottle plus the top was 8 cents and the bottle cost 6 cents more than the top, then the top cost 1 cent to make.

75. Digits, Digits and More Digits

The three answers are 39, 78, and 973.

76. Working His Way Through College

Ivor did not attend work for three days out of the 20 days he was employed.

77. Student Life

The smaller of the two rooms that make up Ivor Nodosh's flat measures 12 ft x 12 ft, and the larger measures 13 ft x 13 ft.

78. Think of a Number

The number I am left with after the calculations is 3.

79. Think of a Number (Again)

There are four possible numbers: 21, 42, 63 and 84.

80. Party Time

There were 100 cans of beer to share at the party.

81. The Boatman

The speed of the current was a constant 2 mph. With the current the boat had an overall speed of 8 mph and against the current a speed of 4 mph, so the boatman's journey time would be doubled.

82. The Round Trip

The distance between Southtown and Northtown is 48 km by train.

83. Vacation by the Sea

Mr Mensaman had a vacation that lasted 15 days, but with a little more careful planning it could have lasted 20 days.

84. A Day in the Life of a Greengrocer

Mr B. Troot bought 300 pineapples and sold only 270 at 8 cents each profit. 300 pineapples for $72 means he paid 24 cents each for them. He sold 270 at 32 cents each, giving him $86.40 income. $86.40 less $72 gives a net profit of $14.40. He paid 20 cents per pound for the apples, and bought 80 sacks at $1.50 and 40 sacks at $1.70.

85. More and More Moores

Old Mrs Moore had five children originally.

86. Are You Sitting Comfortably?

The woman had been waiting 36 minutes 49 seconds.

87. Coffee Break Quiz

1. A stitch in time saves nine.

2. To be or not to be. (2B pencil)

3. Red sky at night, shepherd's delight.

4. One swallow does not make a summer.

5. Too many cooks spoil the broth.

Answers to the Bond films:

1. Doctor No

2. Moonraker

3. Golden Eye

4. Octopussy

5. Thunderball

The tie-break answer is: 'The Charge of the Light Brigade'.

88. Take the Train 2

The two trains pass each other at 14:00, 75 miles from Brotherton.

89. How High is the Mountain?

Draw a circle with a small bump on the top. Now draw a line from the top of the bump to the circumference. This line forms a tangent to the circle and hence meets a radius of the circle at 90°. Now draw a line from the center of the circle to the top of the bump, and we have a right-angled triangle. The angle between the two radii is the same as the angle of depression, so we can now calculate the lengths of the sides of the triangle by trigonometry. The radius of the circle (which represents the earth) is half the diameter = 3,957 miles. The distance from the center of the earth to the top of the mountain is found by 3,957/Cos 1.97 = 3,959.34. Subtract the radius of the earth from this figure and we have the height of the mountain. 3,959.34 - 3959 = 2.34 miles. Multiply this by 5,280 = 12,355 ft.

90. What Time is it Over There?

There are 24 hours in a day, and the earth is divided into 360°. If we convert the hours into minutes and divide by 360, we will find that for each degree of movement, east or west, there will be a time difference of four minutes. So 75° west will give an addition of 300 minutes to the time at Greenwich. If it is 12 noon at Greenwich, then it will be 17.00 hours at 75° west or 5 pm.

91. Over a Barrel

The barrel will hold 112.2 gallons. If you calculated the answer correctly without cheating, then there is only one thing I can say to you, and that is CONGRATULATIONS, YOU ARE AMAZING. The method of calculation without calculus is complex, bordering on the ridiculous, but here it is:

Add together 39 x the square of the larger diameter, 25 times the square of the smaller diameter and 26 times the product of the two diameters. Multiply all that by the length, and divide by the magic number 26,489.84.

92. Bubbles in the Bath

The scientific explanation is not in doubt. In the shape of a sphere 1 cm^3 is contained by 4.835 cm^2 of surface area. In the shape of a cube 1 cm^3 is contained by 6 cm^2 of surface area.

93. Cannon Balls

The velocity of an 18 lb cannon ball fired with the same charge would be 923.76 ft per second.

94. The Playing Field

If little Billy Wiz ran at 5 m per second for 28.28 seconds he covered a distance of 141.4 m, this being the diagonal length of the field. The area of a square can be found by squaring the diagonal and dividing by two, so the area of the field is 9,997 m^2.

95. The Inscribed Circle

The area available to Nanny the goat is a circle inscribed in an isosceles triangle. The area of the circle is, of course Pi multiplied by the radius squared. The radius of the circle may be found by multiplying half the length of the base of the triangle with the tangent of half the base angle. In this case the area of the circular section of pasture is:

3.142(5 x Tan 35)(5 x Tan 35) = 38.5 m^2.

96. The Circumscribed Circle

The radius of the cutter is found by dividing half the distance between the vertices by the Cosine of half the angle between them. Twice this will give the diameter of the hole it will produce:

2(2.5/cos 30) = 2(2.5/0.8660) = 5.77 cm.

97. The Builder's Conundrum

The only possible way for three services to be connected to three houses without crossing over each other is to introduce a third dimension. All three must follow exactly the same route one above the other. They can then enter the houses and separate in the directions required without ever crossing over one another.

98. There's a Hole in my Bucket

The volume of the bucket (the technical name for this shape is a conical frustum) is best found by the use of this formula: add the square of larger radius to the square of the smaller radius and add to this the product of the two radii. Multiply this by Pi (3.142) and then by the height and divide the total by three. Thus:

(15 x 15) + (10 x 10) + (15 x 10) x 3.142 x 25 divided by 3 = 12,435.5 This gives the answer in milliliters. At the rate of one ml per second, this number represents the number of seconds it will take for the bucket to empty. Changing this into hours, minutes and seconds we have the answer 3 hours 27 minutes and 15.5 seconds.

99. Stop the Leak

You have been asked to find the volume of an elliptical ungulas of a conical frustum made by a section passing diagonally through opposite edges of the ends. First multiply the two diameters together and find the square root of the product. Multiply this by the larger diameter and subtract the square of the smaller diameter. Now divide all this by the difference between the two diameters. Multiply your answer first by the smaller diameter, then by the height of the bucket and then by Pi and divide all that by 12. Your answer will be in milliliters; divide by 1,000 to change it into liters:

4.383 liters.

100. Going into Orbit

One-third of the earth's surface will be visible from a distance away from the earth that is exactly the same as the diameter of the earth, 7,914 miles.

101. The Wicked Queen

Sam put his hand into the bag and drew out a pebble. Without looking at it, he let it fall to the pathway, where it was immediately lost.
'Butterfingers!' Sam said loudly. 'Never mind, we can tell which one I chose by looking at the colour of the one left in the bag.' And they all lived happily ever after.

102. The Pentagon

The length of the side of a pentagon is the same as the hypotenuse of a right-angled triangle whose height is the radius of the circle; the base is 5/8 the radius of the circle. The length can be found using Pythagoras' theorem simplified to the square root of 1.391 x 36 = 7.1 cm. This is the length of the side of a pentagon enclosed in a circle of 12 cm diameter.

103. Squares and Circles

The smaller box, when fitted inside the globe, will touch the circumference with its corners. This means that the diagonal of the box is the diameter of the globe. When the globe is placed in the larger box it too touches the sides, which in turn means that the diameter of the globe is the same as the length of the sides of the larger box. The small box has a volume of 1 liter, which is 1,000 cm^3, so the length of the side of the small box is the cube root of 1,000 = 10. To find the volume of the larger box, take the length of the side of the smaller box, multiply it by the square root of three (this being the length of the side of the larger box) and cube it:

(10 x 1.732)3 = 5,196.1524 cm^3 or

5.196 liters.

104. The Wine Glass and the Crystal Ball

The best way to find the volume of the spilled wine is to find the volume of the part left above the level of the glass. Subtract this from the total volume of the crystal ball, and you will have the volume of the spillage. The volume of the sphere is 4/3 of the radius cubed, multiplied by Pi:

4/3 x 2 x 2 x 2 x 3.142 = 33.515

The volume of the section of the sphere above the glass is found by three times the diameter minus twice the height of the segment, times Pi, times the height squared and all of that divided by six. The height of the segment above the glass is 1.345 in (this can be proved by trigonometry):

[(3 x 4) - (2 x 1.35)] x 3.142 x (1.35 x 1.35) divided by 6 = 8.876

33.515 - 8.876 = 24.639 in³ of spilled wine.

105. Wire It Up

The length of the wire may be found by dividing the cross-sectional area of the wire into the volume of the block of copper. The volume of 1 ft³ of copper is 12 x 12 x 12 = 1,728 in³.

The cross-sectional area of the wire is 3.142 x 0.0125 x 0.0125 = 0.00049087385 in².

1,728/0.00049087385 = 3,520,252.7 in.

Divide by 36 to change it into yards = 97,784.8.

Divide by 1,760 to change it into miles = 55.56 miles.

106. Belt Up

The way to calculate the length of a belt between two pulleys of different sizes is found by first getting the surfaces in contact with the belt: 2øRs and 2(π-ø)Rl, where Rs is the smaller and Rl the larger radii, and ø the angle (in radians) between radii tangent to the belt. To these add 2Dcsinø, the free belt lengths, where Dc is the center distance. The answer, once you've calculated everything out, is 151.73cm.

107. Bridge over Troubled Water

The cost of building the bridge over the center of the pond would be $100 x 140 = $14,000. The length of the bridge at the new position is found by twice the square root of the width of the two sections of pond multiplied together. The pond would be split in a ratio of 3:1 which would give distances of 105 m and 35 m. The length of bridge at this point is twice the square root of 35 x 105 = 121.24 m. At $100 per metre this would incur a cost of $12,124 giving a saving of $1,876.

108. The Legacy

This little problem is best solved by simple algebra. Let x = the amount of the increment. If number eight received $6,000, the shares received by the others will be as follows: the ninth will receive 6,000 - x, the tenth 6,000 - 2x, the seventh 6,000 + x, and the preceding ones 6,000 + 2x, 6,000 + 3x, 6,000 + 4x, 6,000 + 5x, 6,000 + 6x, 6,000 + 7x.

Adding all those together we have 60,000 + 25x. This must equal the total legacy of 100,000, so 60,000 + 25x = 100,000.

Then 25x = 40 000

x = 1600

So the ten grandchildren will receive, in order of preference: $17,200, $15,600, $14,000, $12,400, $10,800, $9,200, $7,600, $6,000, $4,400, $2,800.

109. Fields of Corn

The two fields cover a total area of 30 acres. If we divide this by two we have the average size of the fields. Let X = the difference between the two areas. Then the first field yields (15 + X) x 40 kg of corn and the second (15 - X) x 30 kg of corn. The total difference between the amount the two fields produce is 500 kg:

$40(15 + X) - 30(15 - X) = 500$

$600 + 40X - 450 + 30X = 500$

$150 + 70X = 500$ so $70X = 350$

And $X = 5$

So the areas of the fields are 15 + 5 = 20 acres and 15 - 5 = 10 acres.

110. The Three Wise Women

Let the three amounts that the ladies had in their purses be A, B and C, then we have:

$A + B/2 + C/2 = 170$ or $2A + B + C = 340$ (i)

$A/3 + B + C/3 = 170$ or $A + 3B + C = 510$ (ii)

$A/4 + B/4 + C = 170$ or $A + B + 4C = 680$ (iii)

multiply (iii) by 2 and we have $2A + 2B + 8C = 1360$ (iv)

(iv) minus (i) gives $B + 7C = 1020$.

multiply (ii) by 2 and we have $2A + 6B + 2C = 1020$

subtracting (I), $5B + C = 680$ (V)

if $B+7C = 1020$, $5B + 35C = 5100$.

subtracting (v), $34C = 4420$, so $C=130$

substituting into (v), $B=110$

substituting into (I), $A=50$

111. Fit for a King

The weights of the four metals to meet the king's specifications are:

Gold = 30.5 oz

Silver = 9.5 oz

Copper = 14.5 oz

Platinum = 5.5 oz

TOTAL = 60.0 oz

112. Pipes and Tanks

One way to solve this problem is to choose the size of the tank for yourself. Choose a number that will divide by 2, 3 and 4 – 12, say. Then in one day the first pipe delivers 12 gallons. The second pipe delivers 6 gallons in one day, the third 4 gallons and the smallest 3 gallons. Then in one day all four pipes will deliver 25 gallons when they are all running at once, but the tank that only holds 12 gallons so it will be full in 12/25 of one day.

$12/25$ x 24 hours = 11.52 hours

0.52 x 50 minutes = 31.2 minutes

So the tank will be full in 11 hours 31 minutes and 12 seconds.

113. The Charity Walk

Let x = the distance the first person has to walk and y = the measured amount, then the distances can be illustrated as:

x, x + y, x + 2y, x + 3y, x + 4y

Adding these together we have $5x + 10y = 100$

So $x + 2y = 20$ (i)

Also seven times the first two equal the last three, so $7(2x + y) = 3x + 9y$, which becomes $14x + 7y = 3x + 9y$

So $11x - 2y$ (ii)

Substituting in (i), $12x = 20$, so $x = 1.666$ miles and $y = 9.1666$ miles.

The list would have been as follows:

First walker: 1.666 miles

Second walker: 10.833 miles

Third walker: 20.0 miles

Fourth walker: 29.16666 miles

Fifth walker: 38.333 miles

114. The Owl and the Weasel

Let x be the distance that both the owl and the weasel traveled before the point of interception and y be the distance from the hole. Then, using Pythagoras' theorem and letting the height of the tree equal one unit:

$x^2 = y^2 + 12$, but $y = 3 - x$

So $x2 = (3 - x)(3 - x) + 1$

$x^2 = 9 - 6x + x^2 + 1$

$0 = 10 - 6x$

$6x = 10$

$x = 1.6666'$

So the distance of the point of interception is $3 - 1.666 = 1\ 1/3$ times the height of the tree from the hole.

115. Unit Fractions

There are probably several different ways of solving this problem and possibly many different answers. I have chosen a method that avoids complicated progressions or formulae in order to make it easier to follow.

If we subtract a unit fraction which is as close to 2/103 as we can get from 2/103, then hopefully we should get an answer which is itself a unit fraction. 2/104 is very close to 2/103 and can be reduced to 1/52. Now if we subtract this from our original fraction we should find the second unit fraction.

2	-	1
103		52
104 - 103	=	1
5,356		5,356

So it follows that:

1+1		=	2
52	5,356		103

And to answer the conundrum
x = 52, y = 5,356

116. The Six Brothers

Since the area of the triangle is 3,000 m², we can easily find the length of the base by dividing by the height and multiplying by two. The base is 50 m long and the height 120 m. If the height of the triangle is divided into six equal parts, each section must be 20 m wide.

Now each section decreases in area by the same increment, so it follows that the smallest area must be equal to that increment, since any further decrease by the same amount would result in zero area.

The smallest area itself forms a triangle 1/6 the size of the larger, so its height must be 20 m and its base 50/6 = 8 1/3 m.

Its area is therefore half of 20 x 8 1/3 = 83.333' m². This is the area of the increment.

117. In the Heat of the Sun

For the shadows to be equal in length to the height of the poles the sun must have been at an angle of 45° with the ground. There were no shadows at all when the truck broke down, so the sun would have then been at 90°. The earth rotates at a rate of 1° every four minutes, so 4 x 45 = 180 minutes. Thus help arrived at 3 p.m.

118. Busy Bees

The spiral is created by the circumference of five quarter circles, each one smaller than the last by the radius decreasing in length equal to the size of side of the hive. The centres of each quarter circle are the corners of the hive, starting at the one before the entrance, working anti-clockwise around the hive and finishing back at the same point, so the length of the spiral flight of the bee is found by:

2 x 3.142(2.5 + 2 + 1.5 + 1 + 0.5)

4

= 1/2 x 3.142 x 7.5 = 11.78 m.

The technical term for this type of spiral is the involute of the square.

119. A Roll of Ribbon

The ribbon is wound around a centre core 1 cm in diameter, which has a circumference of 3.142 x 1. The roll is made up of ever-increasing circles up to an overall diameter of 3 cm, so there is a 1 cm thickness of ribbon between the core and the outside edge. The ribbon is 0.01 cm thick, so there must be 100 windings in total, each one increasing in circumference by a constant amount. The overall circumference of the roll is 3.142 x 3 = 9.426 cm.

The length of ribbon for each winding must increase in length by the circumference of the roll minus the circumference of the inner core divided by 100.

(9.426 - 3.142)/100 = 0.06284.

To calculate the overall length of ribbon it is easier if we let x = 3.142 and y = 0.06284.

Overall length of ribbon:

= (x + y) + (x + 2y) + (x + 3y) + + (x + 100y)

= 100x + 5,050y

= 314.2 + 317.34

= 631.54 cm or 6.3154 m.

120. A Pack of Candles

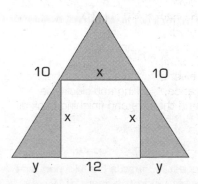

The radius of the inscribed circle of the hexagon is 1.37 times the diameter of the candles. A hexagon is made up of six equilateral triangles, each of which can be divided into two right-angled triangles. Now the radius of the inscribed circle is the height of the triangle, and the base is half the hypotenuse. Since the side of the hexagon is equal to the hypotenuse, we can find this by Pythagoras' theorem.

Let x = the hypotenuse, then:

$x^2 - x^2/4 = 22.992$

$3x2 = 91.968$

$x^2 = 30.656$

x = 5.54 cm, this being the required length.

121. To Catch the Train

Let x = distance from home to garage and y = distance from garage to station, then x + y = distance from home to station.

Time = distance/speed

So x/8 + y/40 = 21/60

40x + 8y = 112

5x + y = 14   (i)

Also x/16 + y/60 = 11 1/2/60

60x + 16y = 184

15x + 4y = 46   (ii)

(i) x 3 gives 15x + 3y = 42   (iii)

(i) minus (iii) gives y = 4

Substitute in (i): 5x + 4 = 14

So x = 2

Distance to station = x + y, so the distance is 6 km.

122. The Travellers

The number of people who took part in the survey was equal to or greater than 137.

123. The Pine Tree

The right triangle formed by the broken tree has a base of 5m and an altitude (a) and hypotenuse (h) which together are 25m. Hence, by Pythagoras, $h^2 - a^2 = 52$, where $h+a = 25$. Solving the equations gives an altitude of 12m, the height at which lightning struck.

124. Sinking a Well

Letting A and B be the two constants for the two known wells, we can form two equations.

For the 10 m depth $100A + 1000B = 60$ (i)

And for the 150 m depth $225A + 3375B = 146.25$ (ii)

Multiplying (i) by 2.25 gives $225A + 2250B = 135$ (iii)

Subtract (iii) from (ii) and we have $1125B = 11.25$ so $B = 0.01$

Substituting in (i): $100A + 10 = 60$

$100A = 50$

$A = 0.5$

So we have the constants $A = 0.5$, $B = 0.01$. Using these we can find the cost of the 20 m well.

$20^2 \times 0.5 + 20^3 \times 0.01 =$ time taken.

$200 + 80 = 280$ hours

280 hours at $50 per hour = $14,000

125. Find the Fraction

Let x = the numerator and y = the denominator, then:

$\dfrac{x+y}{y+7} = \dfrac{5}{6}$ and $\dfrac{x+5}{y+7} = \dfrac{3}{4}$

Cross multiplication gives $6x + 42 = 5y + 35$ and $4x + 20 = 3y + 21$

Rearranging gives:

$5y - 6x = 7$ (i)

$3y - 4x = -1$ (ii)

(i) multiplied by 2 and (ii) multiplied by 3 gives:

$10y - 12x = 14$

$9y - 12x = -3$

Subtraction leads to $y = 17$

Substitute in (ii):

$51 - 4x = -1$

$-4x = -52$

$x = 13$

So the original fraction is $13/17$.

126. The Bowling Green

To raise the green by 1 ft in height, 60,000 ft³ (200 x 300 x 1) of soil are needed. The trench would be 1,032 ft in length, 8 ft wide, and 7.27 ft deep

127. An Old Babylonian Conundrum

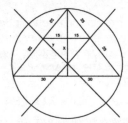

By using Pythagoras' theorem and similar triangles we can find the measurements shown in the diagram above. The radius of the circle is the distance from the intersection of the bisectors of the two sides to the vertices. If we can find a value for x and add it to 20 we have found the radius.

Now $(20 + x)^2 = 25^2 + y^2$, but $y^2 = 15^2 + x^2$

so $(20 + x)^2 = 25^2 + 15^2 + x^2$

$400 + 40x + x^2 = 625 + 225 + x^2$

$400 + 40x = 850$

$40x = 450$

$x = 11.25$

$11.25 + 20 = 31.25$. This is the radius of the circle.

128. De Morgan's Conundrum

The great Augustus De Morgan was 43 years old in the year 1849. He was born in 1806 and died in 1871 at the age of 65.

129. A Square in a Triangle

We can find the length of the side of the lawn if we find the area of the large triangle and subtract it from the areas of the three flower beds. This will leave us with the area of the lawn, and hence we can find the length required. We can find the height of the large triangle by using Pythagoras Theorem. This is 8 m. Calling the length of the side of the lawn x, the area of the upper triangle is 1/2 x (8 - x).

Calling the length of the base of the two lower triangles y, then their areas are 2xy/2, but from the base of the large triangle we can see that x + 2y = 12, so y = 6 - x/2.

So the area of the lower triangles = 2(0.5 x 6 - x/2), which equals x (6 - x/2).

Now the area of the lawn is x², so the area of the large triangle is x + x(6 - x/2) + 1/2x (8 - x) = 48

Removing brackets gives:

x² + 6x - x²/2 + 4x - x²/2 = 48

Collecting terms:

10x = 48

so x = 4.8

The length of the side of the lawn is 4.8 m.

130. Buried Treasure

To answer the cabin boy's question we must add together all the fractions plus 10 plus 1. If we let x = the number of coins found, then:

x/3 + x/4 + x/5 + x/8 + 10 + 1 = x

LCD = 120, so we have 40x/120 + 30x/120 + 24x/120 + 15x/120 = x - 11

Which gives:

109x = 120x - 1320

11x = 1320

x = 120

So the pirates found 120 gold coins.

131. The Farmer's Fields

This problem can be solved by using quadratic equations, but to save you the trouble, the dimensions of the two fields are 30 m² and 10 m².

132. Sharing the Winnings

For $180 to be divided into six parts in such a way as to give a constant difference between the amounts and the sum of the four larger shares to be 53/7 times the sum of the two smaller shares, the sums have to be:

$10, $18, $26, $34, $42 and $50 exactly. This gives a difference between the sums of $8, and 53/7(10 + 18) = (26 + 34 + 42 + 50) = 152.

133. Washing the Blanket

Poor Mrs D. Tergent's blanket is now only 78.75 per cent of its original size, so it has shrunk by 21.25 per cent.

134. Stacking the Shelves

The new shelf would hold 60 packets of cereal. In the ratio of 1:2:3:4 the display would hold six packets of type A, 12 of type B, 18 of type C and 24 of type D.

135. The Three Drunks

Those three foolish men drank a total of 15 liters of beer, which means that they drank 26 imperial pints (32 US pints) between them. Stan drank four more than Bill, and Fred drank four more than Stan. If we let x = the number that Bill drank then:

x + (x + 4) + (x + 8) = 32

3x + 12 = 32

3x = 20

x = 6 2/3

So Bill drank 5 imperial pints (6 2/3 US pints), Stan drank 9 imperial pints

(10 2/3 US pints) and Fred drank 12 imperial pints (14 2/3 US pints).

136. A Cubic Calendar

The numbers on the first cube are 0, 1, 2, 3, 4 and 5, and the numbers on the second cube are 0, 1, 2, 6, 7 and 8.

'But what about number nine?' I can almost hear you cry.

'Turn the six upside down,' is my reply.

137. A Five-Letter Word

A five-letter word containing two vowels and three consonants, all of which are alike, is the word ERROR. There may be more than one answer to this conundrum, so if you have thought of a different word, well done.

138. An Angle in Time

If we take 12 o'clock to be zero°, then for every hour the small hand moves 30°, and for every minute the large hand moves 6°. If it is a quarter past the hour the large hand has moved 90°. For the angle between the two to be 37.5° the hour hand has to have moved either 90 - 37.5° or 90 + 37.5°, that is 52.5° or 127.5°. 52.5° of movement would show a time movement of 1 3/4 hours, making it 1.45. This cannot be correct, as the large hand shows a quarter past the hour, not a quarter to. 127.5° would show a time movement of 4 1/4 hours. So the time is now 4.15. In 20 minutes time the hourhand will move another 10° and the minute hand another 120°, giving angles of 137.5° and 210° respectively, a difference of 72.5°.

139. From an Ellipse to a Circle

An elliptical cylinder whose major axis is twice its minor axis cut by an inclined plane will form a perfect circle when the cut is made at 60° to the horizontal along the major axis.

140. The More You Buy, the More

You Get

The flower seller offered flowers at 10 for $4 to begin with. He then added another seven flowers and increased the price by $1. He then added another nine flowers and $1 to the price. He finally added another 11 flowers and a further $1 to the price, so he was offering 26 flowers for $6.

141. Changing the Patio

The patio measured 26 ft by 22 ft and was made from square flagstones, each one measuring 2 ft x 2 ft. This means there were 143 flagstones in the construction. Anyone attempting to solve this puzzle by making a scale drawing of Mr Mason's patio will probably count that 22 flagstones have to be cut. If the drawing were life-size, they would find that, in reality, 23 would fall under the saw's path, leaving 120 untouched. The diagonal cut divides the patio into two triangles of equal area, so 60 uncut flagstones would be recovered.

142. Cowboy Joe

If Cowboy Joe heads straight to the river at a point 2.5 miles downstream he will cover a distance of 5.59 miles. After watering his horse, if he travels directly to his cabin he will cover a distance of 7.826 miles, a total distance of 13.416 miles. This is his shortest possible route.

143. The Pool Player

The way out is to imagine a mirror is placed against the cushion opposite the red ball. The player should now aim the white ball directly at the reflection of the red. If you make a point on the diagram that represents the position of the reflection of the red ball and draw a straight line from this point to the white ball, you will find the point of contact with the cushion is at position three.

144. The Case of the Different

Areas

On one side of the diagonal line we have an area of 71 cm^2 and on the other 72 cm^2, yet if we ignore the sub-divisions we find that both sides of the diagonal have equal areas of 71.5 cm^2. Obviously something is wrong. Looking at the two triangular sub-divisions we find that the angle the hypotenuse makes with the base is different in each case. A five by six triangle forms a base angle of 39.8°, so the diagonal is not a straight line. This is what is wrong with the diagram.

145. The Dripping Tap

Most people who attempted to solve this puzzle will have calculated the number of minutes between 3.36 and 7.00, multiplied the answer by 60 to find the number of seconds, and divided by 17. They will have found the answer to be 720. Sorry, this is not the right answer. The first drip occurred exactly as I started counting. Yes, there were 720 intervals of 17 seconds each, but I counted 721 drips.

146. The Edges of a Polyhedron

The mathematician Euler made an interesting discovery about the relationship between the number of faces, vertices and edges of polyhedra. If you add the number of faces and the number of vertices together and subtract the number of edges, you always arrive at the answer two. This is true for all the five different possible types of polyhedra. If we let F = faces, V = vertices and E = edges, then:

F + V - E = 2

In this case F = 20 and V = 12, so:

20 + 12 - E = 2

The icosahedron must have 30 edges.

147. The Kingdom of Truth

The wife replied, 'I will be burned alive.'

The king then handed the responsibility of carrying out the sentence over to the court. Her reply caused such confusion and debate among the learned judges that the case was dropped, just as the king had planned.

148. Missing Number

The number I am thinking of is -1.

149. How Old is Grandma?

Grandma is 59 years young.

150. Come Into My Parlour

Simultaneous equations, with x=number of flies (which have six legs) and y=number of spiders (which have eight legs), are 6x + 8y = 166, and x + y = 25. Therefore the solution is that there are 17 flies and 8 spiders.

151. The Cowboy Plumber

The expansion of metal is calculated by multiplying the length of the pipe by the increase in temperature and the co-efficient of expansion. This gives:

Length = 120 ft x 12 = 1440 in

Increase in temperature = 145

Co-efficient of expansion of steel = 0.000012

1440 x 145 x 0.000012 = 2.5056.

The pipe would increase in length by over 2.5 in.

152. The Speed Boat

The original speed of the boat was 12 km per hour.

153. Changing the Fraction

If the fraction 3/5 is written as 15/25 it can easily be seen that the number added to both the numerator and the denominator of 7/17 is 8.

154. Consecutive Numbers

The two consecutive numbers that

have a difference of 53 between their squares are 26 and 27. The difference between the squares of two consecutive integers is always one more than twice the lower number or one less than twice the higher number.

155. Bingo

The probability that neither Alan nor Barry will cross off a number on the first draw is 11/15.

The probability that Alan crosses a number off on both the first and second draws is 2/87.

The probability of only Alan crossing off a number and then only Barry crossing off a number is 3/290.

156. The Cost of a Call

Before the increase 30 seconds were allowed for 1 cent.

157. The Seating Arrangement

The most profitable seating arrangement is to have five rows of each type of chair, which yields $410.

158. From the Mouths of Babes

As water cools it becomes heavier and sinks to the bottom of the pond. When it reaches a temperature of 4°C it is at its heaviest. As the temperature drops below this, the water starts to become lighter and slowly rises to the surface. When it reaches a temperature of zero° it is lighter than the water on the bottom of the pond, and it freezes on the surface.

159. Pythagoras Revisited

Yes. The area of any shape on the hypot-enuse of a right-angled triangle is equal to the sum of the areas of similarly proportioned shapes, such as circles or equilat-eral triangles, drawn on the other sides.

160. A Game of Marbles

The numbers of marbles the boys had at the end of the game are 6, 18, 19, 20, 21 and 36, so the boy who lost the most had only six marbles left at the end of the game.

161. A Tale of Two Ladders

The two ladders cross each other at a distance 10.45 ft above the ground.

162. The Three-Number Problem

The three numbers are 6, 12 and 36.

163. The Genius of Hipparchus

The method here may be a slight simplification, but it contains the essence of Hipparchus' method of calculating the distance from the earth to the moon.

Let us suppose that the calculation was made at a time when a line from the center of the earth to the center of the moon cuts the surface of the earth at a point on the equator. We can then imagine another line from the center of the moon to the earth's surface that forms a tangent to the earth and just touches the surface. The radius of the earth will meet the tangent at 90°, and the three lines form a right-angled triangle. The angle made between the radius of the earth and the line joining the centers of the two bodies is the latitude of the point where the tangent touches the earth's surface. A reasonable value for this latitude is 89.05°, and the radius of the earth is about 3,950 miles. Hence the distance between the center of the earth and the center of the moon is found by 3,950 divided by Cosine 89.05.

Distance = 3,950/0.01658 = 238,000 miles.

164. We Are Sailing

In order to solve this conundrum we need to choose a distance for the voyage. Choose a distance which is divisible by two, three and four – say 12. With the largest sail only in use, the ship travels at a speed of six miles per day. The next largest will drive the ship at a speed of four miles per day, and the smallest three miles per day. With all three sails in use together the ship should make a speed of 13 miles per day. Divide by 24 to find miles per hour, and we have 0.54166˙ mph.

At a speed of 0.54166˙ mph we should cover a distance of 12 miles in 12/0.54166 hours = 22.154 hours or 22 hours nine minutes. This will be true whatever the actual distance of the voyage happens to be.

165. Reducing the Cube

The width of the cube is reduced by 2/3. That means it is 1/3 of its original width. The length of the cube is trebled, so the product of the length and the width is the same for the cuboid as it was for the cube. This leaves us with the height only to consider. The height is reduced by one half; this will reduce the volume by half. The volume of the cuboid is 864 cm^3, so the original volume of the cube must have been 1,728 cm^3.

If we now find the cube root of 1,728 we will have the length of the side of the cube: 12 cm.

166. Disks in a Rectangle

The radius of the second disk is 1.254 cm.

167. Plane for Hire

The original number of people in the party was 30, and the final price each of the remaining passengers had to pay was $45.

168. In the Foundry

In order to find the radius of the original cylinder we must first find the volume. This will be the same as the volume of the hexagon rod. To find this volume we multiply the area of the end of the rod by its length. The end of a hexagon rod is made up of six equilateral triangles, each with sides of length 2 cm. The area of each of these triangles is half the base times the height. The height of each triangle can be found by Pythagoras' theorem and is the square root of three, i.e.. 1.732, so the volume of the rod and hence the cylinder is 1.732 x 1 x 6 x 25 = 10.392.

The radius of the original cylinder is found by dividing this number by the length of the cylinder and by Pi and then finding the square root the answer = 3.437 or 3.5 cm.

The volume of the contents of the tank is found by the radius x radius x Pi x the length of the hexagon rod: 5 x 5 x 3.142 x 25 = 1,963.6 cm^3.

Subtract the volume of the hexagon rod and divide the answer by the radius x radius x Pi:

1,963.5 - 259.8/5 x 5 x 3.142 = 21.7 cm.

This is the depth of fluid before the rod is inserted.

169. The Hikers

There are two ways to solve this and the next two conundrums. One is to draw a scale diagram and measure the distances asked for. The other is by calculation using the Cosine rule. For those people who do not wish to do either, the answer is: Jones and Brown would have to each walk a distance of 1.55 miles to reach Smith.

After Brown has walked back the way he came for half an hour, Jones would have to walk a distance of 2.6 miles to reach him.

Smith would have to walk 1.867 miles to where Brown is waiting.

170. Working with Sheet Metal

There are several ways to work out the dimensions of the width of the 'T' piece, one of which involves quadratic equations. To save you the trouble, the answer is 2.3435 cm.

171. In the Hotel Dining Room

The center of the plane face of the hemisphere lies in the center of the bottom face of the block of cheese. The upper corners of the cheese all lie on the inside surface of the hemisphere, so the distance from the center of the bottom face of the cheese to any of the top corners is the radius of the hemisphere. We use Pythagoras to find the center of the bottom surface, i.e. the square root of 3 x 3 + 2 x 2 = 3.6 in.

Now we use Pythagoras again to find the radius: the square root of 3.6 x 3.6 + 3 x 3 = 4.69 in.

This is the radius of the hemisphere.

172. From Town to Town

Let the car meet the walkers after T hours. So the walkers are then 4T miles form the first town. The car covered the journey between the two towns in 1 1/3 hours, so it meets the walkers in a further (T - 1 1/3) hours; therefore it meets the walkers 30(T - 1 1/3) miles from the next town. However, the two towns are 40 miles apart, so:

4T + 30(T - 1 1/3) = 40

34T = 80

T = 40/17

After picking up the walkers, the car has to cover the distance 30(T - 1 1/3) miles = 30 x 40/17 - 3/4 miles = 520/17 miles in order to get back to the next town. This journey will take 520/17 divided by 30 hours = 52/51 hours. So the total time taken for the party to complete their journey is 40/17 + 52/51 = 172/51 hours.

The party arrives at the next town just after 3.22 p.m.

173. The Tetrahedron

The volume of a tetrahedron is found by the formula: 1/3 x base area x height. Since one of the triangles will form the base we already know the base area = Root 3. To find the height of the tetrahedron we can use Pythagoras. Forming a right-angled triangle, the hypotenuse of which is the height of one of the equilateral triangles, gives us root 3. The base of the right-angled triangle will be the distance from the center of one of the sides to a point directly under the apex of the tetrahedron. This point will be exactly 1/3 of the height of the equilateral triangles, 1/3 root 3, so the volume of the tetrahedron is:

1/3 of the square root of (root 32 minus one third of root 32) multiplied by root three. All this equals 0.9428 centimeters3.

174. The Sum of the Fractions

The number is 120.

175. Percentage Increase

The cost price of producing the goods is 60 cents per kilo.

176. A Six-Shaded Problem

Assigning numbers to letters (A = 1, B = 2, C = 3, etc.), yellow plus brown will equal 164.

177. The Fun Run

Let Alan = A, Bill = B and Charlie = C, then A + B + C = 21.

But A = 5B and C = 2A - 3; therefore C = 10B - 3

5B + B + 10B - 3 = 21

16B = 24

B = 1.5; therefore A = 7.5 and C = 12

If Charlie dropped out of the race 1 km short of the finish, then the course must have been 13 km long.

178. Murder at the Manor House

The butler concluded that the maid was responsible for the deaths of

Romeo and Juliet. There was no one else in the house and the bowl could not have fallen over by itself.

The maid was immediately dismissed for being so careless and for lying about the accidental death of the two goldfish. They were both beloved family pets.

179. The Cost of Silver Plating

If C is the cost, and x cm is the side of the square, then C divided by x2 is constant. Since the cost varies as a square of the length, we can assume that the cost of plating a round tray will vary with the square of the diameter, this being the length of a round tray.

15/64 = C/144 and C = 144 x
15/64 = $33.75

180. The Diet

The cheapest way of buying the food is 1 kg of A for every 2 kg of B.

181. The School Concert

There were 300 seats in the hall, 15 rows of 20 seats each.

182. Investments in Shares

The decrease in the investor's annual income would be just $1 per year.

183. Across the Desert

75 miles.

184. A Tale of Two Trees

This problem is best solved using algebra:

Let x = oak and y = ash

Then x = 1 1/4y or x = 5y/4

and x - 3 = 4(y - 3)/3

So substituting for x:

5y/4 - 3 = 4(y - 3)/3

= 15y/4 - 9 = 4(y - 3.

= 15y - 36 = 16(y - 3)

= 15y - 36 = 16y - 48

= 12 = y

So the oak was 12 m high. Putting this into our original equation:

x = 5(12)/4

4x = 60

x = 15

So the ash was 15 m high before the woodcutter came along.

185. Barrels of Beer

Let x = the second barrel and y = the first barrel:

9x/28 + 2 1/2 = x/2

9x/28 + 70/28 = x/2

18x + 140 = 28x

140 = 10x

14 = x

So the second barrel held 14 liters.

Now 9/28 of 14 + 1/3y - 2 1/2 = y/2

so 4 1/2 - 2 1/2 = y/2 - y/3

2 = 7/6

12 = y

So the first barrel held 12 liters.

186. The Stronghold

The castle was 50 yards on each side, so it occupied 2,500 yd² of land. The area that the moat occupied was 100 yd² less, so it covered 2,400 yd². The total area was thus 4,900 yd². Therefore the square section of land must have measured 70 yd x 70 yd, making the moat 10 yd wide.

187. The Swimmer

He should head at an angle of 78° to the bank, and it will take him 102 seconds.

188. Going Shopping

The answer is 2.5 km.

189. Three Fat Ladies

Let Annie = A, Betty = B and Cally = C, then:

A + B + C = 900

But A = 2B, and C = B + 100

So 2B + B + B +100 = 900

4B = 800

So B = 200, which means A = 400, and C = 300

Annie weighs 400 lb; Betty 200 lb, and Cally weighs 300 lb.

190. Changing Dimensions

The best method to find the answer to this puzzle would be the use of quadratic equations, but to save you the trouble, the length of the original section of land would have been 18 m and the width 16 m.

191. The Farmer's Daughters

Let the ages of the three girls be x, y and z, then:

x + y + z = 33

But 2 (x + 1) = y + 1

And 3y/2 = z + 1

So x + 2 (x + 1) - 1 + 3(2(x +1))/2 - 1 = 33

6x - 5 = 35

x = 5, so 2(5 + 1) = y + 1 and 3(2(5 + 1))/2 = z +1

The ages of the three daughters now are five, 11 and 17.

192. The Ramblers

Average speed is calculated by distance divided by time. The ramblers had spent only two hours 40 minutes of the four hours walking, and one hour 20 minutes resting, so their average walking speed was eight miles divided by two hours 40 minutes, which is three miles per hour.

193. Dirty Pool

15 is a triangular number, so the triangle is an equilateral, giving angles of 60°. As most schoolchildren know, a right-angled triangle with a base angle of 60° has sides in the ratio of

2:root 3:1.

Placing the balls into the frame, a right-angled triangle is formed by the center line of the balls. When all the balls are touching each other, the hypotenuse of this triangle is the diameter of 4 balls = 8 in, or 2 x 4 in. This means the height of the triangle is root 3 x 4 in.

Now the height of the frame will be exactly 1 1/2 diameters higher than the height of the triangle formed by the center line of the balls, so the height of the frame is 4 x root 3 + 3 = 9.9282.

The length of the side of the frame is found by the height divided by Sin 60 = 11.4644, so the area of the inside of the frame is 1/2(11.4644 x 9.9282) = 56.91 in2.

194. The Ballad of Shamus Magee

The range of any projectile on a horizontal plane is found by squaring the velocity, multiplying it by the Sine of twice the angle and dividing by gravitational acceleration. So at a speed of 50 m per second and an angle of 60° we have:

50 x 50 x Sin 120 ÷ 9.8

= (2,500 x 0.866)/9.8 = 220.92 m

So the arrow hit the ground almost 221 m from where Shamus fired it.

Mind Mayhem

Now for yet another style of puzzles. We got a whole team of the best and most experienced puzzle-setters to work on this book. They tend to be people with a nasty sadistic streak. Making life difficult for the readers is their main enjoyment. This section will stretch you in some entirely new ways - a bit like a rack, really.

1. What letter appears once only in each of the first two words but not at all in the last two words?

1. FRUITAGE INTERPLAY *but not in* INTERMISSION OSTEOPOROSIS
2. RIPCORD SHIELDING *but not in* WISTFUL OCTAGONAL
3. PINNACLE COMPLAISANT *but not in* PINCERS MATCHBOX
4. IMPLICATION MULTIFORD *but not in* STAMINA WARDSHIP
5. YEOMANLY VALENCE *but not in* SPADEWORK CARAMELIZE
6. RAMSHACKLE MARSHMALLOW *but not in* STARDUST OCCUPATION
7. PAWNBROKER SINKAGE *but not in* WONDERFUL SACRIFICE
8. WINDSCREEN IMPARTIAL *but not in* FICTITIOUS CAMPAIGN
9. INCRIMINATE FINGERPRINT *but not in* ALPINE BLUEBELL
10. COBBLESTONE ESTIMATE *but not in* GRANITE IGNORANCE
11. JAVELIN ABRASIVE *but not in* PROMPTITUDE RHOMBUS
12. PICTURESQUE IMMACULATE *but not in* SITUATION HIDEOUS
13. EDUCATIONAL MUNDANE *but not in* STEADILY RIDGEPOLE
14. RICOCHET GEOLOGICAL *but not in* OSPREY POLYCARBON
15. ROBUSTIOUS SPELLBOUND *but not in* THUNDERCLAP MOUTHPIECE
16. LYRICISM HAMSTRING *but not in* THISTLEDOWN WORDLESS
17. SORTILEGE DISGRACED *but not in* PRIESTHOOD SOPRANO
18. GRAPEFRUIT ACIDIFIES *but not in* HEADLAND INVENTIVE
19. SPECIFY INVARIABLE *but not in* LAMINATION STANDARD
20. AROMATHERAPY INSPECTION *but not in* MAGNIFICENT DIRECTOR

See answer page 615

2. Remove one letter from the first word and place it into the second word to form two new words. You must not change the order of the letters in the words and you may not use plurals. What letter needs to move?

1.	SALLOW	BAIL		11.	WRING	FIST
2.	PITCH	SALE		12.	TWINE	COME
3.	PRIDE	SLOE		13.	PROUD	BOND
4.	SWAMP	CLAP		14.	DARTED	BEACH
5.	STILL	FACE		15.	CURVED	SHOE
6.	THREE	NICE		16.	CREASE	BAND
7.	VALUE	CASE		17.	BUNGLE	CATER
8.	WHEAT	FAST		18.	BRIDGE	FINER
9.	MONTH	GLAD		19.	TWAIN	hunt
10.	METAL	HOLY		20.	STOOP	FLAT

See answer page 615

3. What word has a meaning related to the first word and rhymes with the second word?

1.	CRACK	—	DRAKE
2.	BOTTOM	—	CASE
3.	RELAX	—	BEST
4.	TRUMPET	—	CUBA
5.	TRUE	—	MEAL
6.	REAR	—	LACK
7.	HOOP	—	SING
8.	CORROSION	—	MUST
9.	GRIT	—	HAND
10.	THREAD	—	GRAND

See answer page 615

4.   Look at the shape below and answer the following questions on it.

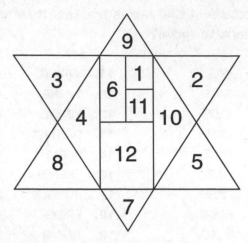

1. How many triangles are there in the diagram?

2. How many rectangles are there in the diagram?

3. How many hexagons can you find?

4. Deduct the sum of the numbers in the rectangles from the sum of the numbers in the triangles.

See answer page 615

5.   In the supermarket, the aisles are numbered one to six from the entrance. Washing powder is next to bottles and it is not the first item you see when entering the supermarket. You will see the meat aisle before the bread aisle. Tins are two aisles before bottles and meat is four aisles after fruit.

1. What is in the last aisle (aisle six)?

2. In which aisle can bottles be found?

3. What is in the first aisle?

4. In which aisle can tins be found?

See answer page 616

6. In a car showroom, the white car is at one end of the showroom and the purple car is at the other. The red car is next to the black car and three places away from the blue car. The yellow car is next to the blue car and nearer to the purple car than to the white one. The silver car is next to the red one and the green car is five places away from the blue car. The black car is next to the green car.

1. Is the silver car or the red car nearer to the purple car?
2. Which car is three places away from the white car?
3. Which car is next to the purple car?
4. Which car is between the silver and the blue?

See answer page 616

7. A survey has been conducted on the types of holidays people have taken over the last twelve months. Five more people had one holiday only and stayed in a self-catering accommodation than had one holiday and stayed in a hotel. Eight people had a camping holiday only and five people took all three types of holiday. Fifty-nine people had not stayed in a hotel in the last twelve months. Four times as many people went camping only as had a hotel and a camping holiday but no self-catering holiday. Of the 107 who took part in the survey a total of 35 people took a camping holiday.

1. How many people only had a hotel holiday?
2. How many people stayed in self-catering accommodation and a hotel but did not camp?
3. How many people did not stay in self-catering accommodation?
4. How many people stayed in only two of the three types of accommodation?

See answer page 616

8. In a day at the library, 64 people borrowed books. Twice as many people borrowed a thriller only as borrowed a science fiction only. Three people borrowed a biography only and 11 people borrowed both science fiction and a thriller but not a biography. The same number borrowed a biography and a thriller but no science fiction as borrowed one of each of the three types. Twenty-one people did not borrow a thriller. One more person borrowed a science fiction book and a biography book than borrowed a biography only.

1. How many biographies were borrowed in total?
2. How many people borrowed only two of the three types?
3. How many people borrowed a thriller, a biography and a science fiction?
4. How many people borrowed a thriller only?

See answer page 616

9. Match the word groups below with the given words.

1. EXTRA
2. WALL
3. VENUS
4. BEND
5. NONE

A	B	C	D	E
Mercury	Zero	Arch	Surplus	Fence
Pluto	Nil	Bow	Excess	Gate
Jupiter	Nought	Curve	Residue	Hedge
Saturn	Nothing	Concave	Remainder	Barrier

See answer page 616

10. What word, which is alphabetically between the two given words, answers the clues?

1.	CURIOUS	—	CURRANT	*Twist or roll*
2.	BARRICADE	—	BARROW	*Obstruction*
3.	CABRIOLET	—	CAMPAIGN	*Welsh town famous for cheese*
4.	CALM	—	CALVARY	*Unit of energy*
5.	DAUGHTER	—	DAY	*Beginning*
6.	DUO	—	DUPLICATE	*Deceive*
7.	EPIC	—	EPIGRAM	*Widespread disease*
8.	EPISODE	—	EPITAPH	*Letter*
9.	FAINT	—	FAITH	*Fantasy world*
10.	FALSE	—	FAME	*Waver*
11.	GOLD	—	GONDOLA	*A sport*
12.	GRAFT	—	GRAMMAR	*Cereal*
13.	HEROINE	—	HERSELF	*Fishbone pattern*
14.	HESITATE	—	HEW	*Coarse fabric*
15.	IMMATURE	—	IMMERSE	*Instant*
16.	JOG	—	JOKE	*Junction of two or more parts*
17.	KIOSK	—	KISMET	*Smoked fish*
18.	LEAF	—	LEAK	*An association*
19.	LIMBER	—	LIMIT	*Rhyme*
20.	MEDDLE	—	MEDICAL	*Intervene*

See answer page 616

11. Match the word groups below with the given words.

1. WAYNE
2. FOXGLOVE
3. GARNISH
4. TOUGH
5. TWILIGHT

A	B	C	D	E
Dusk	Brando	Durable	Poppy	Trimmings
Sundown	Bogart	Strong	Crocus	Accessories
Sunset	Travolta	Sturdy	Peony	Frills
Nightfall	Swayze	Hardy	Aster	Extras

See answer page 617

12. Match the word groups below with the given words.

1. JACKET
2. CONSTABLE
3. PUZZLE
4. CHOPIN
5. CUT

A	B	C	D	E
Ernst	Borodin	Reduce	Baffle	Cover
Rembrandt	Vivaldi	Decrease	Bewilder	Wrapper
Dali	Liszt	Lessen	Confuse	Sleeve
Picasso	Elgar	Curtail	Flummox	Envelope

See answer page 617

13. Match the word groups below with the given words.

1. FRANKENSTEIN
2. COUNTRY
3. ANISEED
4. FEELING
5. TRANQUIL

A	B	C	D	E
Calm	Cumin	Kingdom	Werewolf	Theory
Peaceful	Nutmeg	Realm	Demon	View
Restful	Thyme	State	Dracula	Belief
Serene	Saffron	Nation	Vampire	Opinion

See answer page 617

14. In the map below, C is south of A and south-east of D. B is south-west of F and north-west of E.

1. Which town is at point 1?
2. Which town is furthest west?
3. Which town is south-west of A?
4. Which town is north of D?
5. Which town is at point 6?

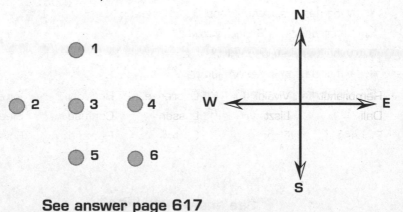

See answer page 617

15. A certain month has five Wednesdays and the third Saturday is the 18th.

1. How many Mondays are in the month?
2. What is the date of the last Sunday of the month?
3. What is the date of the third Wednesday of the month?
4. On what day does the 23rd fall?
5. On what day does the 7th fall?

See answer page 617

16. Three cousins have washing pegged out on the line. On each line there is a shirt, a jumper and a towel. Each has one spotted, one plain and one striped item but none of them has the same item in the same design as their cousins. Sandra's jumper is the same design as Paul's towel and Paul's jumper is the same design as Kerry's towel. Kerry's jumper is striped and Sandra's shirt is spotted.

1. Who has a spotted jumper?
2. What design is Sandra's towel?
3. Who has a striped shirt?
4. What design is Kerry's jumper?
5. What design is Paul's towel?

See answer page 617

17. Three children, Joanna, Richard and Thomas have a pen, a crayon and a pencil-case on their desks. Each has one cat, one elephant and one rabbit design on their item but none has the same item in the same design as the others. Joanna's pencil case is the same design as Thomas's pen and Richard's pen is the same design as Joanna's crayon. Richard has a cat on his pencil case and Thomas has an elephant on his pen.

1. Who has a cat on their pen?
2. What design is Richard's crayon?
3. Who has a rabbit on their pencil case?
4. What design is Thomas's pencil case?
5. Who has a rabbit on their crayon?

See answer page 617

18. The numbers on the right are formed from the numbers on the left using the same formula in each question. Find the rule and replace the question mark with a number.

1.
4 ⟶ 13
7 ⟶ 22
1 ⟶ 4
9 ⟶ ?

2.
6 ⟶ 2
13 ⟶ 16
17 ⟶ 24
8 ⟶ ?

3.
8 ⟶ 23
3 ⟶ 13
11 ⟶ 29
2 ⟶ ?

4.
6 ⟶ 10
5 ⟶ 8
17 ⟶ 32
12 ⟶ ?

5.
18 ⟶ 15
20 ⟶ 16
6 ⟶ 9
14 ⟶ ?

6.
31 ⟶ 12
15 ⟶ 4
13 ⟶ 3
41 ⟶ ?

7.
10 ⟶ 12
19 ⟶ 30
23 ⟶ 38
14 ⟶ ?

8.
9 ⟶ 85
6 ⟶ 40
13 ⟶ 173
4 ⟶ ?

9.
361 ⟶ 22
121 ⟶ 14
81 ⟶ 12
25 ⟶ ?

10.
21 ⟶ 436
15 ⟶ 220
8 ⟶ 59
3 ⟶ ?

11.
5 ⟶ 65
2 ⟶ 50
14 ⟶ 110
8 ⟶ ?

12.
15 ⟶ 16
34 ⟶ 92
13 ⟶ 8
20 ⟶ ?

13.
5 ⟶ 38
12 ⟶ 80
23 ⟶ 146
9 ⟶ ?

14.
7 ⟶ 15
16 ⟶ 51
4 ⟶ 3
21 ⟶ ?

15.
36 ⟶ 12
56 ⟶ 17
12 ⟶ 6
40 ⟶ ?

16.
145 ⟶ 26
60 ⟶ 9
225 ⟶ 42
110 ⟶ ?

17.
25 ⟶ 72
31 ⟶ 108
16 ⟶ 18
19 ⟶ ?

18.
8 ⟶ 99
11 ⟶ 126
26 ⟶ 261
15 ⟶ ?

19.
8 ⟶ 100
13 ⟶ 225
31 ⟶ 1089
17 ⟶ ?

20.
29 ⟶ 5
260 ⟶ 16
13 ⟶ 3
40 ⟶ ?

See answer page 618

19.

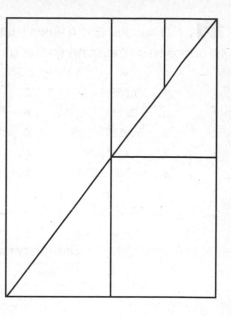

1. How many different sections are there in the drawing?

2. How many triangles are in the drawing?

3. How many rectangles are in the drawing?

4. How many right angles are in the drawing?

5. If the vertical middle line is central, how many similar triangles are there?

See answer page 618

20.

	MONKEYS	LLAMAS	LIONS
WILDLIFE PARK A	42	25	16
WILDLIFE PARK B	35	21	14
WILDLIFE PARK C	48	32	10

1. Which park has twice as many monkeys as Park B has llamas?

2. Which park has one quarter of the total lions?

3. At which park does the sum of the llamas and lions total the number of monkeys?

4. Which park has three times as many monkeys as Park A has lions?

5. Which park has twice as many llamas as one of the parks has lions?

See answer page 618

21. Can you find a word that begins with the letter "A", which is opposite in meaning to the given word?

1.	VANISH	**2.**	BELOW
3.	FORFEIT	**4.**	CONVICT
5.	SWEETNESS	**6.**	PRESENT
7.	IMAGINARY	**8.**	EXTEND
9.	OPPRESSIVE	**10.**	IMMATURE

See answer page 618

See answer page 618

22. Can you find a word beginning with the letter "H", which is opposite in meaning to the following?

1.	EXCEPTIONAL	**2.**	SERIOUS
3.	DIGNIFY	**4.**	FRIENDLY
5.	DOCILE	**6.**	FREE
7.	DESPAIRING	**8.**	PROSPERITY
9.	VILLAIN	**10.**	SATISFIED

See answer page 618

23. In a picture showing a winter scene there are people wearing hats, scarves and gloves. The same number can be seen wearing a hat only as wearing a scarf and gloves only. There are only four people who are not wearing a hat. Five people are wearing a hat and a scarf but no gloves. Twice as many people are wearing a hat only as a scarf only. Eight people are not wearing gloves and seven are not wearing a scarf. One more person can be seen wearing all three than wearing a hat only.

1. How many people are wearing hat, scarf and gloves?
2. How many people are wearing gloves only?
3. How many people are wearing a scarf only?
4. How many people are wearing a hat and gloves but no scarf?
5. How many people are wearing gloves?
6. How many people can be seen in the picture?

See answer page 619

24. In break-time at a shop children can buy chips, candy and soda. Two more children buy candy only than chips only. Thirty-seven children do not buy any candy at all. Two more children buy both chips and soda but no candy than candy only. A total of 60 children buy soda, but only nine of them have soda only. Twelve children buy chips only. One more child buys candy only than candy and soda only, and three more buy both chips and candy but no soda than buy chips and soda but no candy.

1. How many children buy all three items?
2. How many children buy chips and candy but not soda?
3. How many children buy chips and soda but not candy?
4. How many children visit the shop?
5. How many children do not have chips?
6. How many children have candy only?

See answer page 619

25. Sausage, fries and beans are being served to 22 people. The same number have sausage and fries only as sausage and beans only. Only seven do not have fries. The same number have fries and beans only as fries only. Twice as many have beans and sausage but no fries as have sausage only. One person has beans only and one more person has sausage, fries and beans than sausage and fries only.

1. How many people have sausage, fries and beans?
2. How many people have sausage only?
3. How many people do not have beans?
4. How many people do not have sausage?
5. How many people have fries and beans but not sausage?
6. How many people have sausage and fries only?

See answer page 619

26. On sports day the fastest runners are taking part in the sprint, the hurdles and the relay. One more person takes part in the hurdles only than the sprint only. The same number take part in the sprint and the hurdles as take part in the relay and the hurdles. Eleven of the athletes taking some part in these three races do not do the relay. Five people take part in the sprint and the relay and three enter all three races. There are four teams of four runners in the relay. One more person is running in both the relay and the sprint than in the hurdles only.

1. How many people are taking some part in any of the three races?
2. How many people are taking part in the relay only?
3. How many people do not take part in the hurdles?
4. How many people do not take part in the sprint?
5. How many people take part in both the hurdles and relay but not the sprint?
6. How many people take part in two races only?

See answer page 619

27. A survey has been carried out on TV viewing. It shows the percentages of people who watch soaps, documentaries and movies. 26% of people watch all three. 39% of people do not watch documentaries. The percentage of people watching soaps only plus the percentage of people watching movies only is the same as the number who watch both movies and documentaries but not soaps. 27% of people do not watch movies, 14% watch both soaps and documentaries but not movies and 3% watch documentaries only.

1. What percentage of people watch both soaps and movies but not documentaries?
2. What percentage watch soaps only?
3. What percentage watch movies and documentaries but not soaps?
4. What percentage watch movies only?
5. What percentage watch only two out of the three types of show?
6. What percentage watch only one type of show?

See answer page 620

28. At a pick-your-own fruit farm, twice as many people are picking raspberries only as plums only. Three more people pick strawberries, raspberries and plums as pick plums only. Four more people pick strawberries only as pick both raspberries and strawberries but not plums. 50 people do not pick strawberries. Eleven people pick both plums and raspberries but not strawberries. A total of 60 people pick plums. If the total number of fruit pickers is 100, can you answer the questions below?

1. How many people pick raspberries?
2. How many people pick all three?
3. How many people pick raspberries only?
4. How many people pick both plums and strawberries but not raspberries?
5. How many people pick strawberries only?
6. How many people pick only two of the three fruits?

See answer page 620

29. At a college teaching crafts, sciences and humanities, the new intake of students can study a maximum of two of the three subjects. One more student is studying a craft and a humanities than a craft only. Two more are studying both a science and a humanities than are studying both a craft and a science. Half as many are studying both a craft and a humanities as are studying both a craft and a science. 21 students are not doing a craft subject. Three students are studying a humanities subject only and six are studying a science only.

1. How many students are not studying a science?
2. How many students are studying both a science and humanities?
3. How many students are studying two subjects?
4. How many students are studying only one subject?
5. How many students are not doing a humanities subject?
6. How many students are studying a craft only?

See answer page 620

30. At a kennel there are Labradors, Alsatians and Greyhounds and also crosses of these breeds. There are two more true Labradors than true Alsatians. Six dogs are Alsatian and Labrador crosses. Ten dogs have no Labrador or Alsatian in them. Only one dog is a mixture of all three breeds. There are twice as many Labrador and Alsatian crosses than Labrador and Greyhound crosses. There is one more Alsatian and Greyhound cross than Labrador and Greyhound cross. Twenty-two dogs do not have any Alsatian in them. There are 40 dogs in total in the kennels.

1. How many true Labradors are there?
2. How many true Alsatians are there?
3. How many true Greyhounds are there?
4. How many Labrador and Greyhound crosses are there?
5. How many Alsatian and Greyhound crosses are there?
6. How many dogs do not have any Labrador in them?

See answer page 620

31. What word has a similar meaning to the first word and rhymes with the second word?

1.	FRUIT	—	GATE	**2.**	PRICE	—	LOST
3.	STOPPER	—	FORK	**4.**	LEAN	—	SHIN
5.	SPHERE	—	WALL	**6.**	LINK	—	FOND
7.	INSTRUMENT	—	CARP	**8.**	FACE	—	TILE
9.	GROOVE	—	BLOT	**10.**	LOAN	—	SEND

See answer page 621

32. Six children have invented a card game and scoring system. It uses the cards up to 10, at face value, with aces scoring 1. In each round, the value of the card dealt is added to that child's score. Diamonds are worth double the face value. If two or more children are dealt cards with the same face value in one round, they lose the value of that card instead of gaining it (diamonds still doubled). They are each dealt six cards face up as shown below: When the scores are added up, which player:

Player	Card 1	Card 2	Card 3	Card 4	Card 5	Card 6
1	6 ♥	3 ♠	ACE ♦	9 ♣	10 ♥	4 ♠
2	10 ♠	ACE ♠	7 ♥	6 ♦	5 ♠	8 ♣
3	7 ♦	8 ♥	4 ♣	3 ♥	ACE ♣	5 ♣
4	4 ♥	9 ♦	7 ♠	5 ♦	10 ♣	3 ♦
5	8 ♠	5 ♥	6 ♠	9 ♠	2 ♠	4 ♦
6	3 ♣	2 ♣	9 ♥	7 ♣	10 ♦	8 ♦

1. Came third?
2. Won?
3. Came last?
4. Was winning after the fourth cards had been dealt?
5. Had even scores?
6. Had a score divisible by 3?
7. What was the second highest score?
8. What was the sum of all of the scores?

See answer page 621

33. A farmer keeps only four types of animals. He has a total of 560 animals. If he had 10 sheep less he would have twice as many sheep as he has cows. If he had 10 cows less he would have three cows for every pig, and he has two and one half pigs to every horse.

1. How many pigs does he have?
2. How many horses does he have?
3. If he swaps 75% of his cows for 7 sheep per cow, how many animals will he have in total?
4. How many sheep will he have after the swap?

See answer page 621

34. What number should replace the symbols in this grid if only the numbers 1 to 7 can be used?

□	□	△	○	★	14
★	○	△	○	●	19
□	○	●	○	○	23
○	★	●	★	★	9
○	○	★	■	○	23
16	15	19	18	20	?

See answer page 621

35. What numbers should replace the question marks in the series below?

1.	7	9	16	25	41	?		
2.	4	14	34	74	?			
3.	2	3	5	5	9	7	14	?	?
4.	6	9	15	27	?			
5.	11	7	−1	−17	?			
6.	8	15	26	43	?			
7.	3.5	4	7	14	49	?		

See answer page 621

36. What numbers are missing from these number grids?

1.

A	B	C	D	E
7	5	3	4	8
9	8	8	8	8
6	4	9	3	5
8	3	6	?	9

2.

A	B	C	D	E
7	8	7	9	7
5	5	8	5	9
6	3	7	3	9
4	4	8	6	?

3.

A	B	C	D	E
3	5	4	6	3
4	8	5	9	7
6	1	5	4	6
2	2	?	1	4

See answer page 621

37. What numbers should replace the question marks?

1.

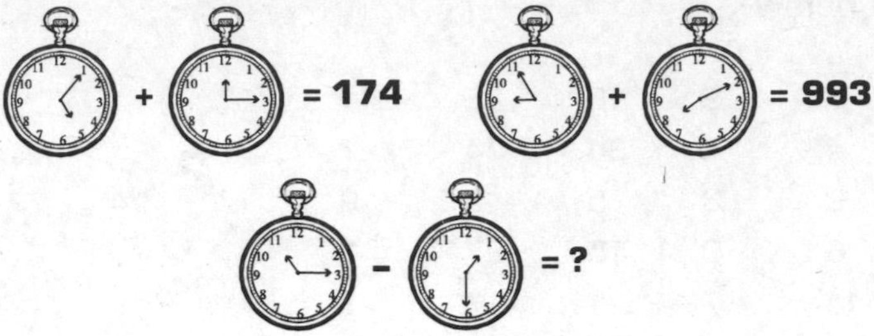

$+$ = 174 $+$ = 993

$-$ = ?

2.

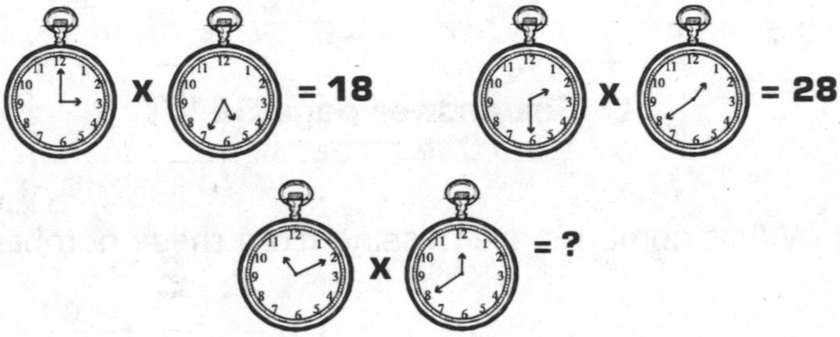

$\times$ = 18 $\times$ = 28

$\times$ = ?

3.

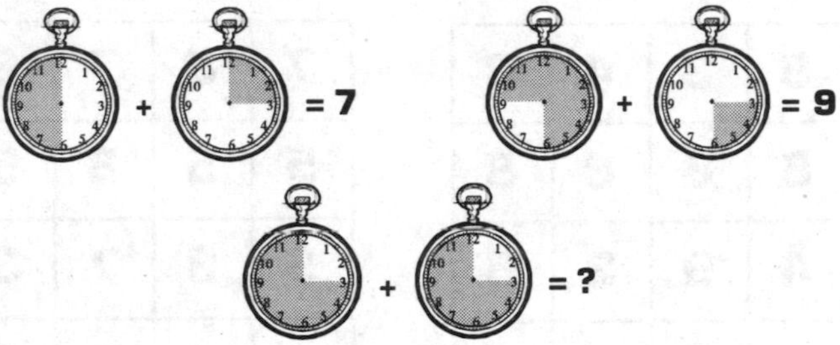

$+$ = 7 $+$ = 9

$+$ = ?

4.

$+$ = 27 $-$ = 6

$\times$ = ?

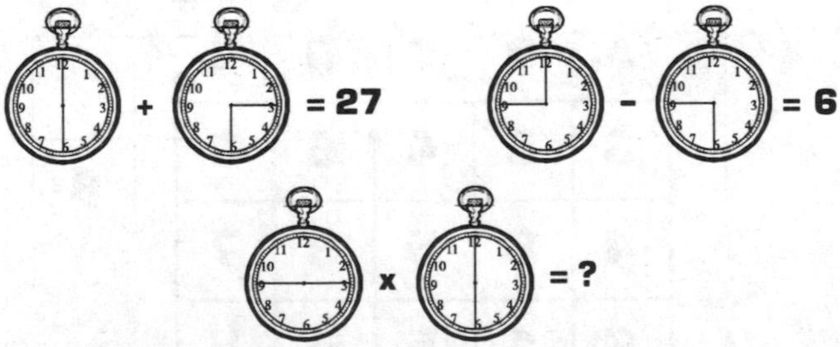

See answer page 621

38. The numbers in box 1 move clockwise to the positions shown in box 2. In which positions should the missing numbers appear?

1.

1

2	6	7
11		1
10	3	5

2

	10	
7		2
	11	

2.

1

22	15	34
12		14
23	21	19

2

14		12
19		23

3.

1

3	5	8
1		6
17	7	9

2

	1	
5		8
	7	

See answer page 622

39.

What numbers should replace the question marks?

1.

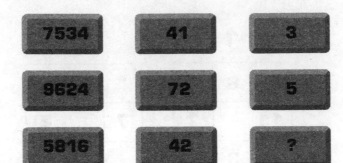

7534	41	3
9624	72	5
5816	42	?

2.

3569	2307	104
7678	5426	380
9925	4185	?

3.

6225	1210	20
7946	6324	188
3483	1224	?

See answer page 622

40. Divide these two grids into four identical shapes. The sum of the numbers contained within each of the shapes must give the totals shown.

1. Totals **120**

8	7	6	8	7	12	9	1
7	12	7	6	4	3	2	14
8	9	7	8	5	7	11	1
8	8	10	7	6	16	10	1
4	9	13	4	12	2	15	6
8	5	2	2	4	9	8	15
6	9	8	14	14	8	2	1
9	6	10	5	12	1	5	17

2. Totals **134**

5	7	8	15	4	7	5	6
11	6	9	8	16	12	10	10
7	12	10	12	3	11	6	8
6	7	2	5	7	7	15	10
12	15	10	8	5	12	8	7
6	7	11	13	9	6	9	6
9	8	10	6	8	8	1	2
3	6	4	10	10	10	15	15

See answer page 622

41. In each line below match the first given word with the word that is closest in meaning, and record your answer on the answer sheet.

	A	**B**	**C**	**D**	**E**
1. RESCUE	Retrieve	Liberate	Salvage	Redeem	Help
2. PROTESTOR	Rebel	Dissenter	Demonstrator	Marcher	Speaker
3. AGGRAVATE	Anger	Insult	Enrage	Provoke	Instigate
4. ETIQUETTE	Custom	Courtesies	Example	Manners	Protocol
5. INVOLVEMENT	Participation	Concern	Responsibility	Implication	Association
6. HERMIT	Solitaire	Recluse	Monk	Loner	Hoarder
7. HASSLE	Problem	Nuisance	Worry	Bother	Trouble
8. FICTIONAL	Legendary	Invention	Informal	Genuine	Imaginary
9. EQUIVALENT	Alike	Twin	Equal	Even	Similar
10. FASCINATE	Catch	Charm	Captivate	Occupy	Win
11. THRIVING	Fit	Strong	Wholesome	Flourishing	Nourishing
12. CONFIDE	Entrust	Limit	Secret	Disclose	Speak
13. WANDER	Saunter	Stray	Veer	Drift	Depart
14. NOURISHING	Good	Wholesome	Healthy	Improving	Worthy
15. ESTIMATE	Guess	Roughly	Calculate	Close	Nearly
16. THANKLESS	Unprofitable	Useless	Ungrateful	Worthless	Unsatisfying
17. TRADITION	Fixed	Custom	Old	Usual	Age-long
18. APPREHENSION	Distrust	Misgiving	Threat	Wariness	Hunch
19. AMAZE	Bewilder	Confuse	Astonish	Startle	Stagger
20. PROFIT	Earnings	Interest	Revenue	Gain	Value

See answer page 623

42. Rearrange the letters given and make as many words as you can that use all of the letters. At least three words are possible from each group.

1. A E G I L N R Y
2. A E E H R T W
3. E N O R S W
4. C E I R R S T T
5. B D E N O R S U
6. A E G I L L S T
7. A C D E I L M S
8. A C H N S T
9. A C E E R R S T
10. E H I R T W
11. E E L R S T W
12. D E E R S T
13. A D E E R R S T
14. A C E L P R
15. A D E L P
16. B E E O R S V
17. A E E N R S T
18. A E L M N Y
19. D E L M O R S U
20. D E G L N O

See answer page 623

43. In each of the following groups of words a hidden common connection is present. Can you identify the connection?

1. NARROWLY   TRAILER   GULLIBLE   JAYWALKING
2. MARIGOLDS   JADEDNESS   EPISCOPAL   CHAMBER
3. DISEASE   BETIDE   UNWAVERING   THREEFOLD
4. CHROME   CORNICE   CLIMATE   BONNIEST
5. BARNACLE   CHUTNEY   CRUSHED   CONTENTED
6. COOKING   SHOOTER   MICROWAVE   ACRYLIC
7. NARROWLY   GLANCED   HOAXERS   BURGUNDY
8. ISSUE   SKIMPY   PAMPHLET   BANNER
9. COMBATING   APPROXIMATE   OPERATE   PIGMENT
10. CUSTARD   RISKY   HONEYMOON   MISUNDERSTAND

See answer page 624

44. When each of the following words is rearranged, one group of letters can be used to prefix the others to form longer words. Which word is used as the prefix and what does it become?

	A	**B**	**C**	**D**
1.	RILE	COTS	MUSE	STILE
2.	SHORE	DIE	DUST	TEN
3.	FEATS	LOPE	RYE	BANE
4.	DENT	SON	LYRE	REED
5.	MAD	DEN	SAGE	LESS
6.	TOP	MOOR	EAT	LESS
7.	RED	AND	LEG	RIDE
8.	EMIT	BLEAT	STILE	RILE
9.	SHORE	HOSE	FILES	SHELF
10.	GIN	CEDES	COLA	FILED

See answer page 624

45. Rearrange the following to form five connected words or names. What are they?

1. TOUGHDUN	FACETIKUR	BRAGGRINDEE	CAJPALKF	CRANOOMA
2. HETCS	RESSERD	STEETE	BALET	DAWBRORE
3. DIALDOFF	PRONDOWS	FUNERSLOW	CHISUFA	GONEIBA
4. OCAIR	ELOUS	HTAENS	HAGABDD	GANKKOB
5. TREAKA	FOLG	BYGUR	DUOJ	TINDBONAM
6. WOIBE	SORS	SCONKAJ	STRANDISE	PLESREY
7. NARI	LICHE	RUGAPAYA	LISARE	HOLDALN
8. PORIPNEPE	SORTITO	ZAPIZ	MAISAL	PATAS
9. GUTTSTART	MORDDNUT	BRINLE	NOBN	GRELEBIDEH
10. CREMRUIT	NINACNOM	NACEYEN	MUNCI	GRONEAO

See answer page 624

46. Add the vowels in the following groups of letters to form five words, one of which does not belong with the others. Which word is the odd one out?

1. GLV	HT	SCRF	SHWL	BRCLT
2. DNM	KHK	NYLN	SLK	WL
3. PLT	DSH	SCR	CHN	BKR
4. BNGLW	FLT	HS	GRDN	MSNTT
5. QRTT	GTR	ZTHR	TRMBN	PN
6. DNCR	GRCR	SLR	DRVR	STDNT
7. BLTMR	RZN	PHNX	CHCG	HSTN
8. VDK	BRBN	GRVY	DVCT	BRNDY
9. DMNND	LLGR	FRTSSM	HRPSCHRD	CRSCND
10. MRYLND	NDN	NVD	GRG	BSTN

See answer page 624

47. Join the letters of the given words to form a single word using all of the letters.

1. PEER	+	DAMP	**2.** CLUE	+	PAIR
3. MEAL	+	DIVE	**4.** CURE	+	MAIN
5. HALL	+	SEES	**6.** SCENE	+	TEN
7. RATE	+	RUSE	**8.** ENSURE	+	DEBT
9. WALL	+	FREE	**10.** CANE	+	TERN

See answer page 625

48. Each of the following words has the prefix missing. The prefix on each question is the same for all of the words in that question. Can you find the prefixes for the following?

1. _ _ _ DOWY   _ _ _ KING   _ _ _ LLOT   _ _ _ RING
2. _ _ _ ITAN   _ _ _ PLES   _ _ _ POSE   _ _ _ SUIT
3. _ _ _ ADOR   _ _ _ CHED   _ _ _ INEE   _ _ _ URED
4. _ _ _ EVER   _ _ _ DDLE   _ _ _ MACE   _ _ _ PPER
5. _ _ _ AWAY   _ _ _ MING   _ _ _ THER   _ _ _ MERS

See answer page 625

49. For each word shown write another word with the same meaning beginning with the letter "C".

1. PSYCHIC   2. ATROCITY
3. ACCURATE   4. OPPOSE
5. INFORMAL   6. PUNISH
7. SLINGSHOT   8. INEXPENSIVE
9. ANGEL   10. INFANT

See answer page 625

50. Which of the following is the odd one out?

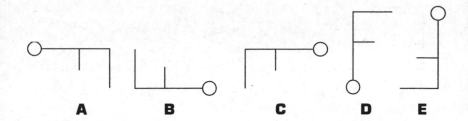

A   **B**   **C**   **D**   **E**

See answer page 625

51. Which of the following is the odd one out?

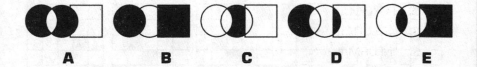

A   **B**   **C**   **D**   **E**

See answer page 625

52. Which of the following is the odd one out?

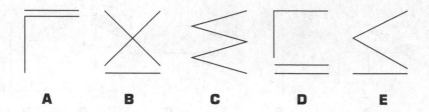

A   B   C   D   E

See answer page 625

53. Which of the following is the odd one out?

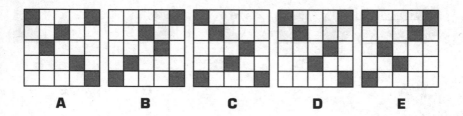

A   B   C   D   E

See answer page 625

54. Which of the following is the odd one out?

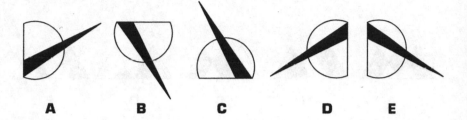

A   B   C   D   E

See answer page 625

55. Which of the following is the odd one out?

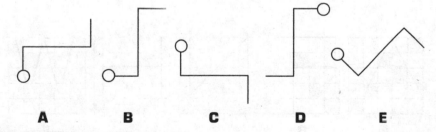

A   B   C   D   E

See answer page 625

56. Which of the following is the odd one out?

A   B   C   D   E

See answer page 625

57. Which of the following is the odd one out?

A   B   C   D   E

See answer page 625

58. Which of the following is the odd one out?

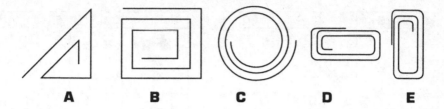

A   B   C   D   E

See answer page 626

59. Which arrangement is missing from this sequence?

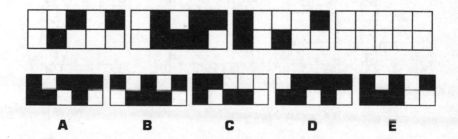

A   B   C   D   E

See answer page 626

60. Which arrangement is missing from this sequence?

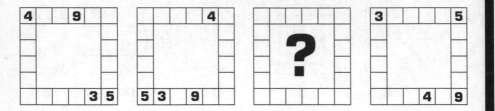

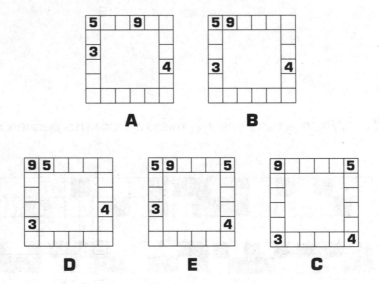

See answer page 626

61. Which arrangement is missing from this sequence?

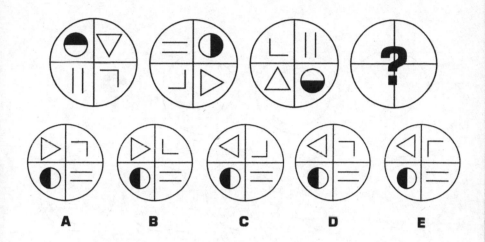

A   B   C   D   E

See answer page 626

62. Which arrangement is missing from this sequence?

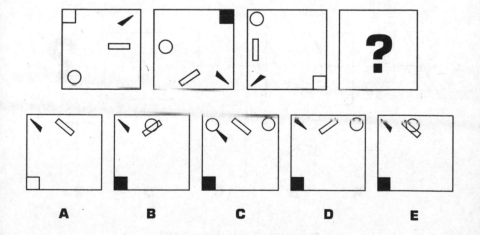

A   B   C   D   E

See answer page 626

63. Which arrangement is missing from this sequence?

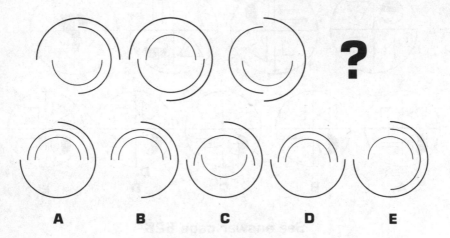

A   B   C   D   E

See answer page 626

64. Which arrangement is missing from this sequence?

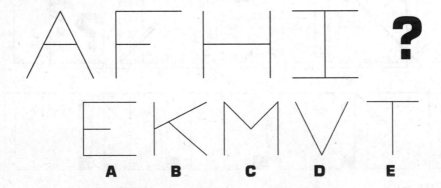

A   B   C   D   E

See answer page 626

65. Which arrangement is missing from this sequence?

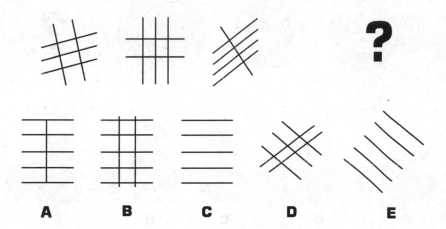

A   B   C   D   E

See answer page 626

66. Which arrangement is missing from this sequence?

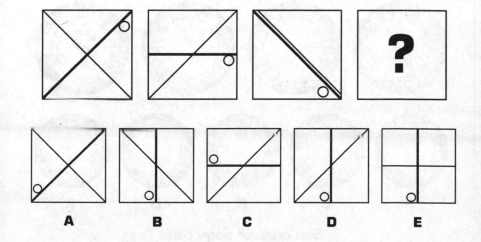

A   B   C   D   E

See answer page 626

67. Which arrangement is missing from this sequence?

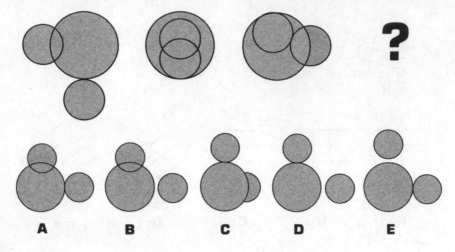

A   B   C   D   E

See answer page 626

68. Which arrangement is missing from this sequence?

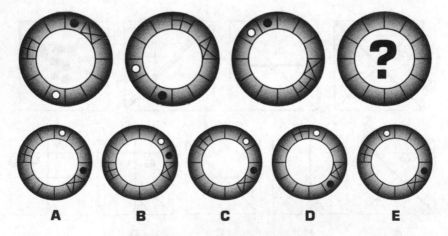

A   B   C   D   E

See answer page 626

69. Which arrangement is missing from this sequence?

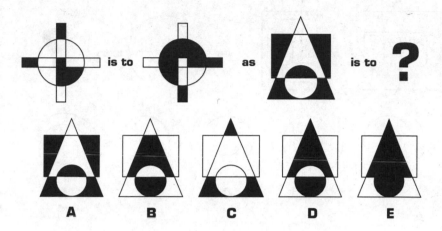

See answer page 626

70. Which arrangement is missing from this sequence?

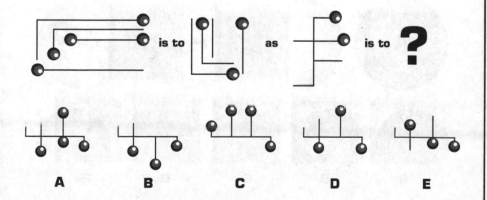

See answer page 626

71. Which arrangement is missing from this sequence?

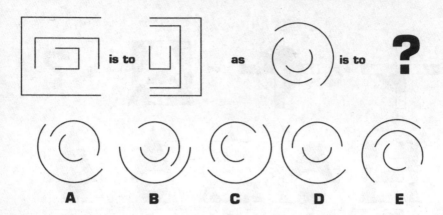

See answer page 626

72. Which arrangement is missing from this sequence?

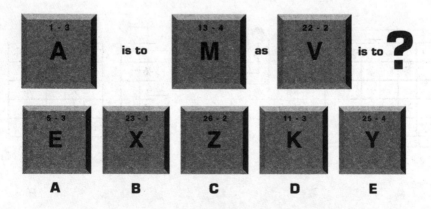

See answer page 626

73. Which arrangement is missing from this sequence?

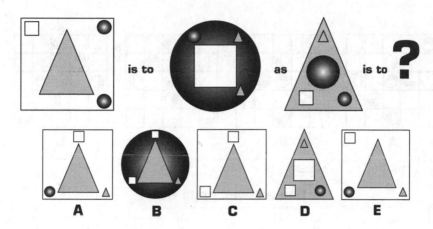

See answer page 626

74. Each one of the next five puzzles is a mirror image problem. Which of A, B, C or D is the odd one out?

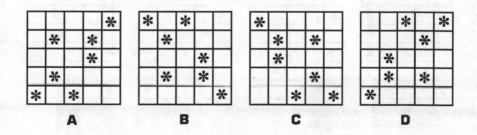

See answer page 626

75. Which of A, B, C or D is the odd one out?

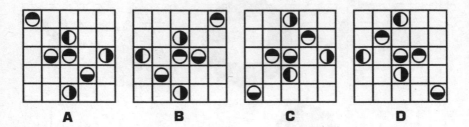

See answer page 626

76. Which of A, B, C or D is the odd one out?

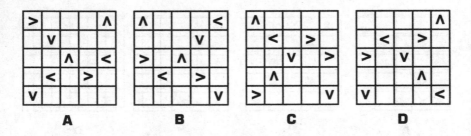

See answer page 626

77. Which of A, B, C or D is the odd one out?

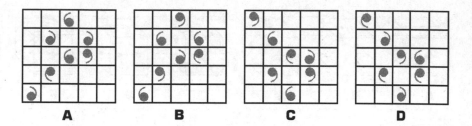

See answer page 626

78. Which of A, B, C or D is the odd one out?

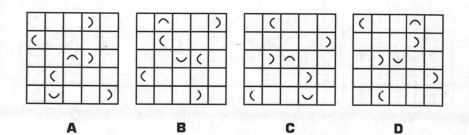

See answer page 626

79. No sign is used on more than one side of the box. Which of these is not a view of the same box?

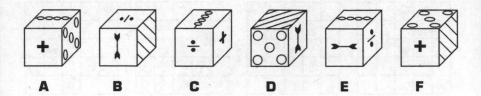

| A | B | C | D | E | F |

See answer page 626

80. No sign is used on more than one side of the box. Which of these is not a view of the same box?

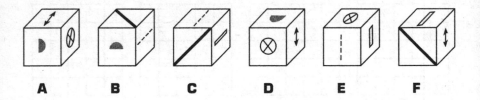

| A | B | C | D | E | F |

See answer page 626

81. No sign is used on more than one side of the box. Which of these is not a view of the same box?

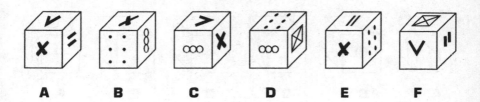

A   B   C   D   E   F

See answer page 626

82. No sign is used on more than one side of the box. Which of these is not a view of the same box?

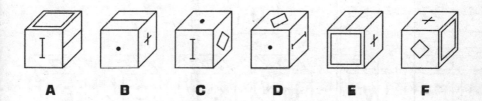

A   B   C   D   E   F

See answer page 626

83. No sign is used on more than one side of the box. Which of these is not a view of the same box?

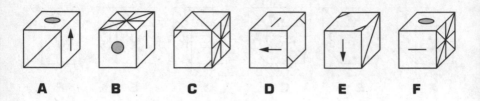

A B C D E F

See answer page 626

84. Which of these boxes can be made from the template?

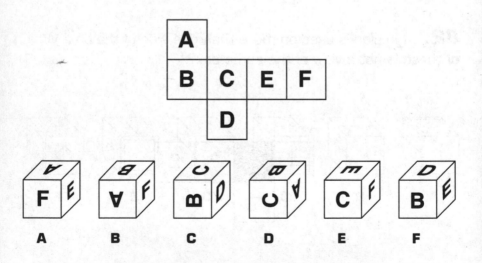

A B C D E F

See answer page 627

85. Which of these boxes can be made from the template?

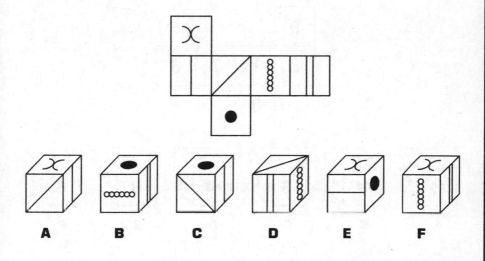

A   B   C   D   E   F

See answer page 627

86. Which of these boxes can be made from the template?

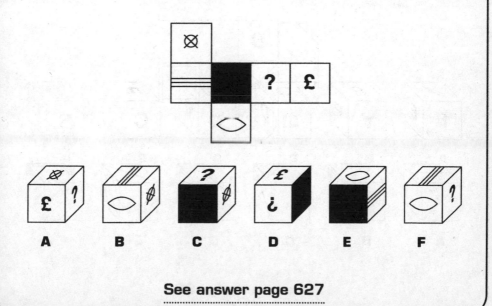

A   B   C   D   E   F

See answer page 627

87. Which of these boxes can be made from the template?

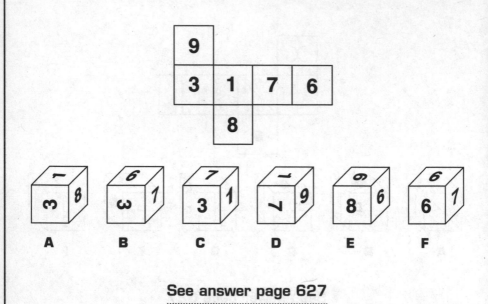

See answer page 627

88. Which of these boxes can be made from the template?

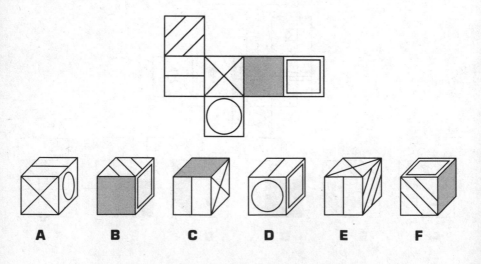

See answer page 627

89. Can you determine which shape has not been used in these questions?

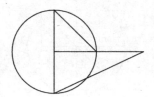

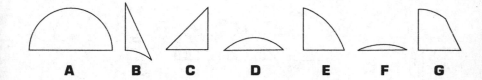

A   B   C   D   E   F   G

See answer page 627

90. Can you determine which shape has not been used in these questions?

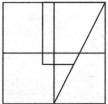

A   B   C   D   E   F   G   H   I   J

See answer page 627

91. Can you determine which shape has not been used in these questions?

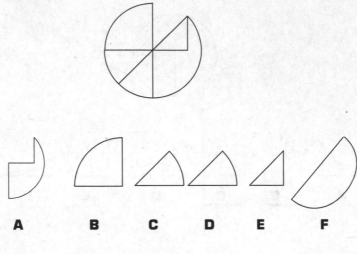

A B C D E F

See answer page 627

92. In the puzzles below, which shape should replace the question mark?

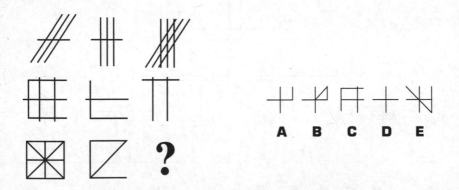

A B C D E

See answer page 627

93. In the puzzles below, which shape should replace the question mark?

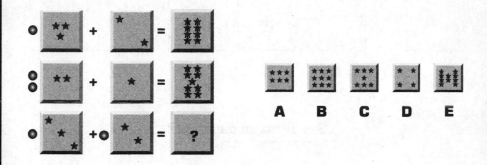

See answer page 627

94. Which of the shapes – A, B, C, D or E – cannot be made from the dots if a line is drawn through all of the dots at least once?

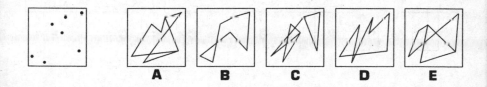

See answer page 627

95. Which of the shapes – A, B, C, D or E – cannot be made from the dots if a line is drawn through all of the dots at least once?

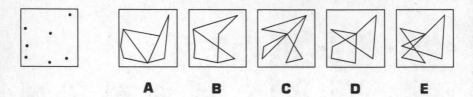

A   B   C   D   E

See answer page 627

96. Which of the shapes – A, B, C, D or E – cannot be made from the dots if a line is drawn through all of the dots at least once?

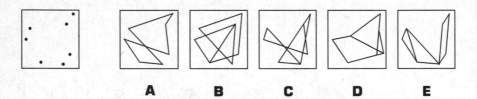

A   B   C   D   E

See answer page 627

97. Which of the shapes – A, B, C, D or E – cannot be made from the dots if a line is drawn through all of the dots at least once?

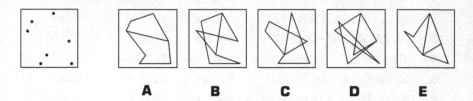

A   B   C   D   E

See answer page 627

98. Which of the shapes – A, B, C, D or E – cannot be made from the dots if a line is drawn through all of the dots at least once?

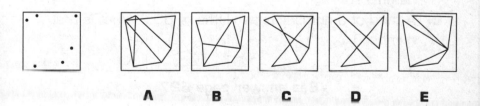

A   B   C   D   E

See answer page 627

99. Which letter occurs once in each of the first two words but not at all in the last two words?

1.	HARMONIOUS	LIBERATE	*but not in*	MELANCHOLY	LIKE
2.	RESPECTABLE	PADDOCK	*but not in*	WATER	PRINT
3.	QUADRUPLE	PLASTIC	*but not in*	STOP	START
4.	CONVERSE	SKATEBOARD	*but not in*	INTERACT	SANDWICH
5.	DANGEROUS	HIGHLAND	*but not in*	CINDER	PARTICLE
6.	CHEMICAL	AMBASSADOR	*but not in*	DANCE	WEEKEND
7.	FIREFIGHTER	MUSHROOM	*but not in*	LENDING	REALITY
8.	GLADIATOR	DATABASE	*but not in*	FORAGE	MEDAL
9.	OCCUPATION	EXCHANGE	*but not in*	CHART	PARCEL
10.	MULBERRY	PENGUIN	*but not in*	MERCENARY	OPENING

See answer page 627

100.

1. Half of a number is three-quarters of 24. What is that number?i
2. A third of a number is two-fifths of 65. What is that number?

See answer page 627

101. Remove one letter from the first given word and place it into the second word to form two new words. You must not change the order of the letters in the words and you may not use plurals. What letter needs to move?

e.g. LEARN — FINE   (LEAN — FINER)

1.	WAIVE	—	NOSE
2.	HONEY	—	EAST
3.	OLIVE	—	CAST
4.	RIFLE	—	LAKE
5.	WAIST	—	HOOT
6.	PAINT	—	BLOT
7.	TRUST	—	DEER
8.	VITAL	—	ABLE

See answer page 628

102. On each line, place a letter in the brackets that can be attached to the end of the word to the left and to the beginning of the word to the right to form another word in each case. No plurals are allowed.

e.g. COME (T) OWN

1.	RUIN	( )	RANT
2.	BOOT	( )	EEL
3.	TAN	( )	NOT
4.	LEAN	( )	HIGH
5.	THEM	( )	VERY
6.	SEE	( )	RAFT
7.	SON	( )	RUNT
8.	EVEN	( )	EACH
9.	LUNG	( )	LAND
10.	CAME	( )	PEN

See answer page 628

103. What word has a similar meaning to the first word and rhymes with the second one?

e.g. AEROPLANE — MET = JET

1.	COIN FACTORY	—	HINT	=
2.	HOME	—	BEST	=
3.	FOG	—	LIST	=
4.	BARGAIN	—	MEAL	=
5.	GRAIN	—	HORN	=
6.	PARTY	—	TALL	=
7.	BRAWL	—	HEIGHT	=
8.	RULER	—	SING	=
9.	LANTERN	—	RAMP	=
10.	BROAD	—	HIDE	=

See answer page 628

104.

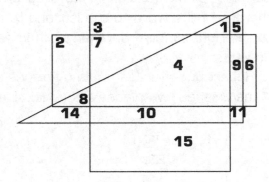

1. How many numbers 1–15 appear in their own triangle?

2. Of the numbers 1–15, which numbers are missing?

3. Which number/s is/are in all three shapes?

4. From the sum of the numbers appearing in only two shapes, deduct the sum of the numbers appearing in only one shape.

5. If each numbered shape is separated from the whole, how many numbers will not be in a square, rectangle, or triangle?

See answer page 628

105. Six people, A, B, C, D, E and F, are in a supermarket queue. F is not at the end of the queue, and he has two people between him and the end of the queue who is not E. A has at least 4 in front of him but is not at the end either. D is not first and has at least two behind him, and C is neither first nor last. List the order of people from the front.

See answer page 628

106. From the information given, find the names and positions of the first eight to finish the marathon. Sean finishes the marathon in fourth place. He finishes after John but before Sandra. Sandra finishes before Robert but after Liam. John finishes after Rick but before Alex. Anne finishes two places after Alex. Liam is sixth to finish the race.

See answer page 629

107. A, B, C, and D take part in school examinations. Only one sits French and that is neither B nor C. B is the only one sitting 3 tests. A sits Math and one other exam. D takes Math and English only. C sits Geography only.

1. Which exam does B not take?
2. Which person sits French?
3. Who takes Math but not English?
4. How many sit two exams?
5. Who sits English but not Geography?

See answer page 629

108. A, B, C, D, and E take part in soccer, baseball, tennis, and swimming, of which soccer is the most popular. More choose tennis than baseball. E only plays one sport. B is the only one to take part in swimming. A and one other of the five play baseball. C does not play soccer. D plays two sports but baseball is not one of them. C plays baseball and tennis.

1. Which sport does A not take part in?
2. Who plays baseball?
3. How many play soccer?
4. Which sport do three of the five take part in?
5. How many play two of the sports only?

See answer page 629

109. What word, which is alphabetically between the two given words, answers the clues?

e.g. FLAP (?) FLASH Distress signal from boat (FLARE)

1.	LUMP	(?)	LUNCH	*Relating to moon*
2.	MILK	(?)	MIME	*Birdseed*
3.	ESTRANGE	(?)	ETHIC	*Endless*
4.	DEPENDENT	(?)	DEPLORE	*Exhaust*
5.	HERALD	(?)	HERD	*Plant-eating animal*
6.	CONTEMPT	(?)	CONTEST	*Satisfied*
7.	BAGEL	(?)	BAHAMAS	*Wind instrument*
8.	NUISANCE	(?)	NUMB	*To render void*
9.	SECTOR	(?)	SEDATE	*Free from danger*
10.	MAGIC	(?)	MAGNOLIA	*Industrialist*

See answer page 629

110. Match the word groups below with the given word.

1. REGAL
2. CROWD
3. PYRENEES
4. MISSISSIPPI
5. ORANGE

A	B	C	D	E
Nile	Elegant	Flock	Rockies	Lime
Amazon	Stately	Litter	Alps	Grapefruit
Rhine	Majestic	Gaggle	Pennines	Lemon

See answer page 629

111. Match the word groups below with the given word.

1. YOGHURT
2. TREACHEROUS
3. LIZARD
4. BERNE
5. SCALES

A	B	C	D	E
Anaconda	Butter	Toaster	Dangerous	Cairo
Alligator	Milk	Colander	Threatening	Paris
Terrapin	Cheese	Skillet	Hazardous	Athens

See answer page 629

112. Match the word groups below with the given word.

1. TEAM
2. OREGANO
3. BUTTERFLY
4. MUSSEL
5. DALMATIAN

A	B	C	D	E
Lobster	Poodle	Cayenne	Earwig	Pack
Prawn	Whippet	Caraway	Ant	Crew
Crab	Doberman	Garlic	Wasp	Herd

See answer page 630

113. Match the word groups below with the given word.

1. TRIANGLE
2. PHYSICS
3. FILE
4. AEROPLANE
5. COPPER

A	B	C	D	E
History	Saw	Train	Beige	Tripod
Biology	Hammer	Bus	Maroon	Trio
Geometry	Chisel	Car	Violet	Triplet

See answer page 630

114. Match the word groups below with the given word.

1. TRAWLER
2. ARTICHOKE
3. CHICKEN
4. TINY
5. HAIL

A	B	C	D	E
Turnip	Snow	Canoe	Minute	Falcon
Pepper	Ice	Dingy	Small	Puffin
Cabbage	Frost	Barge	Short	Pigeon

See answer page 630

115. The map below gives the location of 6 towns A, B, C, D, E and F, but they are not in any given order. D is southwest of B and south of E. C is northeast of A and east of F. E is southeast of F and west of B.

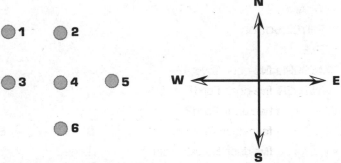

1. Which town is at point 2?
2. Which town is furthest south?
3. Which town is northwest of E?
4. Which town is at point 3?
5. Which town is furthest east?
6. Which town is due south of B?

See answer page 630

116. A certain month has five Thursdays in it and the date of the second Sunday is the 13th.

1. What is the date of the third Tuesday?
2. What is the date of the last Friday in the month?
3. What is the date of the first Monday in the month?
4. How many Saturdays are in the month?
5. What is the date of the second Friday in the month?

See answer page 630

117. Three neighbors, Harry, Fred, and Paul, each have three cars, one two-door, one four-door, and one five-door. They each own a Buick, a Ford, and a Toyota. None of the same make of cars has the same number of doors. Harry's Buick has the same number of doors as Fred's Ford. Paul's Buick has the same number of doors as Harry's Ford. Harry's Toyota is a two-door and Fred's Toyota is a four-door.

1. Who has a five-door Toyota?
2. Who has a five-door Ford?
3. Who has a two-door Ford?
4. Who has a four-door Buick?
5. Who has a five-door Buick?
6. Who has a two-door Buick?

See answer page 630

118. Maria, Peter and Sarah each have a dog, a cat, and a rabbit, one fluffy-tailed, one short-tailed and one long-tailed. None of the same type of animal has a tail the same as another animal, Sarah's cat has the same type of tail as Peter's rabbit. Maria's rabbit has the same tail type as Peter's cat. Sarah's dog has a long tail, and Maria's cat is fluffy-tailed.

1. Who has a dog with a short tail?
2. Who has a rabbit with a long tail?
3. Who has a dog with a fluffy tail?
4. Who has a cat with a short tail?
5. Who has a cat with a long tail?
6. Who has a rabbit with a short tail?

See answer page 630

119. The numbers on the right are formed from the numbers on the left using the same rules. Discover the rule used and replace the question marks.

1.
3 ⟶ 15
5 ⟶ 23
8 ⟶ 35
9 ⟶ ?

2.
3 ⟶ 2
9 ⟶ 6
18 ⟶ 12
24 ⟶ ?

3.
3 ⟶ 8
9 ⟶ 10
15 ⟶ 12
24 ⟶ ?

4.
2 ⟶ 7
5 ⟶ 28
7 ⟶ 52
11 ⟶ ?

5.
2 ⟶ 4
4 ⟶ 32
5 ⟶ 62.5
7 ⟶ ?

6.
2 ⟶ 10
3 ⟶ 13
7 ⟶ 25
11 ⟶ ?

See answer page 630

120. The numbers on the right are formed from the numbers on the left using the same rules. Discover the rule used and replace the question marks.

1. 4 ⟶ 18
6 ⟶ 32
9 ⟶ 53
13 ⟶ ?

2. 1 ⟶ 1.5
4 ⟶ 6
8 ⟶ 12
20 ⟶ ?

3. 2 ⟶ 2
6 ⟶ 4
8 ⟶ 5
14 ⟶ ?

4. 3 ⟶ 2
7 ⟶ 10
9 ⟶ 14
22 ⟶ ?

5. 0.5 ⟶ 14
1 ⟶ 16
3 ⟶ 24
5 ⟶ ?

See answer page 630

121.

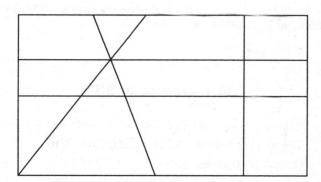

Answer the following questions on the above figure.

1. How many triangles are contained in the drawing?
2. How many right angles can be seen in the drawing?
3. How many sets of parallel lines are there going from side to side or top to bottom?
4. How many different sections are there?
5. How many squares or rectangles are there?

See answer page 630

122. The table below shows the numbers of medals won by different regions at a sports meeting. Assume every event had a gold, silver, and bronze medal-winner with no tied results.

	GOLD	SILVER	BRONZE
REGION A	33	21	63
REGION B	72	8	20
REGION C	27	60	36

1. Which region won half the number of bronze medals as Region B won in gold medals?
2. Which region won three times as many bronze medals as Region A won in silver medals?
3. Which region won one-fifth of its total in bronze medals?
4. The sum of which two regions' gold medals matched the silver medals won by Region C?
5. If there were two other regions competing and they won only 12 gold medals between them, how many silver medals and bronze medals did they get between them?

See answer page 631

123. Find a word that begins with the letter R that is opposite in meaning to the given word.

1. FORGETFUL
2. ORDERED
3. OCCASIONAL
4. UNPREPARED
5. CAPTURE

See answer page 631

124.

1. PARIS *is to* FRANCE *as* LONDON *is to*:

JAPAN   AMERICA   GREECE   ENGLAND

2. NILE is *to* EGYPT *as* MAIN *is to*:

AUSTRIA   FRANCE   ENGLAND   GERMANY

3. TEN *is to* PENTAGON *as* EIGHT *is to*:

HEXAGON   OCTAGON   SQUARE   TRIANGLE

4. FLOOD *is to* RAIN *as* DULL *is to*:

SUN   CLOUD   SNOW   ICE

5. HAND *is to* WRIST *as* FOOT is *to*:

KNEE   ARM   CALF   ANKLE

6. GREEN *is to* EMERALD *as* BLUE is *to*:

DIAMOND   SAPPHIRE   RUBY   GARNET

7. RABBIT *is to* BUCK *as* TURKEY *is to*:

STAG   COCK   ROOSTER   GANDER

8. IRIS *is to* EYE *as* CILIA *is to*:

HAIR   SKIN   BONES   TEETH

9. IO *is to* JUPITER *as* GANYMEDE *is to*:

MERCURY   SATURN   VENUS   URANUS

10. CALORIE *is to* ENERGY *as* LUMEN is to:

ELECTRICITY   PRESSURE   LIGHT   HUMIDITY

See answer page 631

125.

Six children invent a game with dice, where the winner is the person with the highest score. The only rules are that if the same score is obtained by any other person in the round, both their round scores are doubled. Anyone rolling a double has their round score deducted.

Rolling a double and having the same rolled total as another player will give you a minus total that is double the rolled value. A thrown double is denoted by an *.

Player	round 1	round 2	round 3	round 4	round 5
A	7	7	4*	9	10
B	5	8	9	6*	9
C	9	11	5	8*	6
D	8	8*	6	4	11
E	10	9	7	5	6
F	6	4	5	11	8

When the scores are adjusted for the children's rules, which player:

1. Came third?
2. Won?
3. Came last?
4. Was winning after round three?
5. Had an even score?
6. Had a score divisible by 5 (with no remainder)?

See answer page 631

126. A farmer has a total of 224 animals. He has 38 more sheep than cows and 6 more cows than pigs.

1. How many pigs has he?
2. How many sheep has he?
3. If he swaps 75% of his cows for 5 sheep per cow, how many sheep will he have?
4. How many animals will he have when he has made the swap in question 9 above?

See answer page 631

127. The graph below shows the examination results of students taking their schoolleaving exams. 30 children took tests.

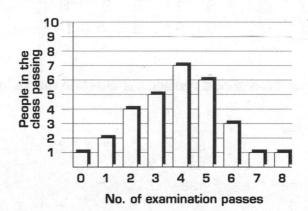

1. What was the average number of exam passes per student?
2. If the top 5 students were not in this class, what would have been the average number of exam passes per student?
3. If 10% took 8 tests, 70% took 6 tests and 20% took 4 tests, how many test papers had a fail mark?

See answer page 631

128. What number should replace the question mark and what are the values of the symbols?

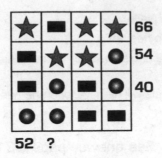

See answer page 631

129. What numbers should replace the question marks in these sequences?

1.	1	5	10	50	100	?	?	
2.	3	8	23	68	?			
3.	3	18	63	198	?			
4.	8	5	4	9	1	7	?	?	?
5.	4	10	22	46	94	?			
6.	6	9	14	21	30	?			

See answer page 631

130. What number should replace the question mark?

1.

2764	1424	48
9534	4512	202
6883	4824	?

2.

7935	2765	1755
6188	5368	3604
9856	5488	?

3.

6459	5204	200
7288	5168	360
9768	7422	?

See answer page 631

131. What numbers should replace the question marks in these boxes?

1.

A	B	C	D	E
3	1	4	7	9
7	0	2	8	6
6	5	1	4	7
2	2	3	9	?

2.

A	B	C	D	E
8	2	6	3	4
5	3	4	2	3
9	1	7	3	5
7	6	8	3	?

3.

A	B	C	D	E
1	5	6	2	7
4	1	5	8	9
7	3	2	6	9
6	2	?	4	?

See answer page 632

132. How many circles are missing from the boxes with the question mark?

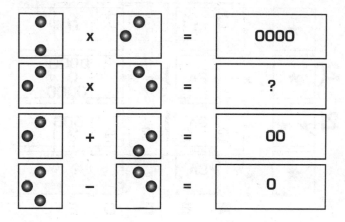

See answer page 632

133. How many circles are missing from the boxes with the question mark?

z	+	w	=	00
z	x	w w w	=	00000
z z	–	w	–	000
z z z	x	w w w	=	?

See answer page 632

134. How many circles are missing from the boxes with the question marks?

$$\star \div n = O$$

$$2(\; \star \times 2n \;) = \begin{matrix} OOOO \\ O \\ OOOO \end{matrix}$$

$$2(\; \star\star - 2n \;) = OOO$$

$$\star + 6n = \;?$$

See answer page 632

135. What numbers should replace the question marks?

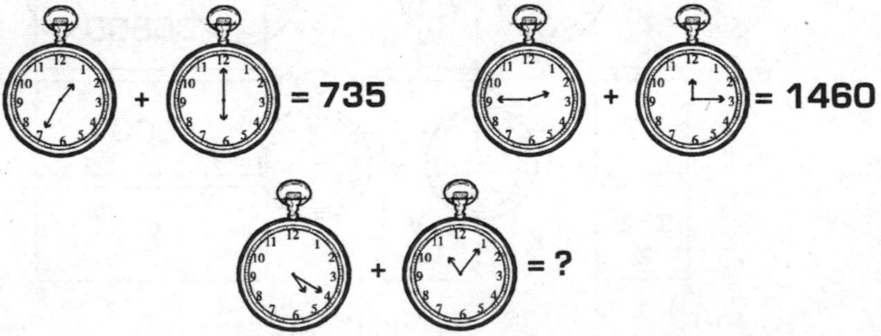

+ = 735

+ = 1460

+ = ?

See answer page 632

136. What numbers should replace the question marks?

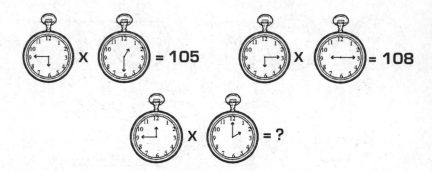

See answer page 632

137. What numbers should replace the question marks?

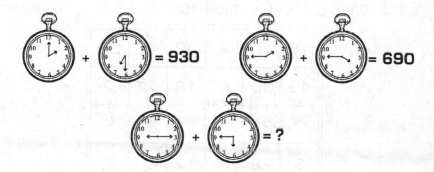

See answer page 632

138. What numbers should replace the question marks?

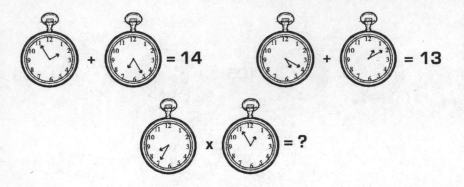

See answer page 632

139. Divide this grid into SIX identical shapes. The sum of the numbers in each section must give the total shown.

Total 100

18	6	4	30	47	29
45	30	6	18	17	2
1	21	1	42	23	5
3	28	7	17	1	6
44	4	32	43	30	40

See answer page 632

140. Divide this grid into SIX identical shapes. The sum of the numbers in each section must give the total shown.

Total 18

6	2	3	4	4	3
3	5	5	2	6	2
5	3	1	3	5	0
2	4	5	3	0	5
3	3	4	6	6	5

See answer page 632

141. Divide this grid into FOUR identical shapes. The sum of the numbers in each section must give the total shown.

Total 45

3	6	3	4	4	6
4	4	7	2	8	3
5	8	5	5	6	7
6	5	3	7	8	2
8	3	1	6	5	4
2	7	8	7	5	3

See answer page 633

142. Divide this grid into FOUR identical shapes. The sum of the numbers in each section must give the total shown.

Total 55

3	6	4	4	8	6
9	6	6	7	9	2
5	6	5	6	2	7
7	6	7	5	9	3
8	9	4	8	9	7
4	9	6	8	4	6

See answer page 633

143. What number should replace the question mark in this grid?

6	4	6	5	8
2	9	8	2	1
5	0	3	4	7
3	2	1	3	1
4	7	?	4	3

144. What number should replace the question mark in this grid?

3	8	7	4	5
5	9	2	6	1
3	2	5	3	7
6	9	3	7	2
1	4	?	1	8

See answer page 633

145. What number should replace the question mark in this grid?

1	5	3	1	2
7	6	7	6	9
2	2	3	1	9
9	9	5	9	4
4	3	?	3	7

146. What number should replace the question mark in this grid?

7	9	7	8	6
3	5	6	4	1
3	2	3	3	5
7	7	2	7	9
5	6	?	5	8

See answer page 633

147. The numbers in the left-hand box move clockwise around the square to the positions shown in the box on the right. In which positions should the missing numbers appear?

1.

11	16	34
23		55
14	63	21

16		11
63		23

2.

5	2	6
7		9
12	4	3

	6	
7		12
	9	

3.

26	32	15
48		83
52	19	41

83		32
15		26

See answer page 633

148. The values of grids A and B are given. What is the value of the C grid?

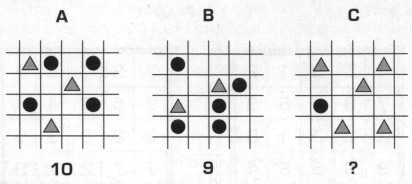

149. The values of grids A and B are given. What is the value of the C grid?

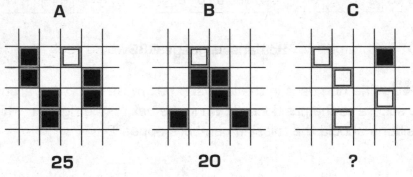

150. The values of grids A and B are given. What is the value of the C grid?

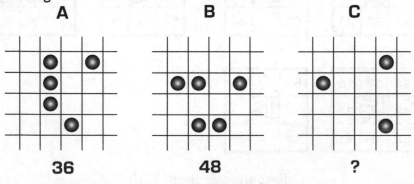

See answer page 634

151. In the number grids below each of the symbols represents a different value. The value of this symbol is also given to all its adjacent squares, including its diagonals. Half that value is also added to the squares adjacent to them (see examples below). Where two or more symbols have overlapping values the sum of those numbers are used. Values of symbol squares are not affected by such numbers from other symbols.

	A	B	C	D	E	F
1	2	2	2	2	0	0
2	4	4	4	2	0	0
3	4	✕	4	2	0	0
4	4	4	4	2	0	0
5	2	2	2	2	0	0
6	0	0	0	0	0	0

+

	A	B	C	D	E	F
1	0	5	5	5	5	5
2	0	5	10	10	10	5
3	0	5	10	△	10	5
4	0	5	10	10	10	5
5	0	5	5	5	5	5
6	0	0	0	0	0	0

=

	A	B	C	D	E	F
1	2	7	7	7	5	5
2	4	9	14	12	10	5
3	4	✕	14	△	10	5
4	4	9	14	12	10	5
5	2	7	7	7	5	5
6	0	0	0	0	0	0

If ✕ = 4 and △ = 10, the grid value would look like the example.

See over

See answer page 634

You are faced with the matrix shown below. Can you calculate the values of each of the symbols and then answer the following questions?

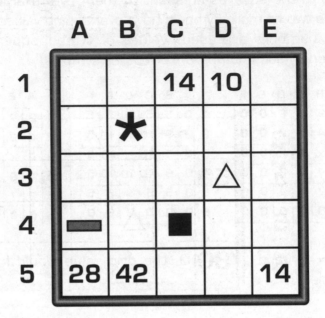

1. What is the value of square B4?
2. What is the value of square C3?
3. What is the value of square A3?
4. How many squares have the value 20?

See answer page 634

152. Now try this more difficult grid. Can you calculate the values of the symbols?

	A	B	C	D	E	F
1			31			
2		■				17
3		★		△		
4	53				■	
5		★	△			
6	30					

1. What is the value of square C2?
2. What is the value of square D4?
3. What is the value of square B6?
4. What is the value of the highest square?
5. What is the sum of the boxes in row 1 and column A combined? Count box A1 only once.

See answer page 635

153.

1. If David gives Mary $4, he will have twice as much as Mary. If Mary gives David $2, David will have 11 times as much as Mary. What did they have at the start?

2. Using each of the symbols +, −, x and ÷ once only, how can you make the following sum work?   2 ? 6 ? 7 ? 4 ? 9 = 24

3. √64 is to 1/8 as 4 is to ?

4. If C J is 310 and L P is 1216, what does G R equal?

5. If D J = 40 and F K = 66, what does H Q equal?

6. A car has a hole in the base of its fuel tank that leaks petrol at a rate of 1.5 gallons per hour. The car starts with a full tank of fuel (10 gallons) and averages 60 miles per hour until it runs out of fuel. The average fuel consumption, without losses caused by the leak, is 30 miles per gallon. How far will the car travel before it runs out of fuel?

7. If the hole in the tank on the car above was halfway up the tank, how far would the car have gone?

8. If it is 26 miles to London and 23 miles to Rome, how many miles is it to Moscow?

9. What three consecutive numbers when squared add up to 365?

10. What three cubed numbers when added = 93 (nine cubed)?

11. What number is next in this sequence?

10   6   13   1   13   ?

See answer page 635

153. continued

12. What are the values of A, B and C in this sum if B is less than twice C and zero cannot be used?

A	B	C
A	A	B	+

| B | A | A |

13. Three-quarters of a number is two-thirds of 63. What is that number?

14. Two-fifths of three-quarters of a number is 19.2. What is that number?

15. The square root of a number is twice the cube root of 125. What is that number?

16. The square root of a number minus 10 is the fourth root of 16. What is that number?

17. Six times a number is half the square root of 144. What is that number?

18. Three-fifths of two-thirds of a number is twice the square root of 81. What is that number?

19. Half of a number is three times the cube root of 125. What is that number?

20. Five times a number is two-thirds of 60. What is that number?

21. Half of one-quarter of a number is eight times the square root of 8. What is that number?

22. Two-thirds of three-quarters of a number is 17. What is that number?

See answer page 635

154. Start at the top left circle and move clockwise to find the value of the circle with the question mark in it.

1.

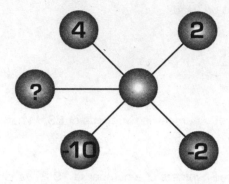

2.

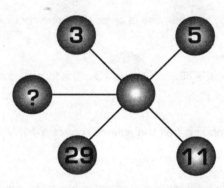

3.

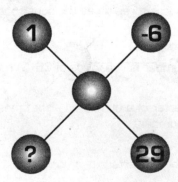

See answer page 635

155. Start at the top left circle and move clockwise to find the value of the circle with the question mark in it.

1.

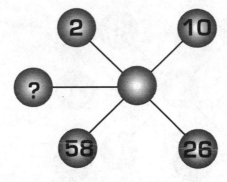

2.

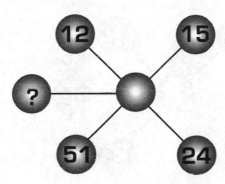

3.

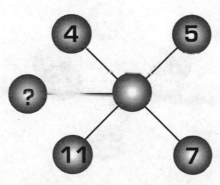

See answer page 635

156. Start at the top left circle and move clockwise to find the value of the circle with the question mark in it.

1.

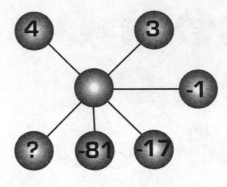

2.

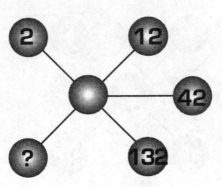

3.

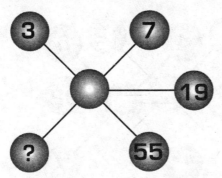

See answer page 635

157. Start at the top left circle and move clockwise to find the value of the circle with the question mark in it.

1.

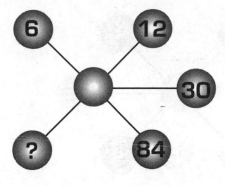

2.

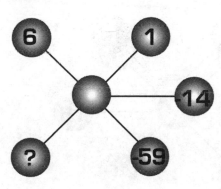

3.

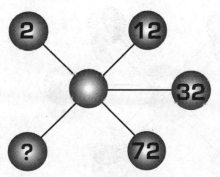

See answer page 635

158. Start at the top left circle and move clockwise to find the value of the circle with the question mark in it.

1.

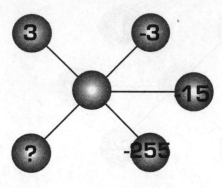

2.

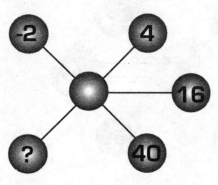

3.

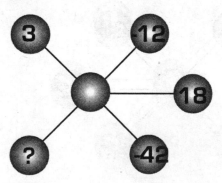

See answer page 636

159. Start at the top left circle and move clockwise to find the value of the circle with the question mark in it.

1.

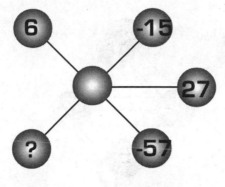

2.

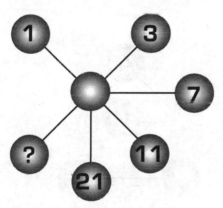

3.

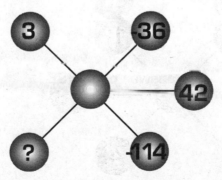

See answer page 636

160. Start at the top left circle and move clockwise to find the value of the circle with the question mark in it.

1.

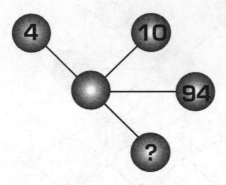

2.

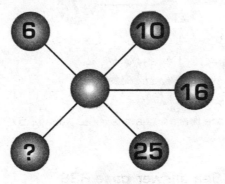

See answer page 636

161. Select a route that takes you from the top number to the bottom number, which always follows a track downwards.

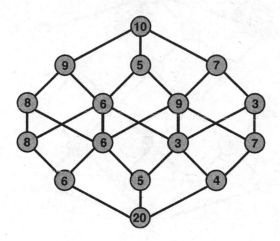

1. Can you find a route that gives you a sum of 49?
2. Can you find a route that gives you a total of 54?
3. What is the highest route value possible?
4. What is the lowest route value possible?
5. How many ways are there to have a route value of 57?

See answer page 636

162. Select a route that takes you from the top number to the bottom number, which always follows a track downwards.

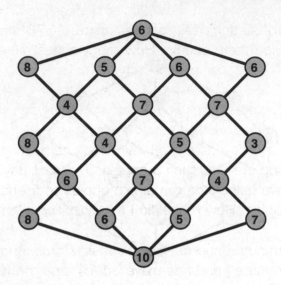

1. Can you find a route which gives you a total of 50?
2. What is the lowest possible route value?
3. What is the second highest route value?
4. How many routes give a value of 43?
5. Can you find a route to give a route value of 49?

See answer page 636

163.

1. A blacksmith had a surplus of horseshoes. He had bids from between 80 and 100 stables for the 1078 shoes. He wished to divide them equally. How many shoes did each stable get and how many stables were there?

2. My apple tree yielded a good load this year. I swapped half of the apples collected for other fruits and ate 4 apples myself. The next day I swapped half of the remaining apples for some wine and ate a further 3 apples. The next day I ate one apple and gave half of the remaining apples to friends. This left me with 5 apples. How many did I have to start with?

3. The minute hand on your clock is 7 cms long. If the point of the minute hand has travelled 14 cms, how much time has elapsed to the nearest second?

See answer page 636

See answer page xx

164. In the grid below the intersections have a value equal to the sum of the 4 adjacent numbers.

	A	B	C	D	E	F	G
	17	34	20	23	21	19	27	25
1
	21	23	22	24	21	32	26	24
2
	18	27	19	27	30	26	19	17
3
	26	35	19	21	25	18	26	22
4
	19	21	24	19	16	28	28	21
5
	24	27	17	29	17	29	18	26
6
	23	25	22	32	20	26	27	22
7
	27	18	20	23	24	29	20	22

1. Can you find two of the four intersections that have values of 100?
2. Which intersections have the lowest value?
3. What is the highest intersection value?
4. What is the highest intersection value on row 7?
5. What is the lowest intersection value on column B?
6. Which row or column has the most intersection values at 100 or more?
7. Which row or column of intersections has the lowest total value?

See answer page 636

165.

1.   What day of the week has an alphabetical value of 100, if A=1, B=2, and Z=26, when all of the letter values are added together?

2.   Dave had $5 plus one half of what Mary had. Mary had 40% of what Dave had. How much did Dave have?

See answer page 636

166. What numbers should replace the question marks?

1.

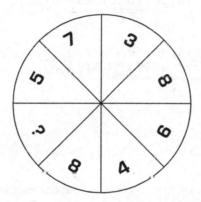

2.

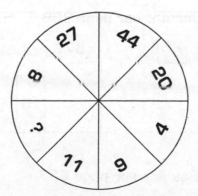

See answer page 636

167. What numbers should replace the question marks?

1.

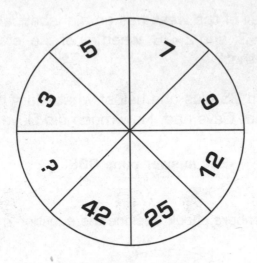

See answer page 637

2.

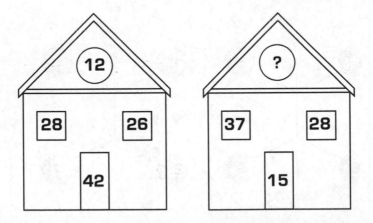

See answer page 637

168. What numbers should replace the question marks?

1.

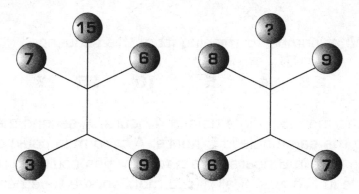

See answer page 637

2.

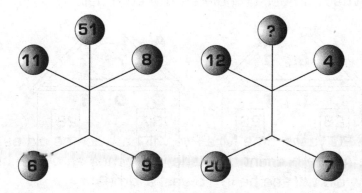

See answer page 637

169.

1. If FACE – DIED = – 67, what does HIDE – BEAD equal?

2. What number is missing from this sequence:

| 2.5 | 4 | 5 | 10 | 25 | ? |

3. One man can dig a hole in 4 hours. A second man could dig the same hole in 5 hours. A third man could dig the same hole in 6 hours, and a fourth man could dig the same hole in 7 hours. If all of the men worked together to dig the hole, how long would it take to dig to the nearest minute?

4. Which number completes this sequence:

7   49   441   ?

5. What number completes the sum below?

```
    D  A  M              A  I  L
 +  8  8  7           +  ?  ?  ?
 _____          _____
    L  I  T              G  O  T
```

6. In 20 years' time Mrs Pye will be twice as old as her son. At the present time she is 7 times as old as her son. How old will she be in 15 years' time?

7. If SHELL = 77345 what number represents HOLES?

See answer page 637

170. Using all of the outer circled numbers once only, can you find the missing numbers in the following questions?

1.

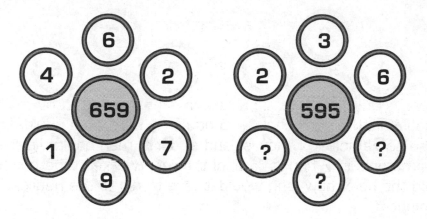

See answer page 637

2.

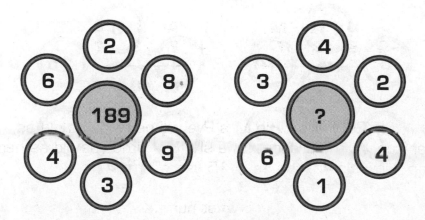

See answer page 637

171. Using all of the outer circled numbers once only, can you find the missing numbers in the following questions?

1.

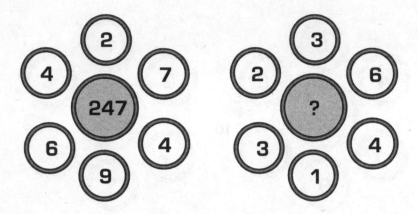

See answer page 637

2.

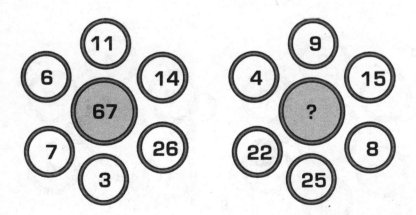

See answer page 637

172. Calculate the values of the black, white, and shaded circles and the sum of the final set in each question.

1.

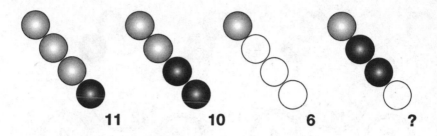

11   10   6   ?

2.

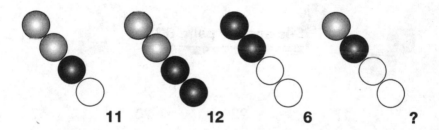

11   12   6   ?

3.

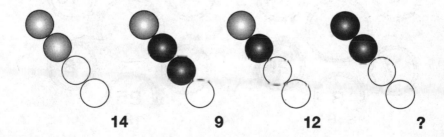

14   9   12   ?

See answer page 637

173. Calculate the values of the black, white, and shaded circles and the sum of the final set in each question.

1.

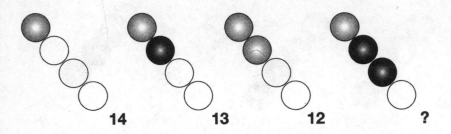

14   13   12   ?

2.

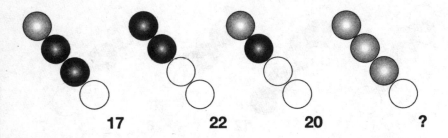

17   22   20   ?

3.

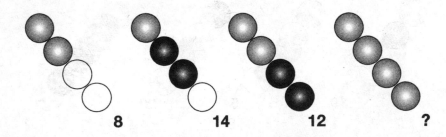

8   14   12   ?

See answer page 638

174. Calculate the values of the black, white, and shaded circles and the sum of the final set in each question.

1.

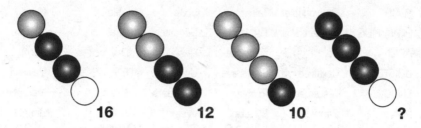

16   12   10   ?

2.

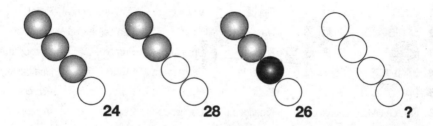

24   28   26   ?

3.

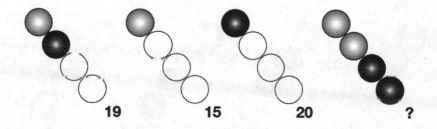

19   15   20   ?

See answer page 638

175. Which word is closest in meaning to the given word? Is it A, B, C, D, or E?

		A	B	C	D	E
1.	FLAIR	Fashionable	Talent	Style	Able	Quality
2.	BONA-FIDE	Correct	Factual	Genuine	Real	Precise
3.	ARID	Cold	Desolate	Deserted	Dry	Burnt
4.	BOISTEROUS	Carefree	Excessive	Unruly	Evil	Devilish
5.	ENDOW	Testament	Probate	Bequeath	Payment	Insurance
6.	PUNY	Petite	Minute	Weak	Soft	Simple
7.	DEMEAN	Arguable	Cheat	Defraud	Degrade	Libel
8.	ATTEST	Protect	Save	Vouch	Warrant	Defend
9.	MEDITATE	Wonder	Consult	Ruminate	Trance	Rest
10.	FLABBY	Soft	Elastic	Unctuous	Waxy	Flaccid
11.	WILD	Feral	Fierce	Violent	Temperamental	Rural
12.	ACRID	Sharp	Nasty	Tart	Bad-tempered	Pungent
13.	MERGE	Coalition	Fusion	Union	Combine	Incorporate
14.	STABLE	Constant	Durable	Permanent	Static	Unalterable
15.	RAPID	Brisk	Fast	Flying	Hasty	Prompt
16.	GOODWILL	Benevolent	Kindliness	Generous	Zealous	Virtue
17.	IMPLORE	Ask	Begged	Plead	Force	Solicit
18.	DORMANT	Asleep	Comatose	Hibernating	Inactive	Latent
19.	OPACITY	Cloudiness	Dullness	Obscurity	Transparent	Unclear
20.	UPKEEP	Aid	Maintenance	Preserve	Conserve	Promote

See answer page 638

176. Rearrange each group of letters to form three words using all of the letters.

1.	D	E	E	I	R	S	V	
2.	E	I	L	M	S			
3.	A	D	E	L	S	T		
4.	A	B	E	D	R			
5.	E	O	R	R	S	T		
6.	A	D	E	G	N	R		
7.	A	C	E	P	R	S		
8.	A	C	E	N	R	T		
9.	A	C	G	I	N	O	S	T
10.	A	G	I	N	P	R	S	
11.	A	C	E	L	R	T		
12.	A	C	G	I	N	R		
13.	E	O	Q	R	T	U		
14.	I	N	O	P	S	T		
15.	I	L	O	P	S	T		
16.	E	G	I	N	S	T	W	
17.	A	E	E	L	M	S	S	T
18.	E	E	K	L	S			
19.	D	E	I	N	N	T		
20.	A	E	E	G	L	N	R	

See answer page 638

177. In each of the following groups of words there is a hidden common connection. Can you identify the connection?

1.	IMPORTED	COLANDER	FORSAKE	ANTEATER
2.	MINUTES	SELFISHNESS	TRIBUNAL	SHOWPIECE
3.	EXPANSE	RADISH	MUTINY	DEPOT
4.	ENTWINE	VALET	STEAL	SPORTY
5.	ROMANTIC	GRUFFLY	MOTHER	BEEFBURGER
6.	TRACTOR	DOVETAIL	CRISPY	STATUTORY
7.	BRANCH	UNICORN	WAISTCOATS	AVARICE
8.	ACCENT	DIMENSION	BRANDISH	HYENA
9.	CLIMATE	BARITONE	NICEST	CORKAGE
10.	TUSSOCK	ADDRESS	SHATTERED	COATING

See answer page 638

178. What am I?

1. My first is in FIRE but not in GRATE
   My second is in EARLY but not in LATE
   My third is in MUSIC and also in TUNE
   My fourth is in DISTINCT but not in SOON
   My last is in FROST and also in SLEET
   When ripe, I am juicy and sweet.
   What am I?

2. My first is in LAMP but not in LIGHT
   My second is in MAY but not in MIGHT
   My third is in DART and also in BOARD
   My fourth is in STRING but not in CORD
   My last is in SEE but not in GLANCE
   I am a city renowned for romance.
   Where am I?

3. My first is in ACT but not in PLAY
   My second is in APRIL but not in MAY
   My third is in NOBLE and also in LORD
   My fourth is in CARD but not in BOARD
   My last is in STACK but not in HAY
   You look at me every single day.
   What am I?

See answer page 639

179. What am I?

1. My first is in PASS but not in FAIL
   My second is in SHOP but not in SALE
   My third is in HAIR and also in FACE
   My fourth is in CARRY but not in CASE
   My last is in ASK but not in PLEA
   You wouldn't want to swim with me.
   What am I?

2. My first is in CASH and also in CHEQUE
   My second is in COLLAR but not in NECK
   My third is in FINGER and also in RING
   My fourth is in SONG but not in SING
   My last is in WATER but not in MOAT
   I am a narrow paddle boat.
   What am I?

3. My first is in JUNE and also in JULY
   My second is in CLEVER but not in SLY
   My third is in PLANT and also in FLOWER
   My fourth is in MUSCLE but not in POWER
   My last is in GLOOMY but not in MOOD
   My whole is a brightly coloured food.
   What am I?

See answer pages 701-704

180. What am I?

1. My first is in HOT and also in COLD
   My second is in BRASH but not in BOLD
   My third is in GANG and also in GROUP
   My fourth is in ARMY but not in TROOP
   My last is in LOAN and also in RENT
   I am a musical instrument.
   What am I?

2. My first is in MOCK but not in FAKE
   My second is in BOIL but not in BAKE
   My third is in ROCK and also in ROLL
   My fourth is in WINDOW but not in POLE
   My last is in BASIN but not in BATH
   I do tricks to make children laugh.
   What am I?

3. My first is in SPRING but not in SUMMER
   My second is in BAND but not in DRUMMER
   My third is in ORANGE and also in RED
   My fourth is in TALK but not in SAID
   My last is in FROSTY but not in SNOW
   I am a fun place to go.
   What am I?

4. My first is in SPRINT but not in RUN
   My second is in BREAD but not in BUN
   My third is in TALL and also in SHORT
   My fourth is in BOAT but not in PORT
   My last is in STEEPLE but not in TOWER
   I am a delicate part of a flower.
   What am I?

See answer pages 701-704

181.

1. There have been orders for 200 Rolls Royces, 115 Vauxhalls, and 500 Hondas. How many orders have there been for Renaults?

2. Donna has won 500 dance competitions, Patricia has won 102, and Charlotte has won 150. How many competitions has Louise won?

3. A model shop has ordered 100 kits of cars, 1000 monster kits, and 600 doll kits. How many space-rocket kits did they order?

4. In a studio audience 8 of the guests are from Virginia, 56 are from Pennsylvania, 1 is from Arizona, and 10 are from Texas. How many guests are there from New Mexico?

5. A price list in a London pottery and china store shows the price of a cup in its various departments. How much should a Wedgewood cup cost?

Royal Doulton	£6.00
Denby	£5.00
Royal Worcester	£1.50
Wedgewood	£?

See answer page 639

182. When each of the following words is rearranged, one group of letters can be used as a prefix for the others to form longer words. Which is the prefix and what does it become?

	A	B	C	D	E
1.	LET	BUS	MILE	RUB	DENT
2.	CHAR	MATS	DIES	NIPS	OPT
3.	SHINES	HIRE	DIE	TIP	SON
4.	EAT	SET	LAP	TAPE	TAME
5.	NIP	LIES	NAT	NOD	NET
6.	TESS	SHIN	LAID	NOTE	ROC
7.	STEM	SINES	RAW	SEND	MITE
8.	BALE	DICE	NIGH	TON	RAY
9.	LEST	SUB	TIES	GINS	DIE
10.	HAS	NET	TOP	OAT	GATE

See answer page 639

183. Rearrange the following to form five connected words. What are they?

1.	ZAMAD	NERTOIC	GUPEETO	TRULEAN	SHIMSTIBUI
2.	NIGEAU	KEELSH	TEESAP	COCKEP	ODESUC
3.	CUGIC	AGEREJ	DINOM	LENCAH	DIDLELOF
4.	TAJECK	HIRST	PRUMEJ	STRUSORE	HOSES
5.	MONZAA	GEANGS	SMATHE	TAZEGYN	BAZZEMI
6.	TALAM	CRIPA	ZAIBI	CYLISI	SHEDOR
7.	BREANCAR	SLEBURSS	SONLIB	RADDIM	TOPRIERA
8.	DAZBUZR	CLOFNA	GEALE	TULRUVE	KHAW
9.	MANDOTBIN	SABBELLA	SKATBEALLB	GOXNIB	COHYEK
10.	STOBERL	WRANP	ROTUT	SMOLAN	CLAIPE

See answer page 639

184. Add the vowels in the following groups of letters to form five words, one of which does not belong with the others. Which word is the odd one out?

	A	B	C	D	E
1.	WLKG	JGGNG	RNNNG	SPRNTNG	STTNG
2.	MSM	MSQ	TMPL	CTHDRL	SYNGG
3.	NSHVLL	SVNNH	LNDN	DTRT	DNVR
4.	MNDY	WDNSDY	JNRY	SNDY	STRDY
5.	RD	YLLW	CRCL	CRMSN	PRPL
6.	ND	TLY	KNY	DLLS	CLND
7.	NGN	CLTCH	GRS	WHLS	LMN
8.	TWNTY	KYBRD	SCRN	MMRY	PRCSSR
9.	CRPHLLY	GRGNZL	STLTN	BR	BLGNS
10.	PLM	PTT	STSM	PRCT	DMSN

See answer page 640

185. Join the letters of the given words to form a single word using all of the letters.

1.	DRUM	+	MIMES	
2.	REPAY	+	LIT	+ SON
3.	DANCE	+	SIT	
4.	SPITE	+	ANTIC	
5.	MEAN	+	ATE	
6.	MONSTER	+	RATE	
7.	CLEMENT	+	RAPE	
8.	DEAD	+	CITE	
9.	NIECE	+	GILL	+ NET
10.	SHINE	+	SUIT	+ CAT

See answer page 640

186. In each of the questions below, 3 pairs of words are given. Match the pair to form 3 longer words.

1.	MAIDEN	VENDOR	HAND	MASTER	NEWS	SHIP
2.	MAN	PAWN	MASTER	LIVERY	PAY	BROKER
3.	SHOOTER	HOUSE	WRITER	SHARP	MASTER	SIGN
4.	PLAY	REEL	NEWS	SCREEN	LIGHT	FOOT
5.	EVER	DAY	DOMES	WHEN	TAIL	WHITE
6.	SPUR	DROP	LILY	LARK	WATER	SNOW
7.	LESS	EARTH	LIST	SACK	QUAKE	RAN
8.	RAM	PEACE	WORD	PART	PASS	ABLE
9.	CRACK	AGE	FOR	BLOCK	WISE	WARD
10.	NAP	HOOD	KID	SOME	FALSE	TROUBLE
11.	MAKER	BOY	LOCK	FRIEND	PEACE	DEAD
12.	TOP	SET	FREE	CARE	MOST	BACK
13.	WHOLE	WIRE	HAY	BAT	SALE	TEN
14.	NECK	ABLE	EYE	BOTTLE	BREAK	SORE
15.	LOVED	GOOD	WILD	BE	LIFE	WILL
16.	SOME	HARDY	FOOL	RAGE	HAND	BAR
17.	ION	AND	LEDGE	REFLECT	KNOW	BRIG
18.	CON	WORK	SIGN	GUESS	POST	TRIBUTE
19.	AGE	HOD	BOND	MAN	SHOW	SLIPS
20.	OUR	FALL	TEN	ROT	RUM	WIND

See answer page 640

187. For each word shown write another word with the same meaning beginning with the letter G.

1.	COLLECT	_ _ _ _ _ _ _
2.	HEREDITARY	_ _ _ _ _ _ _ _
3.	PERMIT	_ _ _ _ _
4.	DISTRESS	_ _ _ _ _
5.	ELEGANCE	_ _ _ _ _
6.	WOLVERINE	_ _ _ _ _ _ _
7.	STUCK	_ _ _ _ _
8.	INORDINATE	_ _ _ _ _
9.	LAMENT	_ _ _ _ _ _
10.	OPENING	_ _ _
11.	PLEASE	_ _ _ _ _ _ _
12.	RAPT	_ _ _ _ _ _ _
13.	BLUSTERY	_ _ _ _ _ _
14.	STOCK	_ _ _ _ _
15.	STOMACH	_ _ _
16.	WILDEBEEST	_ _ _
17.	TRICKERY	_ _ _ _ _
18.	HAMMER	_ _ _ _ _ _
19.	CARGO	_ _ _ _ _ _
20.	RELIGIOUS	_ _ _ _ _

See answer page 641

188. Which of the following is the odd one out?

1.

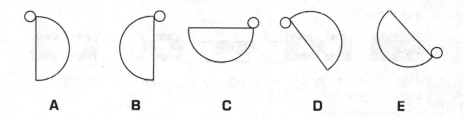

A   B   C   D   E

2.

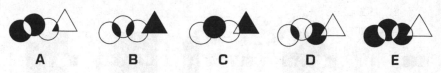

A   B   C   D   E

3.

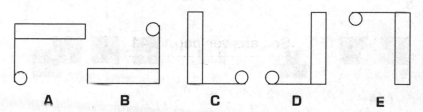

A   B   C   D   E

See answer page 641

189. Which of the following is the odd one out?

1.

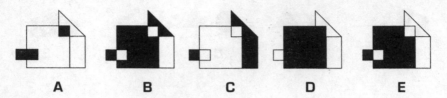

A   B   C   D   E

2.

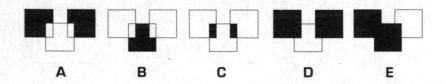

A   B   C   D   E

3.

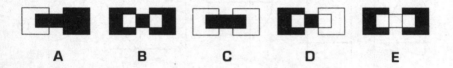

A   B   C   D   E

See answer page 641

190. Which of the following is the odd one out?

1.

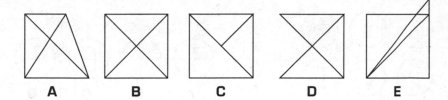

A   B   C   D   E

2.

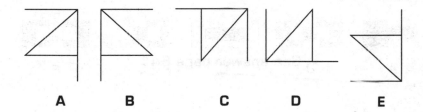

A   B   C   D   E

3.

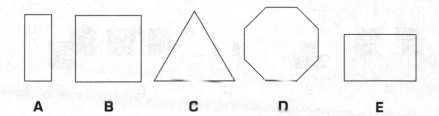

A   B   C   D   E

See answer page 641

191. Should A, B, C, or D fill the empty circle?

1.

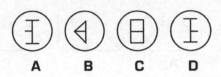

See answer page 641

2.

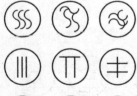

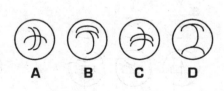

See answer page 641

192. Should A, B, C, or D fill the empty circle?

1.

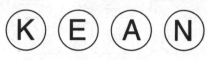

A   B   C   D

See answer page 641

2.

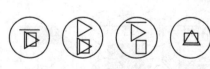

A   B   C   D

See answer page 641

193. No symbol is used on more than one side of the box. Which of these is not a view of the same box?

1.

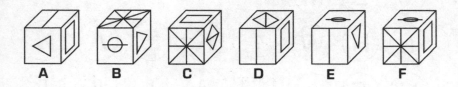

A   B   C   D   E   F

2.

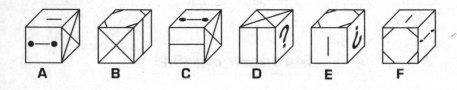

A   B   C   D   E   F

3.

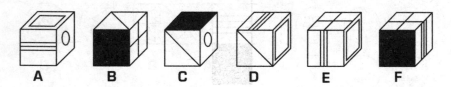

A   B   C   D   E   F

See answer page 642

194. Which of these boxes can be made from the template? Is it A, B, C, D, E, or F?

1.

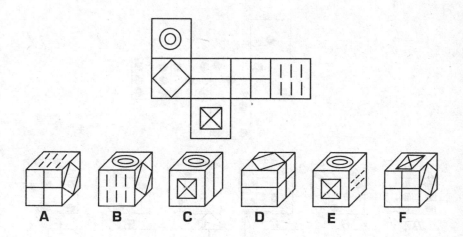

See answer page 642

2.

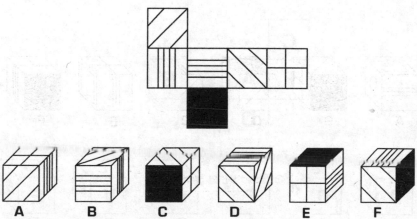

See answer page 642

195. Which of these boxes can be made from the template? Is it A, B, C, D, E, or F?

1.

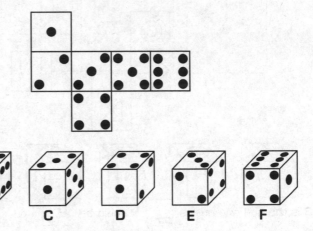

See answer page 642

2.

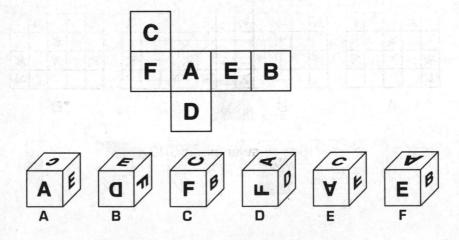

See answer page 642

196. These are mirror image problems. One of the 4 given images has an error on it.

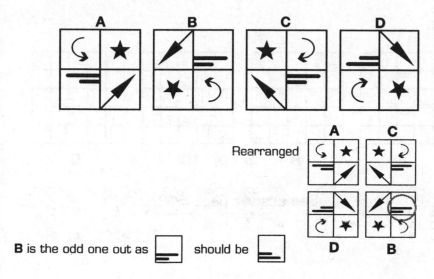

Rearranged

B is the odd one out as [image] should be [image]

1.

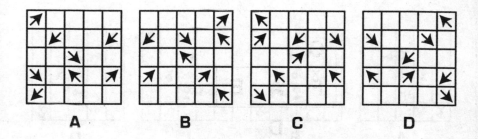

A   B   C   D

See answer page 642

197. These are mirror image problems. One of the 4 given images has an error on it.

1.

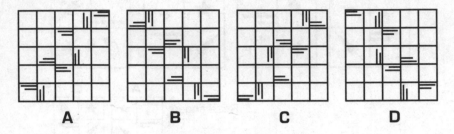

A   B   C   D

See answer page 642

2.

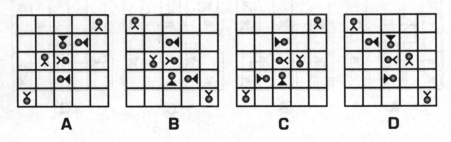

A   B   C   D

See answer page 642

198. These are mirror image problems. One of the 4 given images has an error on it.

1.

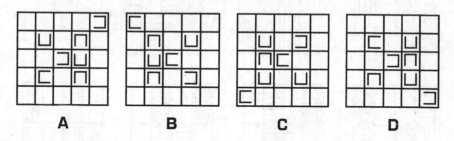

A   B   C   D

See answer page 642

2.

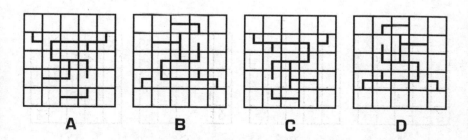

A   B   C   D

See answer page 642

199.

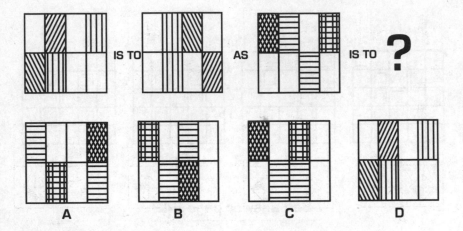

A B C D

See answer page 642

200.

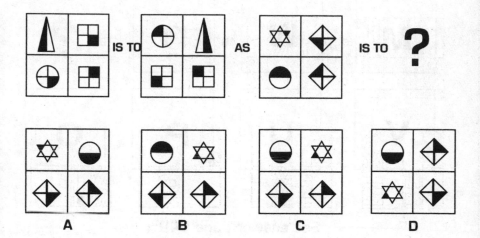

IS TO ... AS ... IS TO ?

A   B   C   D

See answer page 642

201.

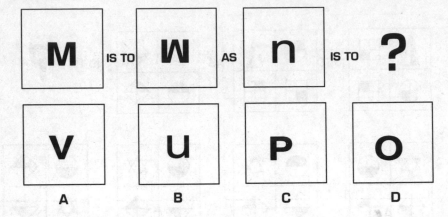

M IS TO W AS n IS TO ?

V	U	P	O
A	B	C	D

See answer page 642

202.

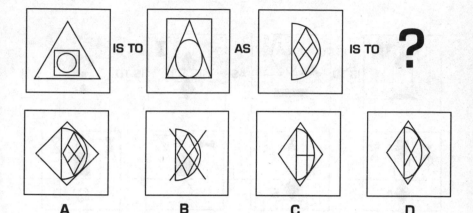

A   B   C   D

See answer page 642

203.

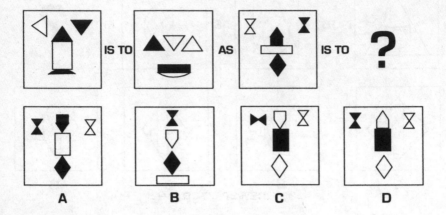

See answer page 642

204. Which of the shapes, A, B, C, D, or E cannot be made from the dots if a line is drawn through all of the dots at least once?

1.

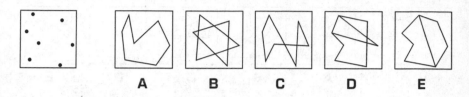

A   B   C   D   E

See answer page 642

2.

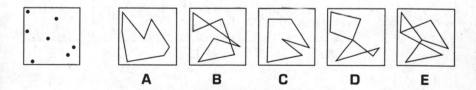

A   B   C   D   E

See answer page 642

205. Which of the shapes, A, B, C, D, or E cannot be made from the dots if a line is drawn through all of the dots at least once?

1.

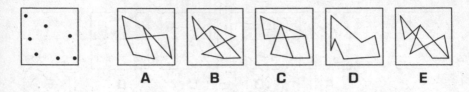

See answer page 642

2.

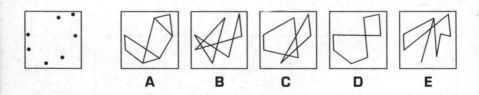

See answer page 642

206. Should A, B, C, or D come next in this series?

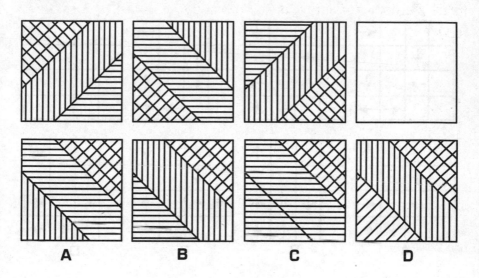

A   B   C   D

See answer page 642

207. Should A, B, C, or D come next in this series?

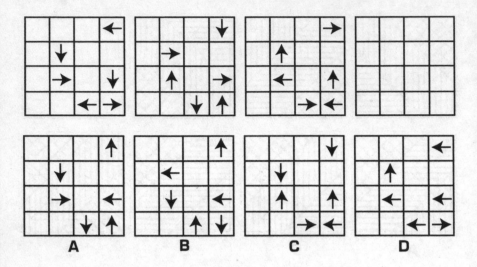

See answer page 642

208. Should A, B, C, or D come next in this series?

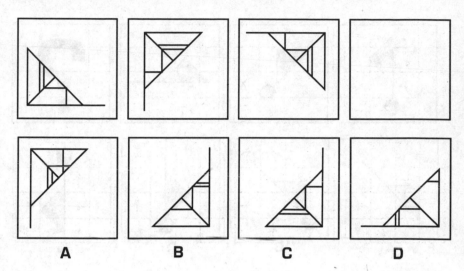

A   B   C   D

See answer page 642

209. Should A, B, C, or D come next in this series?

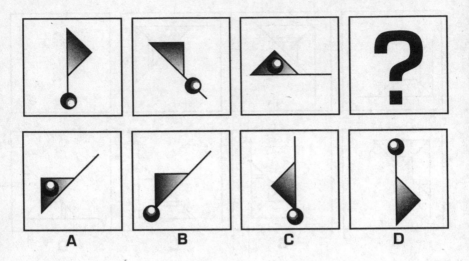

See answer page 642

210. Should A, B, C, or D come next in this series?

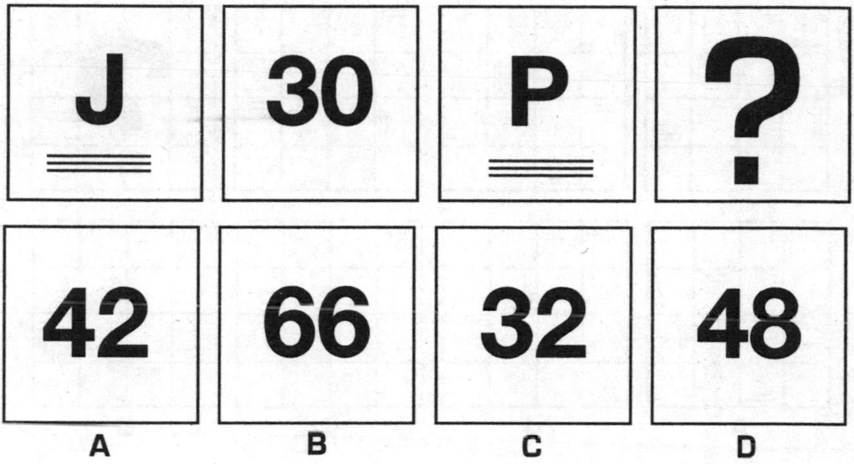

J

30

P

?

42

66

32

48

A   B   C   D

See answer page 642

211. Should A, B, C, or D come next in this series?

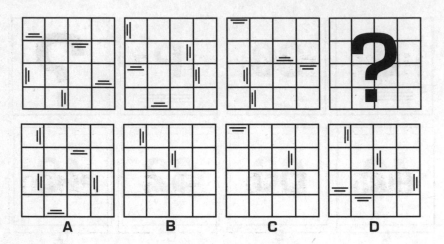

A   B   C   D

See answer page 642

212. Should A, B, C, or D come next in this series?

| HB28 | DC34 | GA17 | **?** |

| EI95 | EI90 | EI85 | EI100 |
| A | B | C | D |

See answer page 642

213. Should A, B, C, or D come next in this series?

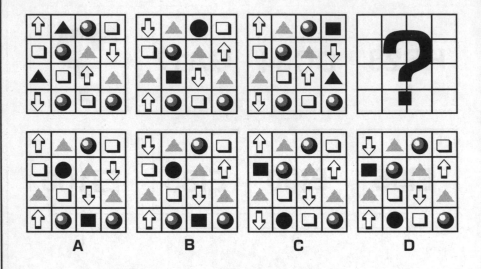

A   B   C   D

See answer page 642

214. Should A, B, C, or D come next in this series?

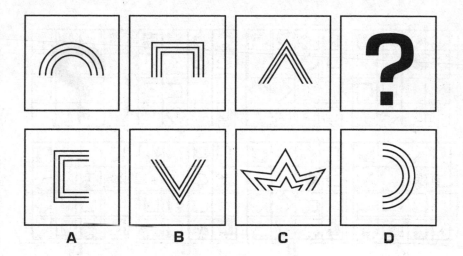

A   B   C   D

See answer page 642

215. Should A, B, C, or D come next in this series?

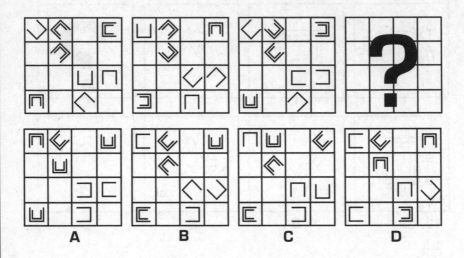

A   B   C   D

See answer page 642

1.

   1. A.

   2. D.

   3. L.

   4. O.

   5. N.

   6. H.

   7. K.

   8. R.

   9. T.

   10. S.

   11. V.

   12. C.

   13. U.

   14. I.

   15. B.

   16. M.

   17. G.

   18. F.

   19. E.

   20. P.

2.

   1. S, to make Allow, Basil.

   2. C, to make Pith, Scale.

   3. P, to make Ride, Slope.

   4. M, to make Swap, Clamp.

   5. T, to make Sill, Facet.

   6. H, to make Tree, Niche.
      Or R, to make Thee, Nicer.

   7. U, to make Vale, Cause.

   8. E, to make What, Feast.

   9. N, to make Moth, Gland.

   10. T, to make Meal, Hotly.

   11. R, to make Wing, First.

   12. T, to make Wine, Comet.

   13. U, to make Prod, Bound.

   14. R, to make Dated, Breach.

   15. V, to make Cured, Shove

   16. R, to make Cease, Brand.

   17. N, to make Bugle, Canter.

   18. G, to make Bride, Finger.

   19. A, to make Twin, Haunt.

   20. O, to make Stop, Float.

3.

   1. Break.

   2. Base.

   3. Rest.

   4. Tuba.

   5. Real.

   6. Back.

   7. Ring.

   8. Rust.

   9. Sand.

   10. Strand.

4.

   1. 14.

   2. 7.

   3. 2 (using segment numbers 1, 6, 7, 9, 11, 12 and 1, 4, 6, 10, 11, 12).

   4. 18.

5. The aisle order is: 1. fruit, 2. tins, 3. washing powder, 4. bottles, 5. meat, 6. bread.
> **1**. Bread.
>
> **2.** Four.
>
> **3.** Fruit.
>
> **4.** Two.

6. From one end or the other, the order is: white, green, black, red, silver, yellow, blue, purple.
> **1.** Silver.
>
> **2.** Red.
>
> **3.** Blue.
>
> **4.** Yellow.

7.

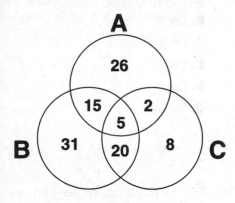

A = Hotel, B = Self-Catering, C = Camping.
> **1.** 26.
>
> **2.** 15.
>
> **3.** 36.
>
> **4.** 37.

8.

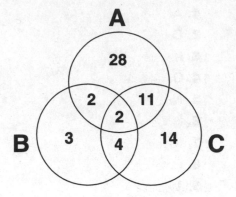

A = Thriller, B = Biography, C = Science Fiction.
> **1.** 11.
>
> **2.** 17.
>
> **3.** 2.
>
> **4.** 28.

9.
> **1.** D.
>
> **2.** E.
>
> **3.** A.
>
> **4.** C.
>
> **5.** B.

10.
> **1.** Curl.
>
> **2.** Barrier.
>
> **3.** Caerphilly.
>
> **4.** Calorie.
>
> **5.** Dawn.
>
> **6.** Dupe.
>
> **7.** Epidemic.
>
> **8.** Epistle.
>
> **9.** Fairyland.
>
> **10.** Falter.

11. Golf.

12. Grain.

13. Herringbone.

14. Hessian.

15. Immediate.

16. Joint or Join.

17. Kipper.

18. League.

19. Limerick.

20. Mediate.

11.

1. B.

2. D.

3. E.

4. C.

5. A.

12.

1. E.

2. A.

3. D.

4. B.

5. C.

13.

1. D.

2. C.

3. B.

4. E.

5. A.

14.

1. F.

2. B.

3. E.

4. F.

5. C.

15.

1. Four.

2. 26th.

3. 15th.

4. Thursday.

5. Tuesday.

16. Kerry has a striped jumper, plain shirt and spotted towel; Paul has a spotted jumper, striped shirt and plain towel; Sandra has a plain jumper, spotted shirt and striped towel.

1. Paul.

2. Striped.

3. Paul.

4. Striped.

5. Plain.

17. Joanna has a cat on her pen, a rabbit on her crayon and an elephant on her pencil case; Richard has a rabbit on his pen, an elephant on his crayon and a cat on his pencil case; Thomas has an elephant on his pen, a cat on his crayon and a rabbit on his pencil case.

1. Joanna.

2. Elephant.

3. Thomas.

4. Rabbit.

5. Joanna.

18.

1. 28. (x 3) + 1.

2. 6. (– 5) x 2.

3. 11. (x 2) + 7.

4. 22. (x 2) – 2.

5. 13. (÷ 2) + 6.

6. 17. (– 7) ÷ 2.

7. 20. (– 4) x 2.

8. 20. (squared) + 4.

9. 8. (√) + 3.

10. 4. (squared) – 5.

11. 80. (+ 8) x 5.

12. 36. (– 11) x 4.

13. 62. (x 6) + 8.

14. 71. (x 4) – 13.

15. 13. (÷ 4) + 3.

16. 19. (÷ 5) – 3.

17. 36. (– 13) x 6.

18. 162. (+ 3) x 9.

19. 361. + 2, then squared.

20. 6. – 4, then √.

19.

1. 6.

2. 6.

3. 5.

4. 14.

5. 14.

20.

1. A.

2. C.

3. B.

4. C.

5. C.

21.

1. Appear.

2. Above.

3. Acquire.

4. Acquit.

5. Acerbity.

6. Absent.

7. Actual.

8. Abbreviate.

9. Airy.

10. Adult.

22.

1. Humdrum.

2. Humorous.

3. Humiliate.

4. Hostile.

5. Headstrong.

6. Hold.

7. Hopeful.

8. Hardship.

9. Hero

10. Hungry.

23.

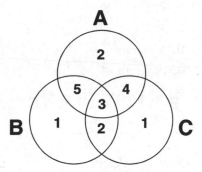

A = Hat, B = Scarf, C = Gloves.
- **1.** 3.
- **2.** 1.
- **3.** 1.
- **4.** 4.
- **5.** 10.
- **6.** 18.

25.

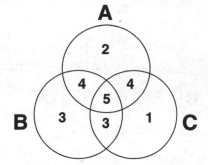

A = Sausage, B = Fries,
C = Beans.
- **1.** 5.
- **2.** 2.
- **3.** 9.
- **4.** 7.
- **5.** 3.
- **6.** 4.

24.

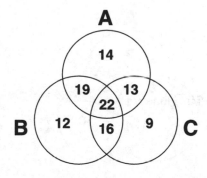

A = Candy, B = Chips, C = Soda.
- **1.** 22.
- **2.** 19.
- **3.** 16.
- **4.** 105.
- **5.** 36.
- **6.** 14.

26.

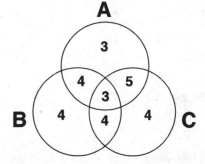

A = Sprint, B = Hurdles, C = Relay.
- **1.** 27.
- **2.** 4.
- **3.** 12.
- **4.** 12.
- **5.** 4.
- **6.** 13.

27.

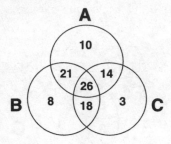

A = Soaps, B = Movies,
C = Documentaries.
  1. 21.
  2. 10.
  3. 18.
  4. 8.
  5. 53.
  6. 21.

29.

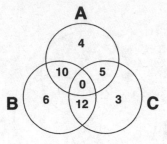

A = Craft, B = Science,
C = Humanities.
  1. 12.
  2. 12.
  3. 27.
  4. 13.
  5. 20.
  6. 4.

28.

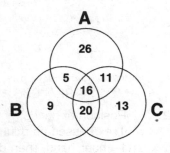

A = Raspberries, B = Strawberries,
C = Plums.
  1. 58.
  2. 16.
  3. 26.
  4. 20.
  5. 9.
  6. 36

30.

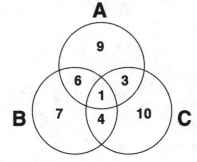

A = Labrador, B = Alsatian,
C = Greyhound.
  1. 9.
  2. 7.
  3. 10.
  4. 3.
  5. 4.
  6. 21.

31.
1. Date.
2. Cost.
3. Cork.
4. Thin.
5. Ball.
6. Bond.
7. Harp.
8. Dial.
9. Slot.
10. Lend.

32.
1. Player 2.
2. Player 3.
3. Player 6.
4. Player 3.
5. Players 1 and 5.
6. Players 1, 4 and 6.
7. 21.
8. 46.

33.
1. 50.
2. 20.
3. 1280.
4. 1170.

34.

☐ = 3 △ = 5 ◯ = 2 ◯ = 7

● = 4 ★ = 1 ■ = 6

35.
1. 66. Two previous numbers added.
2. 154. $(n + 3) \times 2$.
3. 9, 20. Two series $+ 3, + 4, + 5$, etc., and $+ 2$ each time.
4. 51. $(2n - 3)$.
5. –49. $(2n - 15)$.
6. 70. $(2n - 1^2)$, $(2n - 2^2)$, etc.
7. 343. $(n \times \text{previous } n) \div 2$.

36.
1. 2. $(A \times B) - (D \times E) = C$
2. 6. $(BC) + A = DE$
3. 5. (Top row – 3rd row) + 2nd row = 4th row.

37.
1. 97. Position of hands (not time) with hour hand, first, expressed as a sum.

    $113 - 16 = 97$.

    Others are: $51 + 123 = 174$, $911 + 82 = 993$.

2. 36. Position of hands (not time), expressed as minute hand – hour hand, then do sum. $(2 - 11) [-9] \times (8 - 12) [-4] = 36$.

    Others are: $(12 - 3)[9] \times (7 - 5) [2] = 18$, $(6 - 2) [4] \times (8 - 1) [7] = 28$.

3. 16. Sum of segment values of shaded parts.

4. 216. Position of hands (not time), added together, then do sum.

(3 + 9) [12] x (12 + 6) [18] = 216.

Others are: (12 + 6) [18] + (6 + 3) [9] = 27, (12 + 9) [21] – (9 + 6)[15] = 5.

38.

1. Move clockwise by the number of letters in the written number.

5		**3**
1		**6**

2. Move clockwise by the given numbers minus 1.

	21	
15		**34**
	22	

3. Move clockwise by the given number plus 1.

17		**6**
9		**3**

39.

1. 2. Make sums: First 2 digits – Second 2 digits, then First – Second.

2. 280. First digit x Fourth digit = First and Fourth digits, Second digit x Third digit = Second and Third digits.

3. 28. First digit x Second digit = First and Second digits, and Third digit x Fourth digit = Third and Fourth Digits.

40.

1.

8	7	6	8	7	12	9	1
7	12	7	6	4	3	2	14
8	9	7	8	5	7	11	1
8	8	10	7	6	16	10	1
4	9	13	4	12	2	15	6
8	5	2	2	4	9	8	15
6	9	8	14	14	8	2	1
9	6	10	5	12	1	5	17

2.

5	7	8	15	4	7	5	6
11	6	9	8	16	12	10	10
7	12	10	12	3	11	6	8
6	7	2	5	7	7	15	10
12	15	10	8	5	12	8	7
6	7	11	13	9	6	9	6
9	8	10	6	8	8	1	2
3	6	4	10	10	10	15	15

41.

1. C.
2. B.
3. D.
4. D.
5. A.
6. B.
7. D.
8. E.
9. C.
10. C.
11. D.
12. A.
13. D.
14. B.
15. C.
16. C.
17. B.
18. D.
19. C.
20. D.

42.

1. Relaying, Layering, Yearling.
2. Wreathe, Weather, Whereat.
3. Owners, Worsen, Rowens.
4. Stricter, Critters, Restrict.
5. Bounders, Rebounds, Suborned.
6. Legalist, Stillage, Tillages.
7. Decimals, Medicals, Declaims.
8. Stanch, Snatch, Chants.
9. Retraces, Terraces, Caterers.
10. Whiter, Wither, Writhe.
11. Wrestle, Swelter, Welters.
12. Rested, Desert, Deters.
13. Serrated, Treaders, Retreads.
14. Parcel, Carpel, Placer.
15. Paled, Pedal, Plead.
16. Observe, Obverse, Verbose.
17. Earnest, Eastern, Nearest.

18. Namely, Meanly, Laymen.

19. Remoulds, Smoulder, Moulders.

20. Dongle, Golden, Longed.

43.

1. Owl, Rail, Gull, Jay.

2. Gold, Jade, Opal, Amber.

3. Sea, Tide, Wave, Reef.

4. Rome, Nice, Lima, Bonn.

5. Barn, Hut, Shed, Tent.

6. Coo, Hoot, Crow, Cry.

7. Arrow, Lance, Axe, Gun.

8. Sue, Kim, Pam, Anne (or Ann).

9. Bat, Ox, Rat, Pig.

10. Star, Sky, Moon, Sun.

44.

1. Cost, which makes Costlier, Costumes, Costliest.

2. Stud, which makes Studhorse, Studied, Student.

3. Bean, which makes Beanfeast, Beanpole, Beanery.

4. Tend, which makes Tendons, Tenderly, Tendered.

5. Dam, which makes Damned, Damages, Damsels.

6. Tea, which makes Teapot, Tearoom, Teasels.

7. Dan, which makes Dander, Dangle, Dandier.

8. Time, which makes Timetable, Timelist, Timelier.

9. Horse, which makes Horseshoe, Horseflies, Horseflesh.

10. Coal, which makes Coaling, Coalesced, Coalfield.

45.

1. Doughnut, Fruitcake, Gingerbread, Flapjack, Macaroon.

2. Chest, Dresser, Settee, Table, Wardrobe.

3. Daffodil, Snowdrop, Sunflower, Fuchsia, Begonia.

4. Cairo, Seoul, Athens, Baghdad, Bangkok.

5. Karate, Golf, Rugby, Judo, Badminton.

6. Bowie, Ross, Jackson, Streisand, Presley.

7. Iran, Chile, Paraguay, Israel, Holland.

8. Pepperoni, Risotto, Pizza, Salami, Pasta.

9. Stuttgart, Dortmund, Berlin, Bonn, Heidelberg.

10. Turmeric, Cinnamon, Cayenne, Cumin, Oregano.

46.

1. Bracelet. Others are Glove, Hat, Scarf, Shawl.

2. Khaki. Others are Denim, Nylon, Silk, Wool.

3. China. Others are Plate, Dish, Saucer, Beaker.

4. Garden. Others are Bungalow, Flat, House, Maisonette.

5. Quartet. Others are Guitar, Zither, Trombone, Piano.

6. Student. Others are Dancer, Grocer, Sailor, Driver.

7. Arizona. Others are Baltimore, Phoenix, Chicago, Houston.

8. Gravy. Others are Vodka, Bourbon, Advocaat, Brandy.

9. Harpsichord. Others are Diminuendo, Allegro, Fortissimo, Crescendo.

10. Boston. Others are Maryland, Indiana, Nevada, Georgia.

47.

1. Pampered.

2. Peculiar.

3. Medieval.

4. Manicure.

5. Seashell.

6. Sentence.

7. Treasure.

8. Debentures.

9. Farewell.

10. Entrance.

48.

1. Sha.

2. Pur.

3. Mat.

4. Gri.

5. Far.

49.

1. Clairvoyant

2. Cruelty.

3. Correct.

4. Counter.

5. Casual.

6. Chastise.

7. Catapult.

8. Cheap.

9. Cherub.

10. Child.

50. C.

Others rotate into the same shape.

51. D. A & E and B & C form opposite pairs.

52. C.

Others are Roman numerals rotated 90° anti- (counter) clockwise.

53. D.

Others rotate into the same shape.

54. E.

Others rotate into the same shape.

55. A.

Others rotate into the same shape.

56. B. A & D and C & E form opposite pairs.

57. E.

It contains four lines; the others have only three.

58. D.

The pattern inside does not go clockwise.

59. A.

Binary system, start at 5 and add 3 each time. You can also find the answer by treating the images as a negative and mirror-imaging them.

60. B.

Numbers rotate clockwise by the number given.

61. E.

The triangle rotates one sector at a time.

62. B.

Shapes rotate in sequence. Outside line alternately extends and rotates.

63. A.

Shapes rotate in sequence. Outside line alternately extends and rotates.

64. B.

All use three lines.

65. C.

Rotates and lines are subtracted from one and added to the other.

66. D.

Rotating shapes.

67. D.

Small circles move left to right and bottom to top. Lower circle touches large circle in 1st figure, so upper figure will touch it in last.

68. A.

Each shape rotates in a set sequence.

69. D.

Matched opposite pairs.

70. A.

Whole figure rotates 90° anti-(counter) clockwise and circles are reversed at end of lines.

71. C.

Rotations in sequence.

72. D.

First number is alpha-numeric position (eg, A=1).

73. A.

Square becomes circle, triangle becomes square, circle becomes triangle.

74. D.

75. B.

76. C.

77. A.

78. A.

79. D.

80. B.

81. B.

82. E.

83. C.

84. C.

85. F.

86. E.

87. A.

88. F.

89. E.

90. G.

91. F.

92. E.

Duplicated lines on first two of each row are deleted in third figure.

93. E.

Hollow/shaded circle

= (numbers of stars x 2) + numbers of stars = number of stars in column 3.

94. E.

95. A.

96. D.

97. E.

98. B.

99.
  1. R.

  2. C.

  3. L.

  4. O.

  5. G.

  6. M.

  7. H.

  8. T.

  9. N.

  10. U.

100.
  1. 36.

  2. 78.

101.

1. I. (Wave – Noise).

2. Y. (Hone – Yeast).

3. O. (Live – Coast).

4. F. (Rile – Flake).

5. S. (Wait – Shoot).

6. A. (Pint – Bloat).

7. T. (Rust – Deter).

8. T. (Vial – Table).

102.

1. G. Makes Ruing and Grant.

2. H. Makes Booth and Heel.

3. K. Makes Tank and Knot.

4. T. Makes Leant and Thigh.

5. E. Makes Theme and Every.

6. D. Makes Seed and Draft.

7. G. Makes Song and Grunt.

8. T. Makes Event and Teach.

9. E. Makes Lunge and Eland.

10. O. Makes Cameo and Open.

103.

1. Mint.

2. Nest.

3. Mist.

4. Deal.

5. Corn.

6. Ball.

7. Fight.

8. King.

9. Lamp.

10. Wide

104.

1. 3.

2. 12 and 13.

3. 4.

4. –21.

5. 2, 3, 4, 5, 14.

105. 1st, E; 2nd, C; 3rd, F; 4th, D; 5th, A; 6th, B.

106. 1st, Rick; 2nd, John; 3rd, Alex; 4th, Sean; 5th, Anne; 6th, Liam; 7th, Sandra; 8th, Robert.

107.

   1. French.

   2. A.

   3. A.

   4. Two.

   5. D.

108.

   1. Swimming.

   2. A and C.

   3. Four.

   4. Tennis.

   5. Three.

109.

   1. Lunar.

   2. Millet.

   3. Eternity or Eternal.

   4. Deplete

   5. Herbivore.

6. Content.

7. Bagpipes.

8. Nullify.

9. Secure.

10. Magnate.

110.

   1. B.

   2. C.

   3. D.

   4. A.

   5. E.

111.

   1. B.

   2. D.

   3. A.

   4. E.

   5. C.

112.
1. E.
2. C.
3. D.
4. A.
5. B.

113.
1. E.
2. A.
3. B.
4. C.
5. D.

114.
1. C.
2. A.
3. E.
4. D.
5. B.

115.
1. C.
2. D.
3. F.
4. A.
5. B.
6. None.

116.
1. 15th.
2. 25th.
3. 7th.
4. Four.
5. 11th.

117.
1. Paul.
2. Fred.
3. Paul.
4. Paul.
5. Harry.
6. Fred.

118.
1. Maria.
2. Maria.
3. Peter.
4. Sarah.
5. Peter.
6. Peter.

119.
1. 39. (x 4) + 3.
2. 16. (x 2) ÷ 3.
3. 15. (÷ 3) + 7.
4. 124. n**2 + 3.
5. 171.5. n**3 ÷ 2.
6. 37. (x3) + 4.

120.
1. 81. (x 7) – 10.
2. 30. (x 6) ÷ 4.
3. 8. (÷ 2) + 1.
4. 40. (– 2) x 2.
5. 32. (+ 3) x 4.

121.
1. 6.
2. 24.
3. 9.

4. 12.

5. 18.

122.

1. C.

2. A.

3. B.

4. A and C.

5. 55 silver, 25 bronze.

123.

1. Retentive.

2. Random.

3. Regular.

4. Ready.

5. Release.

124.

1. England.

2. Germany.

3. Square.

4. Cloud.

5. Ankle.

6. Sapphire.

7. Cock.

8. Hair.

9. Saturn.

10. Light.

125.

1. C.

2. E.

3. D.

4. B and C.

5. C.

6. Nobody.

126.

1. 58.

2. 102.

3. 342.

4. 416.

127.

1. 3.87. There were a total of 116 passes for 30 students.

2. 3.32. There would have been 83 passes for 25 students.

3. 58.

128. 42. ★=17 ●=5 ■=15

129.

1. 500, 1000. Two methods. Either consecutive Roman numerals or an alternating series, x 5, x 2.

2. 203. Two methods. Either multiply previous number by 3 and deduct 1, or + 5, + 15, + 45, + 135.

3. 603. (previous + 3) x 3.

4. 6, 3, 2. Numbers 1 to 9 in alphabetic order.

5. 190. (+ 1 (x 2).

6. 41. Two methods. $5 + 1^2$, $5 + 2^2$, $5 + 3^2$, or series + 3, + 5, + 7, etc.

130.

1. 328. Along each row multiply first two digits of first number to get first two digits of second number. Multiply last two digits of first number to get last two of second number and join them. 4 x 8 = 32, 2 x 4 = 8; 328.

2. 4752. In each number the first two digits are multiplied by the last two digits to give the next number along the row. 54 x 88 = 4752.

3. 184. In each row the two outer digits of the first number are multiplied to give the two outer digits of the second number. The two middle of the first number are multiplied to give the middle digits of the second number. 7 x 2 =14; 4 x 2 = 8; 184.

131.
1. 3. (A + B) x C = D + E.
2. 3. (A + C) – (D x E) = B or A – B + C ÷ D = E.
3. O and 6. B + D = E; E – A = C.

132. 3 white circles. Black circle values are: Top = 1, right = 2, bottom = 3, left = 4. Values are then added. White circle = 5. Sums are (1 + 3) x (4 + 1) = 20. (4 + 1) x (1 + 2) = 15. (4 + 1) + (2 + 3) = 10. (3 + 4 + 1) – (1 + 2) = 5.

133. 15 circles: Z = 5W, 3W = circle.

134. 6 circles. ★ = 3, n = 1½, ◯ = 2.

135. 1625. Add times as numbers. 135 + 600 = 735; 245 + 1215 = 1460; 520 + 1105 = 1625.

136. 294. Add numbers on pointers and complete the sum. (6 + 9) [15] x (1 + 6) [7] = 105; (6 + 3) [9] x (9 + 3) [12] = 108; (12 + 9) [21] x (2 + 12) [14] = 294.

137. 1560.

Add times as numbers. 200 + 730 = 930; 245 + 445 = 690; 915 + 645 = 1560.

138. 32.

Multiply the hands by their sector values and complete the sum. (1 x 2) [2] + (3 x 4) [12] = 14; (3 x 3) [9] + (2 x 2) [4] = 13; (4 x 4) [16] x (1 x 2) [2] = 32.

139.

18	6	4	30	47	29
45	30	6	18	17	2
1	21	1	42	23	5
3	28	7	17	1	6
44	4	32	43	30	40

140.

6	2	3	4	4	3
3	5	5	2	6	2
5	3	1	3	5	0
2	4	5	3	0	5
3	3	4	6	6	5

141.

3	6	4	4	8	6
9	6	6	7	9	2
5	6	5	6	2	7
7	6	7	5	9	3
8	9	4	8	9	7
4	9	6	8	4	6

142.

3	6	4	4	8	6
9	6	6	7	9	2
5	6	5	6	2	7
7	6	7	5	9	3
8	9	4	8	9	7
4	9	6	8	4	6

143. 4.

The two-digit number on the left minus the two-digit number on the right gives the middle number.

144. 4.

The two-digit number on the right minus the two-digit number on the left gives the middle number.

145. 6.

The two-digit number on the left minus the two-digit number on the right gives the middle number.

146. 2.

The two-digit number on the right minus the two-digit number on the left gives the middle number.

147.

1. Add the two digits of each number together to give the number of places the numbers move round.

2. Add one to each number to give the amount of places each number moves around.

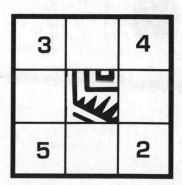

3. The difference between the two digits in each number gives the amount of places each number moves round.

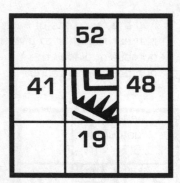

148. Eleven.

The values are totalled in each grid to give the number shown. The sum of the values of triangles and circles gives the answer. $\triangle = 2$, $O = 1$.

149. −15. The sum of the values of white and black squares gives the answer.

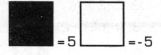

150. 22. The grid values are shown and the sum of the positions gives the answer.

	4	3	2	1
	5	6	7	8
	12	11	10	9
	13	14	15	16

151.
Asterisk = 8, triangle = 12, square = 16, rectangle = 20.

1. 46.
2. 46.
3. 36.
4. 3. E2, E3, E4.

	A	B	C	D	E
1	8	8	14	10	6
2	26	✱	38	24	20
3	36	50	46	△	20
4	▬	46	■	32	20
5	28	42	32	22	14

152. Square = 10, asterisk = 18, triangle = 24.

   1. 57.

   2. 81.

   3. 42.

   4. 94, C4.

   5. 318.

	A	B	C	D	E	F
1	19	31	31	26	12	12
2	28	■	57	43	29	17
3	37	★	78	△	46	22
4	53	77	94	81	■	22
5	39	★	△	64	34	22
6	30	42	47	38	17	5

153.

   1. David has $20, Mary has $4.

   2. (2 + 6) divided by (7 – 4) x 9 = 24.

   3. $\frac{1}{4}$. $\sqrt{64}$ = 8, so $\frac{1}{4}$ is to 4 as $\frac{1}{8}$ is to 8.

   4. 718.

   5. 136.

   6. 171.43 miles.

   7. 235.72 miles.

   8. 36 miles. Add alphabetical positional values of first and last letters.

   9. 10, 11, 12.

   10. 1, 6, 8.

   11. 10. Alphabet values of the first letters of the months.

   12. A = 4, B = 9, C = 5.

   13. 56.

   14. 64.

   15. 100.

   16. 144.

   17. 1.

   18. 45.

   19. 30.

   20. 8.8.

   21. 181.02.

   22. 34.

154. In these answers, n = previous number.

   1. –26. (n x 2) – 6.

   2. 83. (n x 3) – 4.

   3. 834. n∗∗ – 7.

155. In these answers, n = previous number.

   1. 122. (n + 3) x 2.

   2. 132. (n – 7) x 3.

   3. 19. 2n – 3.

156. In these answers, n = previous number.

   1. –337. 4n – 13.

   2. 402. 3 (2 + n).

   3. 163. (n x 3) – 2.

157. In these answers, n = previous number.

   1. 246. 3n – 6.

   2. –194. 3n – 17.

   3. 152. 2(n + 4).

158. In these answers,
n = previous number.
   1. –65535. 2n – n**2.
   2. 88. 2n + 8.
   3. 78. –2(n + 3).

159. In these answers,
n = previous number.
   1. 111. (–2n) – 3
   2. 39. Add previous 3
      numbers.
   3. 198. –2(n + 15).

160. In these answers,
n = previous number.
   1. 8830. n**2 – 6.
   2. 38.5. (1.5n) + 1.

161.
   1. 10—5—6—3—5—20
   2. 10—7—9—3—5—20.
   3. 61: 10—9—8—8—6—20.
   4. 47: 10—7—3—3—4—20.
   5. 3 ways
      10—9—6—6—6—20.
      10—7—9—7—4—20.
      10—7—9—6—5—20.

162.
   1. 6—8—4—8—6—8—10.
   2. 41 (4 ways).
      6—5—4—4—6—6—10
      6—5—4—4—7—5—10
      6—6(rc)—7—3—4—5—10
      6—6(r)—7—3—4—5—10
   3. 48: 6—8—4—8—6—6—
      10.

4. 6 routes.
   6—5—4—4—6—8—10.
   6—6—7—5—4—5—10.
   6—6—7—5—4—5—10.
   6—6—7—3—4—7—10.
   6—6—7—5—4—5—10.
   6—6—7—3—4—7—10.
5. No route gives this total.

163.
   1. 11 horseshoes each for 98
      stables.
   2. 64.
   3. 19 minutes 6 seconds.

164.
   1. There are 4: B3, F4, C6,
      F6.
   2. D4 and D5. Both have 81.
   3. E2. 109.
   4. F. 102.
   5. 7. 85.
   6. Col F. 6.
   7. Col C and Row 5. Both add
      up to 636.

165.
   1. Wednesday.
   2. Dave had $6.25 (Mary had
      $2.50).

166.
   1. 3. Sum of diagonally
      opposite segments equals
      11.

2. 4. Reading clockwise, the lower half numbers are multiplied by 2, 3, 4, 5, respectively to equal diagonally opposite upper sector.

167.

1. 63. Reading clockwise, the upper half numbers are multiplied by 4, 5, 6, 7, respectively to equal diagonally opposite lower sector.

2. 50. (Window + window) – door = roof. (37 + 28) [65] – 15 = 50.

168.

1. 30. (Arm x arm) – (leg x leg) = head. (8 x 9) [72] – (6 x 7) [42] = 30.

2. 4. (Left arm x right leg) – (right arm x left leg) = head. (12 x 7) [84] – (4 x 20) [80] = 4.

169.

1. 140. The alpha positions squared of each letter are added and the sum then completed. The sum for FACE – DIED is $(6^2 + 1^2 + 3^2 + 5^2)$ [71] – $(4^2 + 9^2 + 5^2 + 4^2)$ [138] = –67; for HIDE – BEAD is $(8^2 + 9^2 + 4^2 + 5^2)$ [186] – $(2^2 + 5^2 + 1^2 + 4^2)$ [46] = 140.

2. 125. Multiply the previous two numbers and divide by 2.

3. 79 minutes. (1 hour 19 minutes).

4. 441. Multiply last term in each number by the number. (7 x 7), (9 x 49), (441 x 1).

5. 668. Alpha numeric sum. AIL (1, 9, 12) + 6, 6, 8 = 7 (G), 15 (O), 20 (T).

6. 43 years old. She is currently 28 and her son is 4.

7. 53704 (calculator display shown upside-down).

170.

1. 359. Top number + lower number = middle number. 462 + 197 = 659 236 + 359 = 595

2. –272. Top number – lower number = middle number. 628 - 439 = 189 342 - 614 = 272

171.

1. 88. Sum of top 3 numbers x sum of bottom 3 numbers = middle number.

2. 83. Sum of all numbers in outer circles.

172.

1. 8. Black = 2; white = 1; shaded = 3.

2. 8. Black = 2; white = 1; shaded = 4.

3. 10. Black = 1; white = 4; shaded = 3.

173.
1. 12. Black = 3; white = 4; shaded = 2.
2. 13. Black = 4; white = 7; shaded = 2.
3. 4. Black = 5; white = 3; shaded = 1.

174.
1. 18. Black = 4; white = 6; shaded = 2.
2. 36. Black = 7; white = 9; shaded = 5.
3. 22. Black = 8; white = 4; shaded = 3.

175.
1. B. Talent.
2. C. Genuine.
3. D. Dry.
4. C. Unruly.
5. C. Bequeath.
6. C. Weak.
7. D. Degrade.
8. C. Vouch.
9. C. Ruminate.
10. E. Flaccid.
11. A. Feral.
12. E. Pungent.
13. D. Combine.
14. A. Constant.
15. B. Fast.
16. B. Kindliness.
17. C. Plead.
18. D. Inactive.
19. D. Obscurity.
20. B. Maintenance.

176.
1. Derives, Diverse, Revised.
2. Limes, Miles, Slime, Smile.
3. Deltas, Lasted, Salted, Slated.
4. Bared, Beard, Bread, Debar.
5. Resort, Roster, Sorter, Storer.
6. Danger, Gander, Garden, Ranged.
7. Capers, Pacers, Parsec, Recaps, Scrape.
8. Canter, Carnet, Nectar, Recant, Trance.
9. Coasting, Agnostic, Coatings.
10. Parings, Parsing, Rasping, Sparing.
11. Claret, Cartel, Rectal.
12. Arcing, Caring, Racing.
13. Quoter, Roquet, Torque.
14. Pitons, Pintos, Piston, Points.
15. Pistol, Pilots, Postil, Spoilt.
16. Stewing, Twinges, Westing.
17. Tameless, Mateless, Meatless.
18. Leeks, Keels, Sleek.
19. Indent, Intend, Tinned.
20. Enlarge, General, Gleaner.

177.
1. Port, Cola, Sake, Tea.
2. Nut, Fish, Bun, Pie.
3. Pan, Dish, Tin, Pot.
4. Wine, Ale, Tea, Port.

5. Ant, Fly, Moth, Bee.

6. Actor, Vet, Spy, Tutor.

7. Bran, Corn, Oats, Rice.

8. Cent, Dime, Rand, Yen.

9. Lima, Bari, Nice, Cork.

10. Sock, Dress, Hat, Coat.

178.

1. Fruit.
2. Paris.
3. Clock.

179.

1. Shark.
2. Canoe.
3. Jelly.

180.

1. Organ.
2. Clown.
3. Party.
4. Petal.

181.

1. 50. Letters which are Roman numerals in the names are added together.

2. 51. Letters which are Roman numerals in the names are added together.

3. 200. Letters which are Roman numerals in the names are added together.

4. 1111. Letters which are Roman numerals in the names are added together.

5. £10.00. Letters which are Roman numerals in the names are added together.

182.

1. B. SUB. Subtle, Sublime, Suburb, Subtend.

2. E. TOP. Toparch, Topmast, Topside, Topspin.

3. D. PIT. Pithiness, Pithier, Pitied, Pitons.

4. C. PAL. Palate, Palest, Palpate, Palmate.

5. E. TEN. Tenant, Tenpin, Tendon, Tensile.

6. E. COR. Cordial, Coronet, Cornish, Corsets.

7. C. WAR. Wardens, Wartime, Warmest, Wariness.

8. D. NOT. Nothing, Notary, Notable, Noticed.

9. B. BUS. Busiest, Bussing, Bustles, Busied.

10. C. POT. Pottage, Potash, Potent, Potato.

183.

1. Mazda, Citroen, Peugeot, Renault, Mitsubishi.

2. Guinea, Shekel, Peseta, Copeck, Escudo.

3. Gucci, Jaeger, Mondi, Chanel, Oldfield.

4. Jacket, Shirt, Jumper, Trousers, Shoes.

5. Amazon, Ganges, Thames, Yangtze, Zambezi.

6. Malta, Capri, Ibiza, Sicily, Rhodes.

7. Canberra, Brussels, Lisbon, Madrid, Pretoria.

8. Buzzard, Falcon, Eagle, Vulture, Hawk.

9. Badminton, Baseball, Basketball, Boxing, Hockey.

10. Lobster, Prawn, Trout, Salmon, Plaice.

184.

1. E. Sitting. The others are Walking, Jogging, Running, Sprinting.

2. A. Museum. The others are Mosque, Temple, Cathedral, Synagogue.

3. C. London. The others are cities in the USA; Nashville, Savannah, Detroit, Denver.

4. C. January. The others are days of the week; Monday, Wednesday, Sunday, Saturday.

5. C. Circle. The others are colours; Red, Yellow, Crimson, Purple.

6. D. Dallas. The other countries are India, Italy, Kenya, Iceland.

7. E. Lemon. The others car parts; Engine, Clutch, Gears, Wheels.

8. A. Twenty. The others are Computer parts; Keyboard, Screen, Memory, Processor.

9. E. Bolognese. The others are Caerphilly, Gorgonzola, Stilton, Brie.

10. B. Potato. The others are Plum, Satsuma, Apricot, Damson.

185.

1. Midsummer

2. Personality.

3. Distance.

4. Antiseptic.

5. Emanate.

6. Remonstrate.

7. Replacement.

8. Dedicate.

9. Intelligence.

10. Enthusiastic.

186.

1. Handmaiden, Newsvendor, Shipmaster.

2. Liveryman, Paymaster, Pawnbroker.

3. Signwriter, Sharpshooter, Housemaster.

4. Screenplay, Newsreel, Footlight.

5. Whenever, Domesday, Whitetail.

6. Larkspur, Snowdrop, Waterlily.

7. Listless, Earthquake, Ransack.

8. Rampart, Password, Peaceable.

9. Wisecrack, Blockage, Forward.

10. Kidnap, Falsehood, Troublesome.

11. Deadlock, Peacemaker, Boyfriend.

12. Setback, Topmost, Carefree.

13. Wholesale, Batten, Haywire.

14. Eyesore, Breakable, Bottleneck.

15. Beloved, Wildlife, Goodwill.

16. Handsome, Foolhardy, Barrage.

17. Reflection, Brigand, Knowledge.

18. Contribute, Signpost, Guesswork.

19. Bondage, Slipshod, Showman.

20. Windfall, Rotten, Rumour.

187.

1. Gather.
2. Genetic.
3. Grant.
4. Grief.
5. Grace.
6. Glutton.
7. Glued.
8. Great.
9. Grieve.
10. Gap.
11. Gratify.
12. Gripped.
13. Gusty.
14. Goods.
15. Gut.
16. Gnu.
17. Guile.
18. Gavel.
19. Goods.
20. Godly.

188.

1. C. Others are matched opposite pairs.
2. B. Others rotate into each other.
3. D. Others rotate into each other.

189.

4. E. Has only two segments shaded; the others have three.
5. E. Only one with middle square white.
6. F. Not symmetrical around a vertical middle.

190.

1. D. Others have six lines.
2. A. Others rotate into each other.
3. C. Not symmetrical around horizontal axis.

191.

1. D. Letter reverses, stick moves to the left.
2. C. One vertical line moves to a horizontal position, then two lines move to a horizontal position.

192.

1. B. First letter contains two straight lines, second letter contains three straight lines, and third letter contains four straight lines.

2. B. Vertical object moves 45° clockwise, then a further 45° clockwise, then doubles.

193.
  1. A.
  2. B.
  3. D.

194.
  1. B.
  2. C.

195.
  1. E.
  2. D.

196. B.

197.
  1. D.
  2. D

198.
  1. C.
  2. A.

199. A. Move sections three places clockwise.

200. C. Boxes rotate clockwise and opposite segments are shaded.

201. B. Same upside-down.

202. D. Shapes get longer and outside shape gets narrower.

203. C. White shapes turn 90° clockwise. Black shapes turn 180°. Black becomes white and white becomes black.

204.
  1. E.
  2. C.

205.
  1. D.

206. A. Box rotates 90° anti- (counter) clockwise.

207. B. Each segment rotates 90° anti- (counter) clockwise.

208. C. Turns 90° clockwise.

209. B. Turns 45° anti- (counter) clockwise, circle moves along.

210. D. Alpha position multiplied by the number of lines.

211. D. Short and long lines swap places and rotate clockwise.

212. A. Alpha values reversed.

213. D. Arrows reverse direction. Shading moves one place.

214. C. Lines point down.

215. B. Each shape moves clockwise, 45° with one line, 90° with two.

Puzzle Paradise

• •

If you have successfully fought your way through the previous four sections you are now a rough, tough case-hardened puzzle solver who is not easily scared by the toughest conundrum. Here is another section of IQ puzzles which you will slice through like a hot knife through butter. You hope.

1. Which of the numbers should replace the question mark?

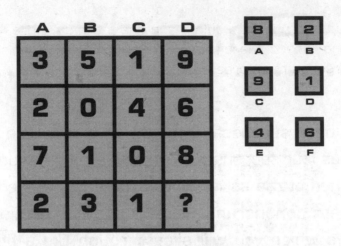

See answer pages 701-704

2. As an entrance test for a University, you are given a corked bottle with a very small coin in it. Your task is to remove the coin without taking the cork out of the bottle or breaking the glass, or boring a hole in the cork or glass.

How do you pass the test and get the coin out?

See answer pages 701-704

3. Here is an unusual safe. Each of the buttons must be pressed only once in the correct order to open it. The last button is marked F. The number of moves and the direction is marked on each button. Thus 1U would mean one move up, while 1L would mean one move to the left. Using the grid reference, which button is the first you must press?

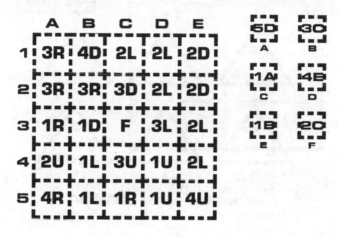

See answer pages 701-704

4. Insert the correct mathematical signs between each number in order to resolve the equation. What are the signs?

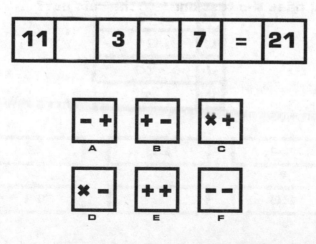

See answer pages 701-704

5. Which triangle continues this series?

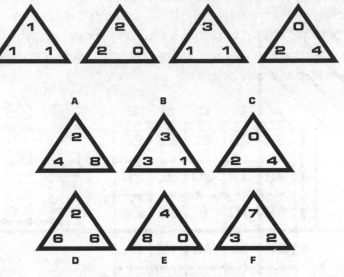

See answer pages 701-704

6. Discover the connection between the letters and the numbers. Which number should replace the question mark?

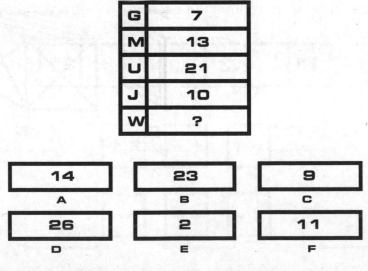

See answer pages 701-704

7. Which of the constructed boxes cannot be made from the pattern?

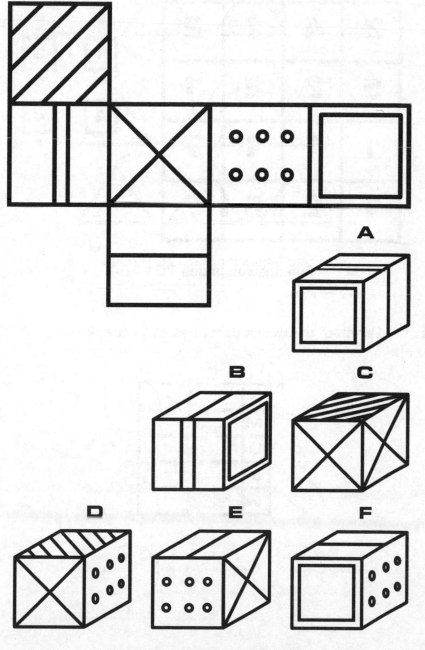

A

B   C

D   E   F

See answer pages 701-704

8. Which of the numbers should replace the question mark?

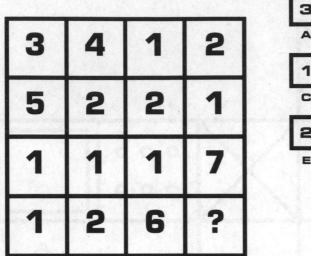

See answer pages 701-704

9. Which of the clocks continues this series?

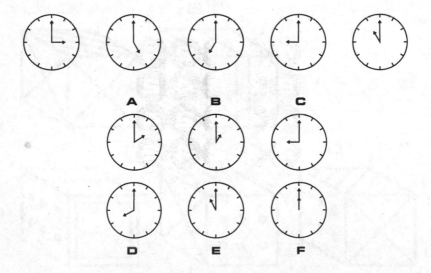

See answer pages 701-704

10. When rearranged the shapes will give a number. Which of the numbers is it?

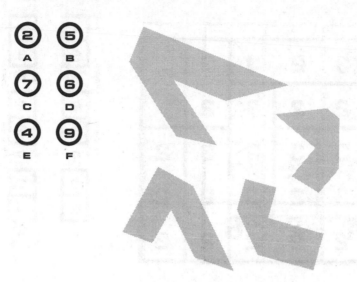

(2) A   (5) B

(7) C   (6) D

(4) E   (9) F

See answer pages 701-704

11. Move from ring to touching ring, starting from the bottom left corner and finishing in the top right corner. Collect nine numbers and total them. Which is the highest possible total?

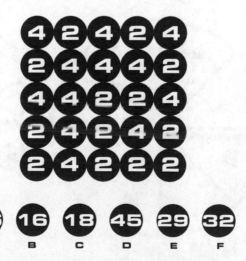

(36) A   (16) B   (18) C   (45) D   (29) E   (32) F

See answer pages 701-704

12. This square follows a logical pattern. Which of the tiles should be used to complete the square?

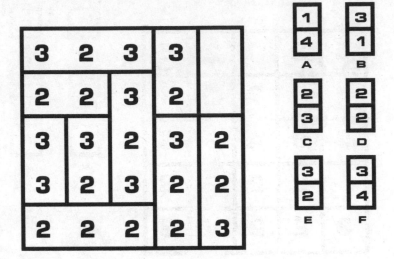

See answer pages 701-704

13. Which of the slices should be used to complete the cake?

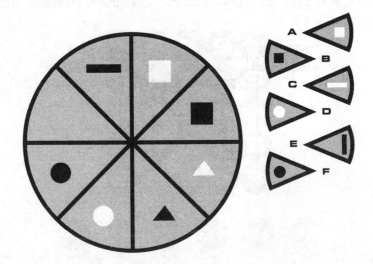

See answer pages 701-704

14. Use the numbers (right) to complete the grid. Each straight line of five numbers should total 20. Which of the numbers will replace the question mark?

5	2		2	5
1		?		1
5	8	4		3
	2	2	2	8
3	2	2	10	3

4	1
A	B

3	6
C	D

5	2
E	F

See answer pages 701-704

15. Start at any corner and follow the lines. Collect another four numbers and total the five. One of the numbers in the squares below can be used to complete the diagram. If the correct one has been chosen, one of the routes involving it will give a total of 28. Which one is it?

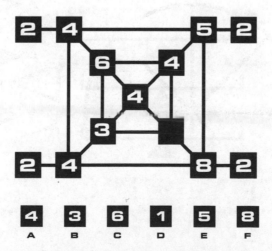

4	3	6	1	5	8
A	B	C	D	E	F

See answer pages 701-704

16. Which of the boxes should be used to replace the question mark?

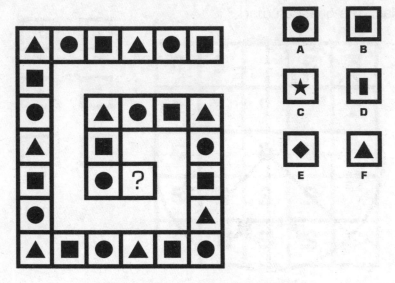

See answer pages 701-704

17. Scales one and two are in perfect balance. Which of these pans should replace the empty one?

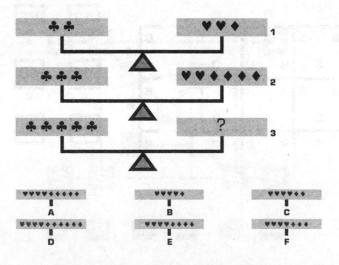

See answer pages 701-704

18. How many ways are there to score 25 on this dartboard using three darts only? Each dart always lands in a sector and no dart falls to the floor.

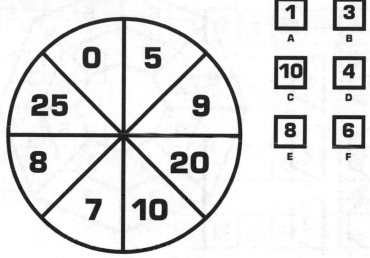

1
A

3
B

10
C

4
D

8
E

6
F

See answer pages 701-704

19. Which square's contents match D1?

	A	B	C	D	
	A A / B	A / B C	D D / D	D C / A	1
	B A A / D	A A / Λ	C C / D	B B / B	2
	B B B / C C A	B C / C	A / C C	A B / D	3
	C / D D	A C / D	D / C	B B / B C	4

A3
A

B2
B

D4
C

C2
D

B1
E

A1
F

See answer pages 701-704

20. Which of the numbers should logically replace the question mark in the octagon?

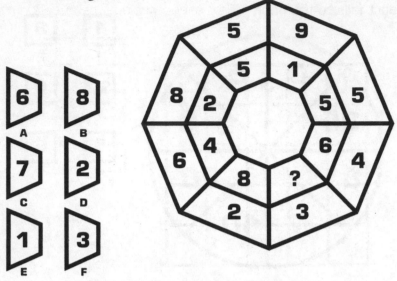

See answer pages 701-704

21. Which number is missing from this series?

See answer pages 701-704

22. Complete the square using the five numbers shown. When completed no row, column or diagonal line will use the same number more than once. What should replace the question mark?

1	2	3	4	5
4	5	1	2	3
?				

1		5
A		B

2		3
C		D

4
E

See answer pages 701-704

23. Which of the numbers should replace the question mark?

3		4
A		B

6		1
C		D

8		2
E		F

6	3	1	4	9
5	1	0	2	8
1	2	1	2	?

See answer pages 701-704

24. Start at 1 and move from circle to touching circle. Collect four numbers each time. How many different routes are there to collect 11? A reversed route counts twice.

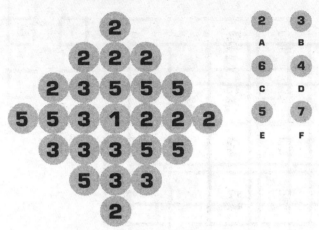

See answer pages 701-704

25. Here is an unusual safe. Each of the buttons must be pressed only once in the correct order to open it. The last button is marked F. The number of moves and the direction is marked on each button. Thus 1i would mean one move in, whilst 1o would mean one move out. 1c would mean one move clockwise and 1a would mean one move anti-clockwise. Which button is the first you must press?

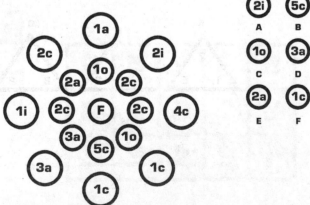

See answer pages 701-704

26. Which of the numbers should replace the question mark?

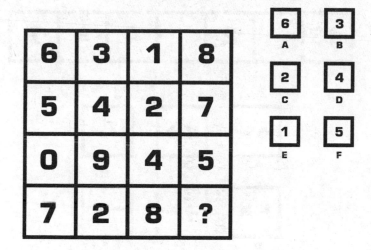

See answer pages 701-704

27. Which triangle continues this series?

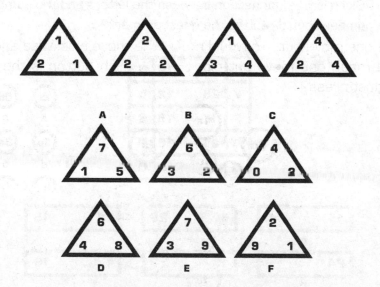

See answer pages 701-704

28. Insert the correct mathematical signs between each number in order to resolve the equation. What are the signs?

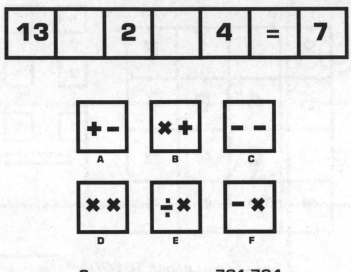

| 13 | | 2 | | 4 | = | 7 |

A $+ -$
B $\times +$
C $- -$
D $\times \times$
E $\div \times$
F $- \times$

See answer pages 701-704

29. Discover the connection between the letters and the numbers. Which number should replace the question mark?

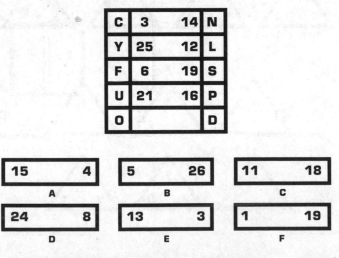

C	3	14	N
Y	25	12	L
F	6	19	S
U	21	16	P
O			D

A | 15 | 4 |
B | 5 | 26 |
C | 11 | 18 |
D | 24 | 8 |
E | 13 | 3 |
F | 1 | 19 |

See answer pages 701-704

30. Which of the constructed boxes can be made from the pattern?

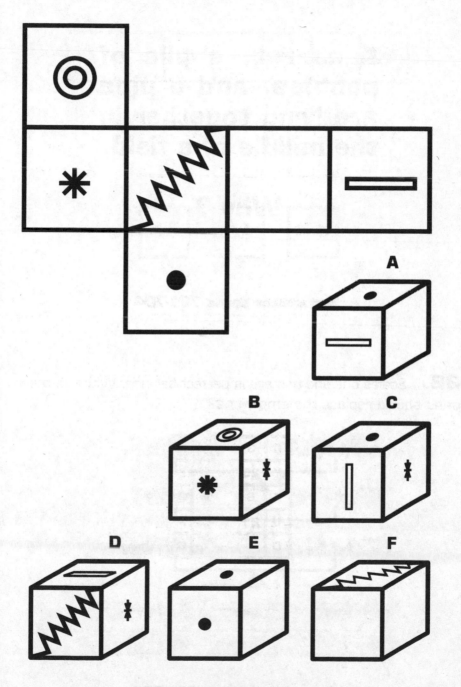

A

B   C

D   E   F

See answer pages 701-704

31.

A carrot, a pile of pebbles, and a pipe are lying together in the middle of a field.

Why ?

See answer pages 701-704

32. Scales one and two are in perfect balance. Which of these pans should replace the empty one?

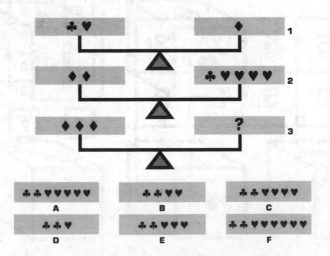

See answer pages 701-704

33. When rearranged the shapes will give a number. Which of the numbers is it?

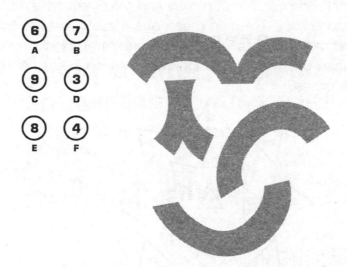

(6) A (7) B

(9) C (3) D

(8) E (4) F

See answer pages 701-704

34. Which of the numbers should replace the question mark?

6	1	7	3
2	5	2	8
3	5	5	1
4	4	1	?

6 A   3 B

4 C   2 D

5 E   1 F

See answer pages 701-704

35. Here is an unusual safe. Each of the buttons must be pressed only once in the correct order to open it. The last button is marked F. The number of moves and the direction is marked on each button. Thus 1i would mean one move in, whilst 1o would mean one move out. 1c would mean one move clockwise and 1a would mean one move anti-clockwise. Which button is the first you must press?

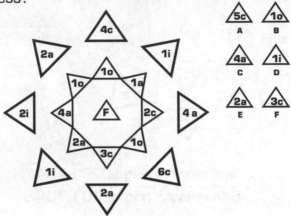

See answer pages 701-704

36. Which number is missing from this series?

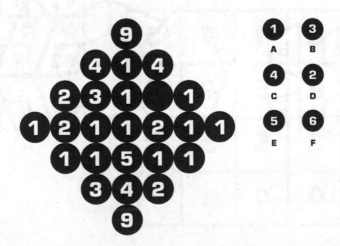

See answer pages 701-704

37. Which triangle should replace the empty one?

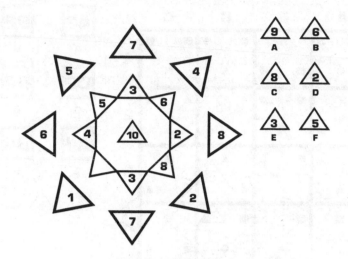

See answer pages 701-704

38. Which of the numbers should logically replace the question mark in the octagon?

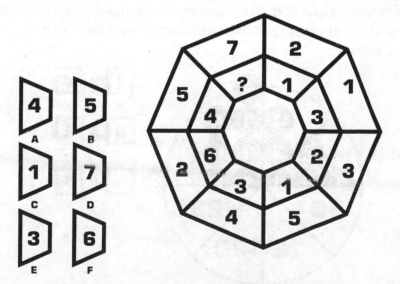

See answer pages 701-704

39. Which square's contents matches C4?

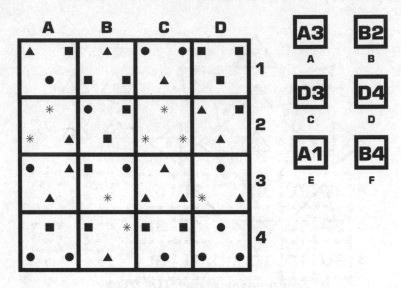

See answer pages 701-704

40. How many ways are there to score 123 on this dartboard using three darts only? Each dart always lands in a sector and no dart falls to the floor. Any sector can be used more than once in any set of throws, but the same set of numbers can be used in one order only.

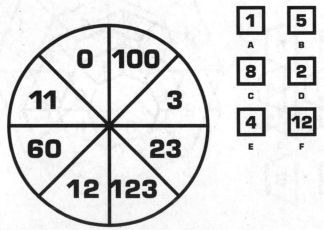

See answer pages 701-704

41. Here is an unusual safe. Each of the buttons must be pressed only once in the correct order to open it. The last button is marked F. The number of moves and the direction is marked on each button. Thus 1U would mean one move up, while 1L would mean one move to the left. Using the grid reference, which button is the first you must press?

	A	B	C	D	E	F
1	2D	4R	F	4D	3D	4D
2	3D	2D	3R	1R	3D	5L
3	5R	1U	2U	2L	1L	3L
4	3U	1R	1D	3U	1L	5L
5	1R	4U	3U	3U	2U	1U

4B	5F
A	B

2C	1E
C	D

4D	3A
E	F

See answer pages 701-704

42. Which of the numbers should logically replace the question mark in the octagon?

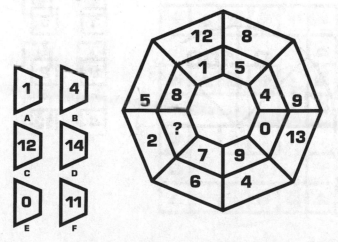

A 1
B 4
C 12
D 14
E 0
F 11

See answer pages 701-704

43. Which of the numbers should replace the question mark?

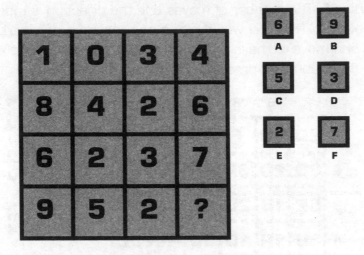

See answer pages 701-704

44. Which of the boxes should be used to replace the question mark?

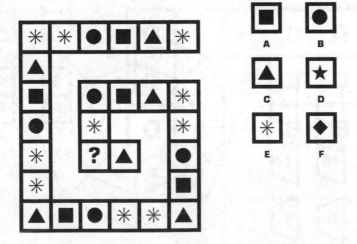

See answer pages 701-704

45. Which of the numbers should replace the question mark?

2	1	2	1	?
5	1	2	7	3
7	2	4	8	6

A 8 **B** 1

C 7 **D** 9

E 3 **F** 4

See answer pages 701-704

46. This square follows a logical pattern. Which of the tiles should be used to complete the square?

A	C	B		D
C	E	B		D
B	B	E	A	D
E	A	A	C	E
D	D	D	E	A

A
B
E

B
A
D

C
E
A

D
C
D

E
C
A

F
D
B

See answer pages 701-704

47. Which of the constructed boxes cannot be made from the pattern?

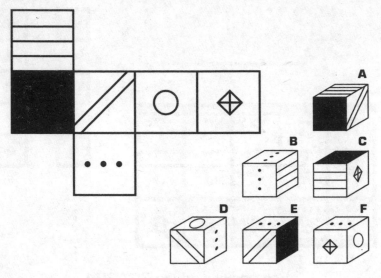

See answer pages 701-704

48. Move from ring to touching ring, starting from the bottom left corner and finishing in the top right corner. Collect nine numbers and total them. Which is the highest possible total?

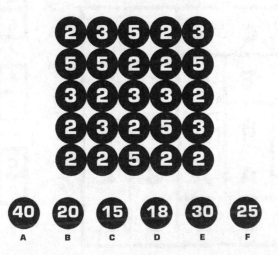

See answer pages 701-704

49. Scales one and two are in perfect balance. Which of the pans should replace the empty one?

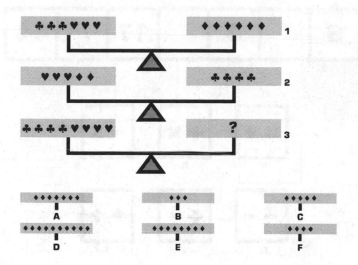

See answer pages 701-704

50. Which of the clocks continues this series?

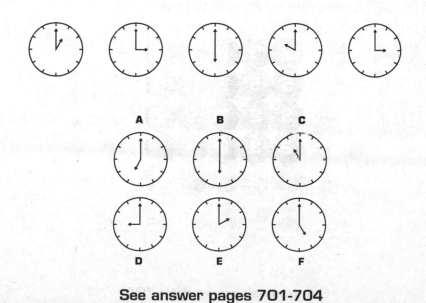

See answer pages 701-704

51. Insert the correct mathematical signs between each number in order to resolve the equation. What are the signs?

| 9 | | 3 | | 17 | = | 44 |

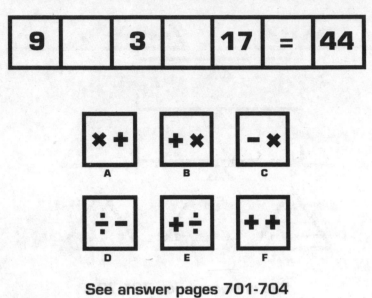

See answer pages 701-704

52. Start at 1 and move from circle to touching circle. Collect four numbers each time. How many different routes are there to collect 12? A reversed route counts twice.

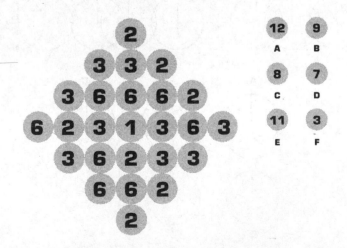

See answer pages 701-704

53. Which triangle belongs to these?

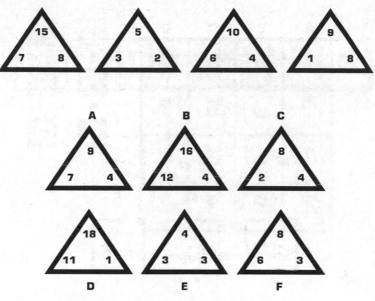

See answer pages 701-704

54. Which of the clocks continues this series?

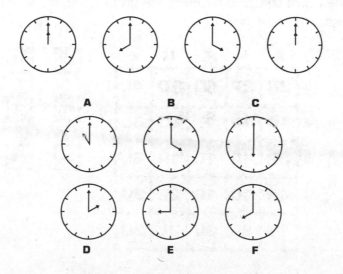

See answer pages 701-704

55. Which of the numbers should replace the question mark?

	A	B	C	D
	7	9	8	8
	3	9	5	7
	1	6	3	4
	2	2	1	?

A	B
4	2

C	D
3	1

E	F
5	6

See answer pages 701-704

56. Here is an unusual safe. Each of the buttons must be pressed only once in the correct order to open it. The last button is marked F. The number of moves and the direction is marked on each button. Thus 1U would mean one move up, while 1L would mean one move to the left. Using the grid reference, which button is the first you must press?

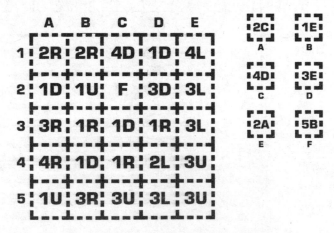

	A	B	C	D	E
1	2R	2R	4D	1D	4L
2	1D	1U	F	3D	3L
3	3R	1R	1D	1R	3L
4	4R	1D	1R	2L	3U
5	1U	3R	3U	3L	3U

A	B
2C	1E

C	D
4D	3E

E	F
2A	5B

See answer pages 701-704

57. Start at any corner and follow the lines. Collect another four numbers and total the five. One of the numbers in the squares below can be used to complete the diagram. If the correct one has been chosen, one of the routes involving it will give a total of 33. Which one is it?

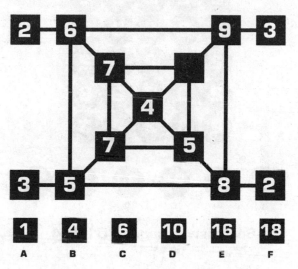

See answer pages 701-704

58. This square follows a logical pattern. Which of the tiles should be used to complete the square?

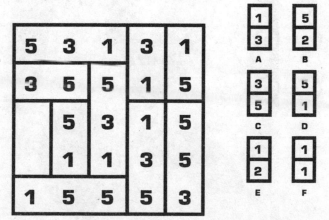

See answer pages 701-704

59. Move from ring to touching ring, starting from the bottom left corner and finishing in the top right corner. Collect nine numbers and total them. Which is the highest possible total?

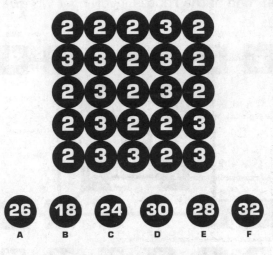

26 **18** **24** **30** **28** **32**
A   B   C   D   E   F

See answer pages 701-704

60. When rearranged the shapes will give a number. Which of the numbers is it?

8 A   **3** B

5 C   **2** D

1 E   **9** F

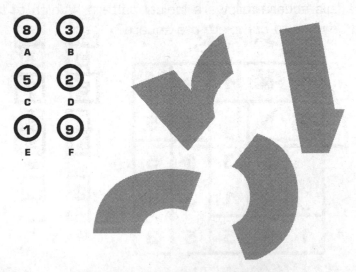

See answer pages 701-704

61. Which square's contents match D1?

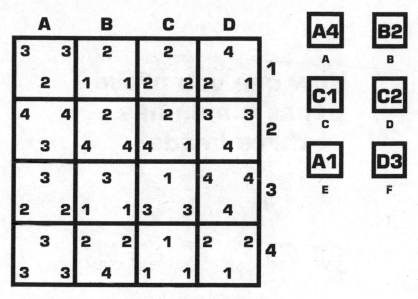

See answer pages 701-704

62. How many ways are there to score 60 on this dartboard using three darts only? Each dart always lands in a sector and no dart falls to the floor.

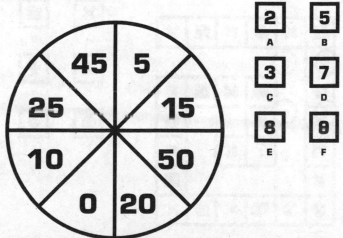

See answer pages 701-704

63.

How can you prove that a man has three heads?

See answer pages 701-704

64. Which of the boxes should be used to replace the question mark?

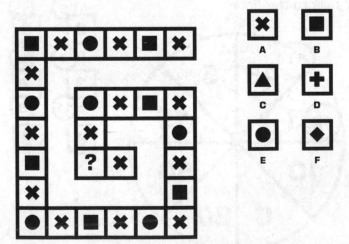

See answer pages 701-704

65. Complete the square using the five numbers shown. When completed no row, column or diagonal line will use the same number more than once. What should replace the question mark?

1	2	3	4	5
		5		
?		2		
		4		
4	5	1	2	3

2
A

4
B

3
C

5
D

1
E

See answer pages 701-704

66. Which circle should replace the empty one?

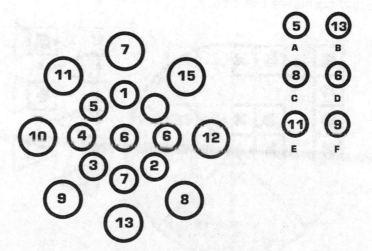

See answer pages 701-704

67. Each straight line of five numbers should total 25. Which of the numbers will replace the question mark?

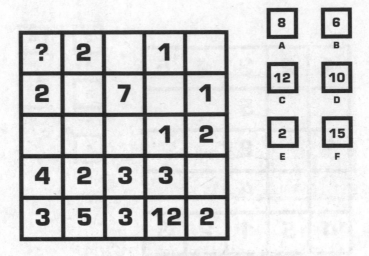

See answer pages 701-704

68. Which of the slices should be used to replace the question mark and complete the cake?

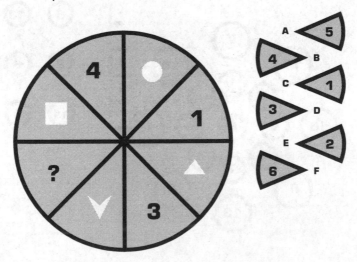

See answer pages 701-704

69. Which of the numbers should replace the question mark?

9	6
A	B

2	7
C	D

4	5
E	F

5	9	1	2	1
8	9	6	4	3
3	0	5	2	?

See answer pages 701-704

70. Discover the connection between the letters and the numbers. Which number should replace the question mark?

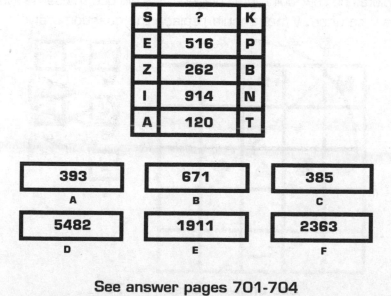

S	?	K
E	516	P
Z	262	B
I	914	N
A	120	T

393	671	385
A	B	C

5482	1911	2363
D	E	F

See answer pages 701-704

71. Here is an unusual safe. Each of the buttons must be pressed only once in the correct order to open it. The last button is marked F. The number of moves and the direction is marked on each button. Thus 1i would mean one move in, while 1o would mean one move out. 1c would mean one move clockwise and 1a would mean one move anti-clockwise. Which button is the first you must press?

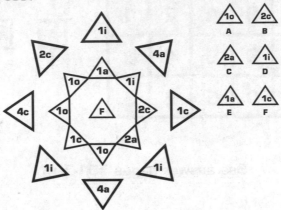

See answer pages 701-704

72. Complete the square using the five symbols shown. When completed no row, column or diagonal line will use the same symbol more than once. What should replace the question mark?

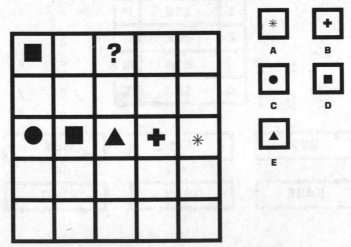

See answer pages 701-704

73. Which of the slices should be used to complete the cake?

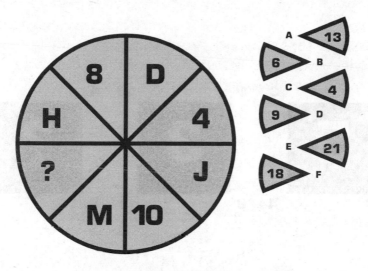

See answer pages 701-704

74. Start at 4 and move from circle to touching circle. Collect four numbers each time. How many different routes are there to collect 24? A reversed route counts twice.

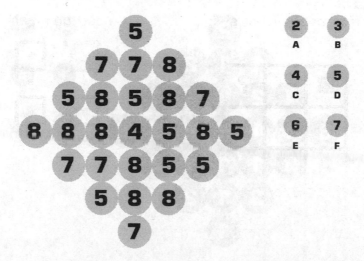

See answer pages 701-704

75. What number should replace the question mark?

8   3   1   13   4   9

5   **3**   **?**

2   4   8   2   5   6

See answer pages 701-704

76. Which number is missing from this series?

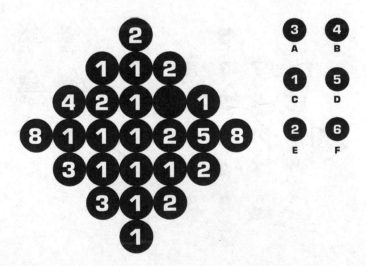

See answer pages 701-704

77. Complete the square using the five symbols shown. When completed no row, column or diagonal line will use the same symbol more than once. What should replace the question mark?

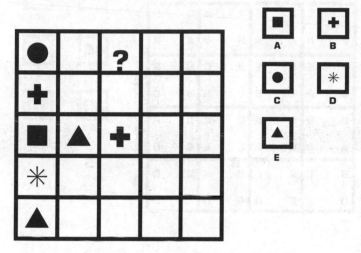

See answer pages 701-704

78. Which triangle should replace the empty one?

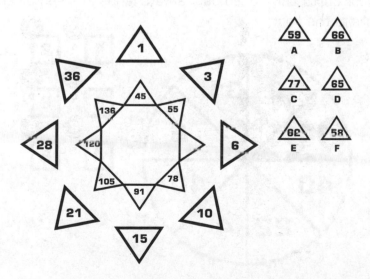

See answer pages 701-704

79. Which square's contents matches C1?

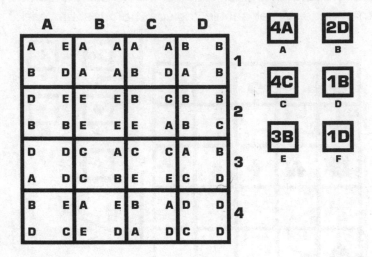

See answer pages 701-704

80. How many ways are there to score 62 on this dartboard using four darts only? Each dart always lands in a sector and no dart falls to the floor.

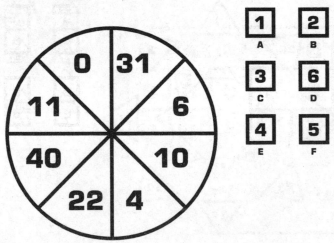

See answer pages 701-704

81. Which of the numbers should logically replace the question mark in the octagon?

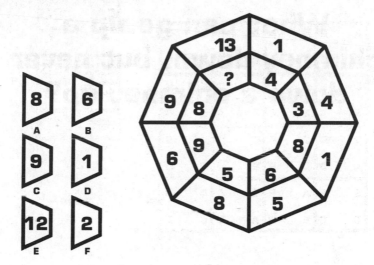

See answer pages 701-704

82. This square follows a logical pattern. Which of the tiles should be used to complete the square?

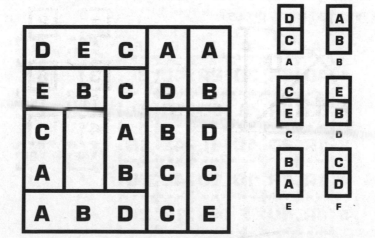

See answer pages 701-704

83.

What can go up a chimney down, but never down a chimney up?

See answer pages 701-704

84. Here is an unusual safe. Each of the buttons must be pressed only once in the correct order to open it. The last button is marked F. The number of moves and the direction is marked on each button. Thus 1U would mean one move up, while 1L would mean one move to the left. Using the grid reference, which button is the first you must press?

	A	B	C	D	E	F
1	4D	3R	3D	2R	4L	3L
2	3R	3R	1L	3D	1D	5L
3	1R	2D	1U	1L	4L	1D
4	1R	2R	1D	1U	4L	2U
5	4R	4U	F	4U	1R	2U

2F A
5C B
4D C
5B D
4E E
3F F

See answer pages 701-704

85. Move from ring to touching ring, starting from the bottom left corner and finishing in the top right corner. Collect nine numbers and total them. Which is the highest possible total?

See answer pages 701-704

86. Which of the numbers should replace the question mark?

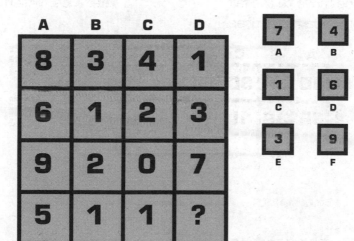

See answer pages 701-704

87. When maggie arrives at work alone, she must walk up the stairs, but when she arrives with a friend she can use the elevator. Why?

Hint: It's not because of any rule or regulation.

See answer pages 701-704

88. Scales one and two are in perfect balance. Which of these pans should replace the empty one?

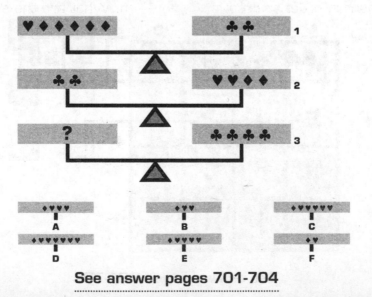

See answer pages 701-704

89. Here is an unusual safe. Each of the buttons must be pressed only once in the correct order to open it. The last button is marked F. The number of moves and the direction is marked on each button. Thus 1i would mean one move in, while 1o would mean one move out. 1c would mean one move clockwise and 1a would mean one move anti-clockwise. Which button is the first you must press?

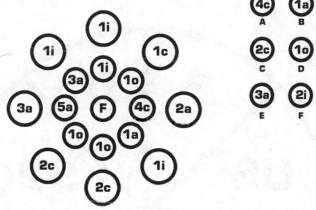

See answer pages 701-704

90. Insert the correct mathematical signs between each number in order to resolve the equation. What are the signs?

| 84 | | 7 | | 3 | = | 36 |

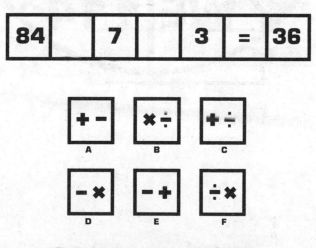

See answer pages 701-704

91. What number should replace the question mark?

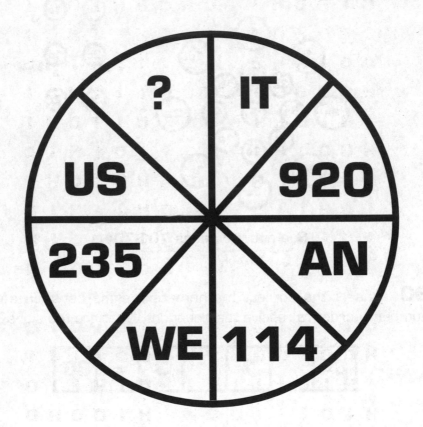

See answer pages 701-704

92. In the grid the word 'Ohio', written without a change of direction, appears only once. It can be written forwards and backwards in a horizontal, vertical or diagonal direction. Can you spot it?

```
H I H O H I I O H O H H I O H I
I H O H O I O I I O H H I H H I
O O I H H O I I O I I O H I H O
H O O O O I O H I H I I I H O I
I O I O H I H O I I O I I O H I
H O O I O I O H O I I O I H I O
O I H H H H I I O H H O I O H I
I O H I I O I I I O H I I H I O
I O I O I I O I I O O I O O I H
H O I I O H O I I O O I I O I H
I O O I O I O I I I I I H O H I H
O I O O I O I O I O I O I O I O
H O O I O O H O H I O O I I O I
I H I O I I I H I O O I H I I O
H I O I I I O O H I H I O O H O
O H O I O O I H I O I H H I H I
```

93. Take one letter from each bottle in order to find 5 insects.

See answer pages 701-704

94. Which dice face should replace the question mark?

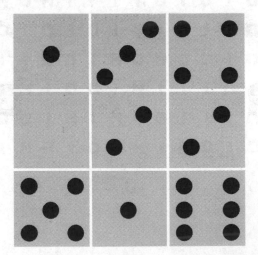

See answer pages 701-704

95. Place the letters in the grid to make a fish and a flower.

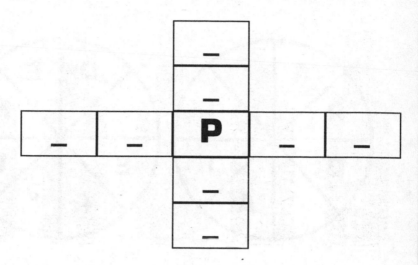

G
I
L
N
P
U
U
Y

96. Place 3 two-letter bits together to form a drink.

AP **CO** **FF**

RI **PA** **GR**

EI

See answer pages 701-704

97. Fill in the blank spaces to find two words that are synonyms.

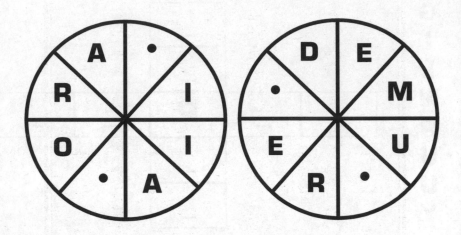

See answer pages 701-704

98. Fill in the missing letters to find an 8-letter word.

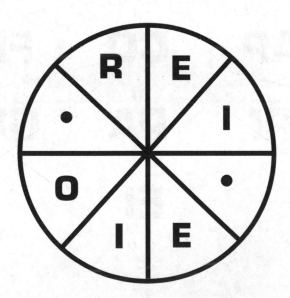

See answer pages 701-704

99. Fill in the missing letters to find food on the menu.

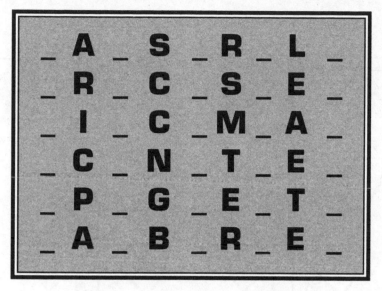

See answer pages 701-704

100. How many triangles are there in this diagram?

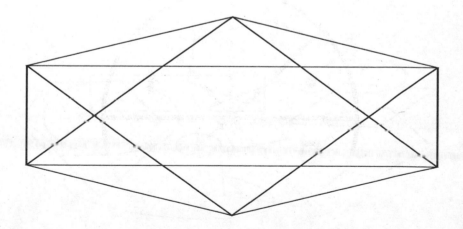

See answer pages 701-704

101. What number should replace the question mark?

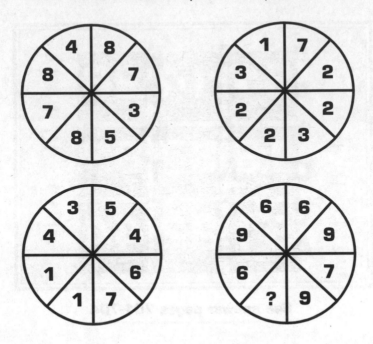

See answer pages 701-704

102. What number should replace the question mark?

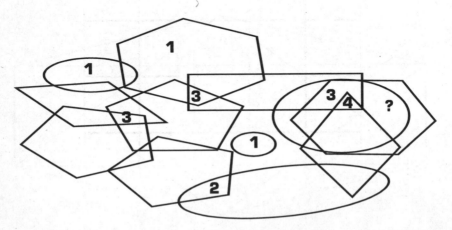

See answer pages 701-704

103. Multiply the largest prime number by the smallest even number.

See answer pages 701-704

104. How many squares are there in this diagram?

See answer pages 701-704

105. If they all worked together on the fence, each working at his same speed as before, how long would it take?

One man can paint a fence in 2 hours

One man can paint a fence in 3 hours

One man can paint a fence in 4 hours

One man can paint a fence in 6 hours

See answer pages 701-704

106. Arrange these 12 objects into 4 sets of three.

LAMPREY	**TARSUS**	**SAFFRON**
CLARET	**HERRING**	**ANISEED**
SCAPULA	**ANCHOVY**	**HEMLOCK**
CYPRESS	**SORREL**	**FIBULA**

See answer pages 701-704

107. Which figure is the odd one out?

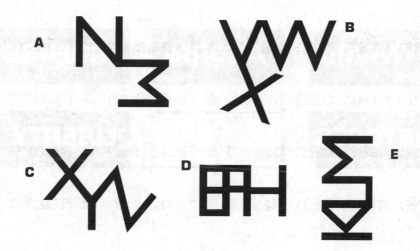

See answer pages 701-704

108. Arrange all of the letters of the newspaper headline below to spell out three musical instruments.

NICE ALLOCATIONS ROBS COP

See answer pages 701-704

109. What word is coded to appear in the middle box?

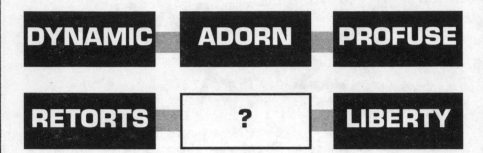

DYNAMIC   ADORN   PROFUSE

RETORTS   **?**   LIBERTY

See answer pages 701-704

110. Which number is the odd one out?

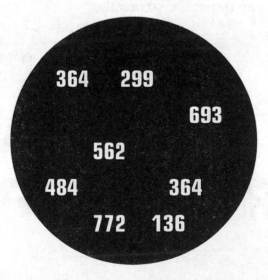

364   299

693

562

484   364

772   136

See answer pages 701-704

1. F.

On each row A + B + C = D.

2. Push the cork *into* the bottle and shake the coin out.

3. F.

4. E.

5. B.

The numbers in the first triangle total 3, the second 4 and so on.

6. B.

The alphanumeric value of each letter is placed next to it.

7. C.

8. C.

Each row totals 10.

9. B.

The hour hand moves forward two hours each time.

10. E.

11. 32.

12. D.

When completed the box reads the same both down and across.

13. C.

14. D.

15. F.

16. F.

17. A.

♣ = 6, ♥ = 5, ♦ = 2.

18. F.

19. E.

20. C.

Each double section totals 10.

21. B.

Two series lead from 1 to 16.

22. C.

23. D.

Deduct row 2 from row 1 to give row 3.

24. C.

25. E.

26. E.

On each row the two squares to the left total 9, as do the two to the right.

27. F.

The numbers in the triangles total 4, 6, 8, 10 etc.

28. C.

29. A.

The alphanumeric value of each letter is placed next to it.

30. A

31. The remains of a melted snowman.

$\alpha=4$, $\beta=7$, $\chi=5$, $\delta=8$.

32. A.

♣ = 2, ♥ = 1, ♦ = 3.

33. E.

34. B.

Each of the four columns of numbers totals 15.

35. C.

4a in the inner ring.

36. D.

The numbers on each row total 9.

37. A.

A large triangle added to the nearest small triangle will give the middle number.

38. E.

Each double section is added together. Reading clockwise from 2 + 1, the totals increase by one each time.

39. B.

40. E.

41. D.

42. F.

Each double section totals 13.

43. A.

On each row the first figure minus the second figure plus the third figure gives the fourth.

44. E.

45. E.

The first row plus the second row gives the third row.

46. C.

The box now reads the same down and across.

47. B.

48. E.

49. E. ♣ = 8, ♥ = 6, ♦ = 7.

50. D.

The hour hand moves forward two hours, then three hours, then four hours etc.

51. A.

52. B.

53. B.

In each triangle the bottom two numbers, when added together, give the top number.

54. F.

The hour hand moves back four hours each time.

55. C.

On each row A + B - C = D.

56. E.

57. D.

58. A.

When completed the box reads the same both down and across.

59. C.

60. C.

61. D.

62. D.

63. No man has two heads. A man has one head more than no man. Therefore a man has three heads.

64. B.

65. D.

66. F.

A large circle minus the nearest small circle will give the middle number.

67. A.

68. B.

Reading clockwise, the numbers relate to the number of line forming the shape in the previous sector.

69. C.

The first row plus the third row gives the second row.

70. E.

The alphanumeric positions of the letters are placed together in the middle.

71. B.

2c in the inner ring.

72. B.

73. A.

Reading clockwise, the number in the sector is the alphanumeric value of the letter in the previous sector.

74 F.

75 2. Add top two numbers and subtract bottom two numbers

76 C.

Each column totals 8.

77 E.

78 B.

From the 1, the numbers increase in a spiral by missing out one number, then two numbers, then three numbers and so on.

79 C.

80 E.

81 B.

Each double section is added together. These totals increase by two each time.

82 F.

When completed the box reads the same both down and across.

83 An umbrella.

84 E.

85 A.

86 E.

On each row A - B - C = D.

87 Maggie is not tall enough to reach to the up button.

88 C. ♣ = 4, ♥ = 3, ♦ = 1.

89 D.

1o in the inner ring, between another 1o and 5a.

90 F.

91 2119. The number following each word clockwise is determined by the position in the alphabet of the letters in each word.

92

```
H I H O H I I O H O H H I O H I
I H O H O I O I I O H H I H H I
O O I H H O I I O I I O H I H O
H O O O O I O H I H I I I H O I
I O I O H I H O I I O I I O H I
H O O I O I O H O I I O I H I O
O I H H H H I I I O H H O I O H I
I O H I I O I I I O H I I H I O
I O I O I I O I I O O I O O I H
H O I I O H O I I O O I I O I H
I O O I O I O I I I I H O H I H
O I O O I O I O I O I O I O I O
H O O I O O H O H I O O I I O I
I H I O I I H I O O I H I I O
H I O I I I O O H I H I O O H O
O H O I O O I H I O I H H I H I
```

93 MIDGE, EMMET, APHID, LOUSE, DRONE

94 4. Opposite dice are subtracted to get middle numbers.

95 GUPPY, LUPIN

96 GRAPPA

97 AROMATIC, PERFUMED

98 HOTELIER

99 CASSEROLE, FRICASSEE, MINCEMEAT, SCHNITZEL, SPAGHETTI, HAMBURGER

100 32.

101 7. In corresponding segments of the wheels (A-B)+C=D

(8-2)+1=7.

102 2. The numbers relate to the number of shapes in which the number is enclosed.

103 1162. 83x14=1162

104 55.

105 0.8 hours. Take reciprocal.

1. 2 hours $\frac{1}{2}$ = 0.5

2. 3 hours $\frac{1}{3}$ = 0.333

3. 4 hours $\frac{1}{4}$ = 0.25

4. 5 hours $\frac{1}{6}$ = 0.166

equals 1.25.

Again take reciprocal $\frac{1}{1.25}$ = 0 8

106

TREES/ BODY/ COLOURS/ FISH

CYPRESS/ TARSUS/ SAFFRON/ ANCHOVY

ANISEED/ SCAPULA/ SORREL/ HERRING

HEMLOCK/ FIBULA/ CLARET/ LAMPREY

107 D. It contains EFH. The others contain consecutive letters of the alphabet.

108 PICCOLO, CLARINET, BASSOON

109 ORBIT. Take corresponding letters from words in the top set.

110 562. In all the others, multiply the first and last digits and divide by 2 to arrive at the middle digit.